Published in celebration of the 125th anniversary of the

founding of the University of Wisconsin-Madison

CONTRIBUTORS

Vernon Carstensen
Merle Curti
Jonathan W. Curvin
Mark Eccles
David Fellman
Mark H. Ingraham
James A. Larsen
Clara Penniman
Chester H. Ruedisili
William B. Sarles
Clay Schoenfeld
William H. Sewell
Kurt F. Wendt
F. Chandler Young
William H. Young

THE UNIVERSITY
OF
WISCONSIN
One Hundred and Twenty-Five Years

EDITED BY

Allan G. Bogue
and
Robert Taylor

The University of Wisconsin Press

Published 1975
The University of Wisconsin Press
Box 1379, Madison, Wisconsin 53701

The University of Wisconsin Press, Ltd.
70 Great Russell Street, London

First printing

Printed in the United States of America

For LC CIP information see the colophon

ISBN 0-299-06840-4

Contents

Preface

WHEN Chancellor Edwin Young of the University of Wisconsin-Madison established a committee to plan the celebration of the 125th Anniversary of the campus during 1974-1975, one of that committee's first concerns was the lack of an up-to-date University history.

In writing their magnificent history of the University for the University Centennial in 1949, Merle Curti and Vernon Carstensen had ended their narrative at the year 1925. Although some biographical and autobiographical studies published more recently tell part of the story since that date, no effort has yet been made to present a balanced account of the University's development between 1925 and 1974, years of great growth and, at times, considerable stress.

Realizing that good histories are not written in a day nor even in a year, members of the 125th Anniversary Committee decided to take only the first step toward bringing the history of the campus through the past fifty years. The result is this book of essays, which places some of the more important campus developments since 1925 within the perspective of the University's longer history.

Merle Curti and Vernon Carstensen agreed to provide an introductory chapter that concisely reviewed the major events and trends described in their earlier work. Dean Emeritus Mark H. Ingraham was willing to undertake a survey of the years between 1925 and 1949. Against this background, other scholars who had served during the last twenty-five years at the University undertook to sketch the major trends and more important developments of the years from 1950 to 1974. The editors take responsibility not only for the areas selected for essays, but also for imposing space limitations on the authors which, some felt, made adequate coverage of their areas impossible. The fact that some authors heeded these limitations to the word, and others bent them, produced a book which differs somewhat in balance from what the editors desired, but must leave to the remedy of some future historian. Nonetheless, the editors hope this volume will serve in lieu of a definitive history of the years 1925-1974 until this need is filled.

In 1894 the Board of Regents of the University of Wisconsin noted that, "In all lines of academic investigation it is of the utmost importance that the investigator should be absolutely free to follow the indications of truth wherever they may lead." Less well known than the famous "sifting and winnowing" passage that immediately followed it and which appears on the plaque bolted to Bascom Hall, this statement not only affirms the right of untrammeled inquiry but outlines in stark simplicity the major purpose that unites all university constituencies in joint endeavor. Modern society, however, is highly complex; the organization, activities, and objectives of large state universities reflect this complexity. Such institutions mean very different things to different people and may indeed mean different things to the same individual at different times. The gifted young woman who later wrote *A Raisin in the Sun* came to the University in 1949 and found that everything but the Wisconsin snow was "a bust." But by 1962 Lorraine Hansberry could write to a young correspondent that the college years spent among mankind's accumulated intellectual treasures should be a period of "perpetual exhilaration." The editors of this book realize therefore that it does not convey a sense of all the complex problems of higher education, but its authors have tried to avoid misleading simplifications like the mischievous distinction between teaching and research, two endeavors that are so intimately and rewardingly joined in this university that separation would paralyze if not destroy both patients.

The editors and authors realize that much of this book is not history in the strict sense. The authors, who sacrificed their leisure hours to prepare these essays, were very much a part of the things they wrote about—indeed, some of them headed committees they describe in the book or played an important role in decisions that have fundamentally shaped the course of the University. Tomorrow's historian will value this autobiographical dimension but must also realize that it shaped the perspectives of our authors to some degree. The problem of perspective has affected the contents of this book in another respect as well. Given the limited lapse of time involved, the editors did not believe that the presidential administrations of this era could be evaluated in the way that Curti and Carstensen have done in their study of the years prior to 1925 or that Dean Emeritus Ingraham was able to do in his survey of the years 1925-1950. However, no author was curbed in this regard and the editors believe that historians will see much of importance in the administrations of the men who have guided the University of Wisconsin at Madison since the retirement of President Fred.

In closing this introduction, all who have been involved in the preparation of this volume thank the University of Wisconsin Foundation, which provided the funds for its publication, Chancellor Edwin Young for his support, and J. Frank Cook and the staff of the University Archives, who have given many hours of their time to the task of assisting the authors and editors.

In addition, the authors and editors have benefited from the assistance and cooperation of many other persons and wish to express their appreciation to Earl M. Aldrich, David A. Baerreis, S. W. Bailey, Tino Balio, Bruce Benward, E. L. Bennett, Steven W. Berkley, Leonard Berkowitz, Edwin Black, E. James Blakely, C. H. Blanchard, Robert M. Bock, Robert R. Borchers, Robert E. Bowman, Robert W. Bray, R. H. Bruck, R. Creighton Buck, George Bunn, Samuel Burns, William C. Burns, Robert H. Burris, Porter Butts, Eugene N. Cameron, Grace Chatterton, Camden A. Coberly, Arthur D. Code, Signe S. Cooper, Joseph J. Corry, Grant Cottam, Ted Crabb, Donald W. Crawford, Ralph D. Culbertson, William Dawson, Don H. Didcoct, Jean Dorman, Wallace H. Douma, L. E. Drake, John A. Duffie, George Dury, Marvin E. Ebel, James V. Edsall, Leon D. Epstein, Mary Fee, Richard F. Fenske, Charlotte Finley, R. Booth Fowler, Edwin B. Fred, Robert E. Frykenberg, Dale Gilbert, Herbert S. Gochberg, T. R. Goldsworthy, Donald W. Greve, John Gruber, Helen M. Guzman, John H. Halton, Theodore S. Hamerow, Richard Hartshorne, Lyndon Harries, Kay Hawkins, Charles Heidelberger, Raymond G. Herb, Lila Hillyer, S. Edward Horkan, Russell J. Hosler, Richard S. Hosman, Herbert M. Howe, J. Willard Hurst, Donald R. Johnson, Joseph Kauffman, Bryant E. Kearl, Donald W. Kerst, Bonnie Kienitz, Robert Kimbrough, William L. Kraushaar, Mary Kreul, Luke Lamb, Robert J. Lampman, E. E. LeMasters, Kenneth Little, Frederick Logan, C. William Loomer, Ian Loram, LeRoy E. Luberg, Elizabeth Madden, Menahem Mansoor, W. Robert Marshall, Russell Merritt, Lorraine V. Meythaler, James L. Miller, Elizabeth C. Miller, Elgin Milligan, Julius Mintz, Theodore Morgan, Karlos Moser, James A. Mott, Harald Naess, H. L. Nelson, Ordean G. Ness, John F. Newman, Eleanore M. Oimoen, Norman C. Olson, Mary Ann Peckham, D. Perlman, Barbara Peterson, Cyrena N. Pondrom, Glenn S. Pound, Robert Ratner, Hugh T. Richards, Arthur H. Robinson, Frederick L. Roesler, Millard Rogers, Roberta Schambow, Alice E. Schroeder, Dorothy Schultz, Charles T. Scott, J. Thomas Shaw, Robert Siegfried, James J. Skiles, George W. Sledge, Newell Smith, W. H. Stone, Martha Sumner, Verner Suomi, Keith R. Symon, Howard M. Temin, Wilson Thiede, Randolph S. Thrush, G. C. Tiao, M. K. Verma, James S. Watrous, Warren Weaver, Charles Wedemeyer, John E. Willard, Coleman Woodbury, and L. C. Young.

Illustration of this volume was aided tremendously by the drawing together of photographs for the Elvehjem Art Center's exhibition, "The University of Wisconsin — 125 Years Through the Camera's Eye."

Photographs were provided by University of Wisconsin Archives, State Historical Society of Wisconsin, U.W. Extension Department of Photography, and the University News and Publications Service.

Photographers represented include Barbara Baenziger, Delmar Brown, Burton Gellman, John Gruber, Duane Hopp, Milton Leidner, Norman Lenburg, Gerhard Schulz, and a number of anonymous artists, among them those who took photographs for Diemer Studio, Kamera Kraft Shop, and Photoart House, three of Madison's early photographic studios.

A. G. B.
R. T.

Madison, Wisconsin
February 1975

THE UNIVERSITY OF WISCONSIN

One Hundred and Twenty-Five Years

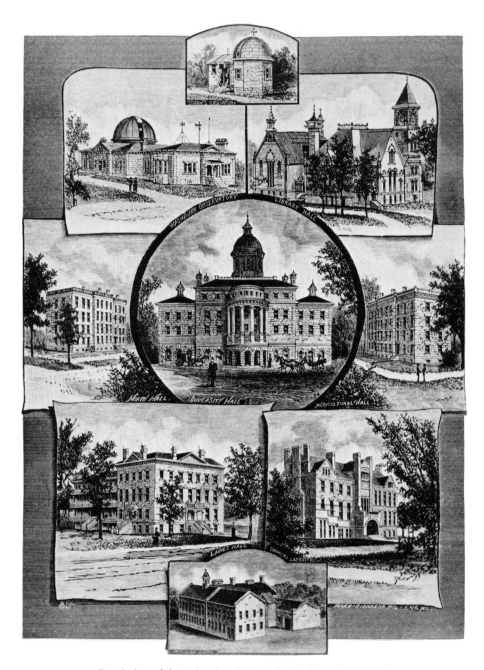

Frontispiece of the University of Wisconsin Catalogue, 1887-1888.

CHAPTER 1

The University of Wisconsin: To 1925

MERLE CURTI
and
VERNON CARSTENSEN

On January 16, 1850, almost all of the 1,500 citizens of Madison took some part, if only as observers, in the inauguration of John H. Lathrop as the first chancellor of the University of Wisconsin. The procession which escorted him to the Legislative Assembly included the governor, the regents, members of the Legislature and Supreme Court, and a brass band. Much was expected of the man who had studied and taught at Hamilton College and Yale University and who had presided over the University of Missouri for seven years. No one seemed disappointed in his two-hour address, phrased in elegant language and replete with evidence of learning. Lathrop defined a university as "the depository and the almoner of the intellectual treasures of the age" and as the true democracy that levels, not downward, but upward.[1] The knowledge it safeguarded and extended was the key to progress. More given to generalities than to specifics, Lathrop did not spell out a program for the realization of such a noble end. He did, to be sure, speak of the importance of a library and scientific apparatus as well as of a faculty composed of men of

Merle Curti, Frederick Jackson Turner Professor at Wisconsin from 1947 to his retirement in 1968, has taught or lectured in many American and foreign universities. He was the winner of the Pulitzer Prize in History and is the author of many books and articles in American social and intellectual history. Among these was *The University of Wisconsin: A History, 1848-1925*, coauthored with Vernon Carstensen. Professor Curti is a past president of the American Historical Association. His honorary degrees include a Doctorate of Humane Letters from the University of Wisconsin-Milwaukee.

Vernon Carstensen was born on a farm in Iowa and received his Ph.D. from the University of Iowa. He joined the Department of history at the University of Wisconsin in 1945 and served as associate dean of the Graduate School between 1960 and 1963. He accepted his present position as professor of history at the University of Washington in 1964 and has been president of the Faculty Senate in that university. He is the author or editor of numerous publications in western American history and in agricultural history and has served as editor of *Agricultural History*.

mature vigor, sound scholarship, aptitude for teaching, and conciliatory demeanor: to such men should be given the internal management of the instruction and discipline of the institution. He advocated free tuition for future teachers and ministers — the special agents for the moral instruction of the popular mind. Lathrop also proclaimed the responsibility of the state for education and admonished the Legislature to make careful provision for the wise, honest, and efficient protection of the land endowment that the federal government had conferred for the support of seminaries of learning when the territory had been organized.

As yet, the blueprint of the new institution had barely been sketched. The Constitution of 1848 had provided for the establishment of a university, free from sectarianism, at or near the seat of government and for the protection of the land grant which was to support the institution. The control over the land endowment was lodged in an ex-officio board of commissioners. The constitution also permitted the university to establish connections with other colleges in the state. It made no mention of its relation to future high schools.

The first Legislature of the new state, meeting in the summer of 1848, implemented the constitutional requirement in a basic law or charter. This vested the government of the University in twelve regents elected by the Legislature and a chancellor, chosen by the regents and serving ex-officio on the board. The regents were authorized to enact laws for the University. to select a faculty as well as a chancellor, and to fix, subject to legislative approval, their salary. The law also stipulated the organization of four departments — Science, Literature, and the Arts; Law; Medicine; and the Theory and Practice of Elementary Instruction — whose faculties were entrusted with the internal management of their departments. The regents were further empowered to regulate the course of instruction, to prescribe, with the advice of the professors, "books and authorities" to be used, and appropriate degrees. The regents were authorized to spend part of the income of the University Fund, derived from the sale of the land grants, for the purchase of a site, buildings, scientific apparatus, and a library, all subject to legislative approval. In accordance with the provision in the constitution the governing board might also admit into a connection with the University, other colleges in the state. It is clear from the terms of the act that the Legislature intended to exercise close supervision over the University. Such, then, was the legislative blueprint that was to guide the regents, chancellor, and faculty, with minor revisions, until 1866.

Under the vigorous leadership of Eleazer Root, a graduate of Williams College and the principal agent in the previous establishment of an academy and Carroll College, the regents proceeded to organize the

University even though they were entirely without funds inasmuch as the Legislature had not yet authorized the sale of University lands. In taking what seemed to some critics an unduly hasty and unrealistic action, the regents replied that the purpose was to prevent the squandering of University funds and, apparently, at the same time to force an early sale of the land endowment. Hence the board committed two thousand dollars annually for the salary of the chancellor and additional sums for the professors. The Preparatory School, deemed necessary in view of the lack of high schools, was to start things off. The regents named Lathrop chancellor. John Sterling, a graduate of Princeton, who had worked with Root in his educational ventures at Waukesha, was appointed professor in charge of the Preparatory School, at a salary of $500, to be paid by student fees. Sterling began his thirty-five years of service to the University by opening the first preparatory class of seventeen boys on February 1, 1849, in a rent-free room of the Madison Female Academy. The Legislature, in approving these steps, also authorized the regents to purchase College Hill and undertake the construction of the first buildings.

These were the chief accomplishments of the regents when John Lathrop was installed as chancellor on January 16, 1850. As a token of the generally shared enthusiasm of the occasion, the Legislature forthwith granted the requests of the regents and the new chancellor. These included approval of the organization of the Department of Science, Literature, and the Arts and of the Department of the Theory and Practice of Elementary Instruction, the plans for the development of the site, legislative action for increasing and safeguarding the fund to be derived from the sale of the University lands, and a loan of $25,000 from the School Fund, to be repaid, with interest, as soon as the University Fund became available.

In the ten years between the arrival and the departure of Chancellor Lathrop in 1859, he enjoyed the respect and affection of the students and, at least initially, the confidence of the regents. The board seldom rejected his recommendations. Yet this cautious and sometimes obstinate man did not succeed in becoming a powerful influence in realizing the objectives of the University that Eleazer Root, the principal founding father, had expressed in welcoming Lathrop. We have, Root had said, called you to preside over the institution which "we believe is destined to exert a great and salutary influence on the moral, intellectual, and social character of the people of this state for all time to come."[2] The failure to approach this objective was the result of the lack of a consensus as to what a state university should be, of national events that no one in Wisconsin foresaw in 1850, and of the lack of money, which Lathrop called "the nerves of learning."

The funds needed for current operating expenses and for the first building — North Hall — were in large part borrowed from private sources and, with legislative approval, from the slowly accumulating University Fund. Thus the slender resources overloaded each professor with the task of covering vast fields of knowledge and limited the possibility of attracting the rare instructor really equipped to teach youths how to apply the sciences to commerce, industry, mining, and agriculture. Nor were all of the professors, traditionally trained as they were, sympathetic to the professed purpose of the University to provide a utilitarian education for all classes of citizens. Even Chancellor Lathrop, despite his admirable rhetoric about the importance of practical education, felt that this should rest on a theoretical basis and thus that the first priority, the core of the University's offerings, should be the traditional curriculum. Hence the gap between what the University professed to be doing in the direct, immediate, and practical interest of all the people and what was actually being done was too great to be overlooked.

Other problems also militated against a smooth road for the University. Lathrop observed that in a pioneer state a university labored under great disadvantages inasmuch as there was not "the same general appreciation of liberal culture in the new country as in the old" and that, moreover, this lack of appreciation was not mitigated by the mere fact of state sponsorship of an institution of higher learning.[3] To make matters worse, the sectarian colleges claimed a share of the revenues from the sale of University lands and found champions in the Legislature who denounced the University as a "godless" institution and maintained, possibly with some justice, that academic standards were higher and a liberal education better exemplified in private colleges. Others insisted that the University was in actuality a mere local academy rather than a state institution and supported their claim by noting the domination of the Board of Regents by its Madison members and by pointing to the large number of students from nearby communities. The frequently reckless handling of public interests and funds in the 1850s created an atmosphere in which suspicion was easily aroused that the regents were mismanaging the finances of the institution.

All these factors help explain the fact that as early as 1854 the University was attacked in the Legislature. A committee reported a bit later that the affairs of the University had been administered with less energy than was commensurate with the expectations of its friends. The Panic of 1857 stimulated a feeling for the need of retrenchment and drastic economy in state institutions. Thus the joint committee appointed in 1857 to look into the finances and needs of the University presented two reports critical of the expansion beyond either need or resources, prevailing low academic standards, and, most of all, the failure to provide the practical training needed by teachers, famers, engineers, and businessmen. Neither report was adopted by both houses of the Legislature.

Nevertheless, sensing what was in the air and no doubt fearful of future legislative action, the regents, with the approval of Chancellor Lathrop, adopted an "ordinance" which presumably aimed to meet the criticisms that had been advanced. The University was "reorganized" from within. The faculty was legislated out of existence, though all but two "recalcitrant" members were reappointed. The Department of Science, Literature, and the Arts was expanded to include new "schools" of Agriculture, Commerce, Engineering, and Applied Science, and the professorships were reshuffled accordingly. A gesture toward making the Department of the Theory and Practice of Elementary Instruction more meaningful by locating it in the Madison high school and the annexation of a private commercial school constituted the principal achievements of the reorganization as far as practical education went, though, to be sure, a Department of Physiology and Hygiene, with a new professor, was established in 1859. Perhaps the most significant result of the reorganization was the institution of the Board of Visitors, whose function was to report to the regents on examinations and on needed changes in the course of study and in the organization of the University.

Sensing the dissatisfaction in many quarters with his leadership, Lathrop cooperated with the regents in opening the way to persuade Henry Barnard, a leading figure in the public school movement and editor of the *American Journal of Education,* to accept the joint positions of chancellor and head of the recently established normal schools. After his resignation as chancellor, Lathrop was reappointed to the professorship of ethics, civil policy, and political economy. He presently accepted an invitation to Indiana University and, shortly afterwards, returned to the University of Missouri as professor and then as president. Although Lathrop got along reasonably well with the regents and was admired and liked by students, he failed to show the leadership needed to carry through his conception of the University as the head of the state's educational system, to balance in a way satisfactory to the interested public his ideas about liberal and professional education, or to emulate the superintendent of the State Historical Society, who persuaded the Legislature to support directly an institution of less value to the people than the University.

Dr. Henry Barnard, who accepted the chancellorship in January 1859, never took an active part in the affairs of the University. His eminent reputation as a leader in the public school movement and as editor of the *American Journal of Education* had raised great expectations, none of which was fulfilled. Plagued by ill health and occupied with editorial tasks, he spent in all only a few months in Wisconsin. He was, to be sure, active in holding teachers' institutes in several parts of the state. Asked by the regents in July 1859 to present a plan by which "the expenses for interest, insurance, instruction etc. . . . . shall be brought within the current income," Barnard instead offered his resignation.[4] The board accepted it the next year. Faced by a critical financial situation, the regents reduced the staff to five professors and a tutor and salaries from $1,500 to $1,000 and, in the case of the professor of modern languages, to $800. The incumbent professors were reappointed, with the exception of Joseph Pickard, who was replaced by John F. Fuchs, a protege of Carl Schurz.

With the depletion of students in the Civil War and the further reduction of salaries to little more than half of what they had once been, it took all the patience and persistence of John Sterling, who was named dean and, in 1865, vice chancellor, to hold things together. Incredibly overburdened by a multitude of tasks, Sterling unsuccessfully urged the regents to rotate the chief administrative position among his colleagues.

With the outbreak of the Civil War the students organized a military company. In 1864 all but one of the graduating class of thirty-two left for voluntary service under the leadership of Charles Allen, director of the Normal Department. The faculty urged the establishment of a military department comparable to those in other state universities, but the Legislature failed to appropriate the annual thousand dollars needed for its support.

The chief innovation during the Civil War was the result of expediency—the need of attracting enough students to keep the doors of the institution from closing. Thus in 1863 the Normal Department was opened to women, who were also allowed to attend other classes. In 1864, of the total 229 students in the University, 162 were enrolled in the Normal Department, and of these, 119 were women. The faculty looked on the sudden appearance of women with mixed feelings. Sterling reported that some felt the admission of women would let down the standard of culture if it did not destroy the character of the institution. Such prejudices seem to have disappeared rather quickly, especially when the six women in the first graduating class of the Normal Department demonstrated an academic ability equal to that of the men. Yet it seems clear that neither the faculty nor the regents would have moved any further toward full coeducation had not the Legislature in 1866 stipulated that the University was to be open to women in all of its departments. That goal, however, was not to be achieved without a long struggle.

The early 1860s were also important in that the foundation was laid for the future state support of the University. In the early years the chief source of income was the University Fund, supplemented by the sale of off-campus town lots on the purchase site and by student fees. The Board of Regents was on the one hand committed to a policy of withholding from sale University lands until demand insured higher prices than those prevailing in the early years, and, on the other, in boldly launching the University regardless of the fact that interest on the University Fund was too small to cover the cost of the first buildings and the meager operations of the miniscule institution. The problem was complicated by the fact that the management of the original federal land grant and that of the supplementary one of 1854 was in the hands of a state commission rather than the regents. Pressure from speculators and land-hungry preemptors and the commissions's decision to lend money from the school funds to small borrowers complicated the picture still further. Rather than postpone the opening of the University the regents withdrew their opposition to selling the lands at a moderate price, and this was done. By 1857 the total value of the University Fund was $316,000, with an annual income of $21,000. But the picture was by no means as bright as these figures suggest. The buyers of University lands owed $260,000 of the purchase price, an alarming figure in view of the impending depression of 1857. Moreover, the regents had borrowed from the capital of the University Fund for the construction of North and South Halls and for the Main Edifice (Bascom Hall). Thus the endowment for the future was depleted by the drain from the capital fund for the first buildings. By 1861 an indebtedness of $97,216.27 and forfeitures of purchases of land resulted in the steady decline in the value of the fund. At the request of the regents the Legislature in 1862 authorized an appropriation of $100,000 from the University Fund to liquidate the debt, but this meant, of course, that the income of the fund was drastically reduced. The University's financial plight was not alleviated.

In 1862 the Legislature responded favorably to the request of the Commissioners of School and University Lands for permission to invest the funds in state and federal bonds in the interest of securing the endowments. In other words, the Legislature now took the position that the credit of the state represented the best security for these funds. This step, together with the sale at reduced prices of the remaining University lands, slowly reconstituted the University Fund. In 1867 it reached almost $194,000, with an annual income of $13,000. This handling of the fund by the regents with legislative approval established a basis from which to launch a campaign to secure financial aid from the state, not by virtue of any inherent claim that higher education might have for state support, but simply because the state, through the action of its agents, the regents, and the Legislature had failed in its trust by permitting the lands to be sold too cheaply and the fund to be dissipated. In 1862 the regents held that had not successive legislatures allowed the use of the fund for other than the original purpose of endowment, it would be sufficient to provide for all the needs of the University. A year later the board asked to be relieved of the costs charged for the administering of the fund and noted that Michigan, with a land endowment half the size of Wisconsin's, enjoyed an annual income from that source of $40,000. The faculty, on its part, submitted to the regents in 1864 a long review of the handling of the land endowment, in which comparisons were made with affairs in other states with federal grants for higher education. The faculty concluded, with confidence, that "it was not to be questioned but the state will sooner or later furnish the means of adequate support."[5]

The first decade and a half of the University's history saw the development of customs and institutions that were in good part to be perpetuated. The chancellor spoke for the faculty, which had little contact with the regents. Although political considerations sometimes influenced appointments and even dismissals from the staff, this was exceptional. The regents could and did hold fairly tight reins over the faculty. Chancellor Lathrop felt it necessary to ask their permission to buy a book and lithographs of Calhoun, Clay, and Webster for University use. Permission also was needed for professors to leave the campus during the term, even for missions closely related to a professor's work. Little was said about academic freedom, but in 1855 a member of the board introduced a resolution condemning Professor O. M. Conover for attending a meeting held to denounce the governor for removing the state geologist from office. The resolution, after some discussion, was withdrawn, but the threat of possible regent censure remained. Nor was the atmosphere within the University democratic. Lathrop seldom consulted other professors on courses of study, organization, or buildings. Some in the faculty regarded him as dictatorial and autocratic.

Of the early faculty, three were trained in theological schools and two held medical degrees. The teaching load was twice that in many eastern colleges, and no professor managed to limit his instruction to what was supposed to be his field of competence. In addition, almost all held classes in the Preparatory School. At Wisconsin, as at most institutions of the time, teaching was largely confined to daily recitations of students from textbooks. Though Ezra Carr talked about laboratory work, his scientific instruction largely took the form of recitations and lectures. While all the professors were men of scholarly taste and culture, few if any were distinguished as scholars or teachers.

At the close of the Civil War the student body, most of which still came from Dane County, was, in size, comparable to that of Wisconsin's private colleges. As late as 1865 only 41 of a total of 331 students were listed as members of the courses leading to degrees. The rest, "irregulars," either did not meet entrance requirements or were not candidates for graduation. The faculty supervised the study room at least once in the morning and once in the afternoon and kept careful records of students' scholarship and deportment, punished misdemeanors, great and small, and generally maintained an exacting discipline. When, in 1865, seven young men attended the Madison German theater, one was permanently dismissed, three for the rest of the term, and the others publicly reprimanded and put on good behavior. Yet the faculty defended students against outside criticism and refuted allegations of a "godless" institution by making it clear that students and professors alike attended compulsory daily chapel and that many students began and ended the day with prayer.

Except for Madisonians, most of the men and, after 1863, the women who were admitted by the back door of the Normal Department, lived in North Hall or South Hall. Some ate at commons presided over by Professor and Mrs. Sterling; others provided their own fare in spartan rooms. There were no organized sports, but wicket, quoits, and baseball were played. The disciplined routine of daily classes was enlivened by the exercises sponsored by the literary society and, in 1856 and 1857, by the student publication, *The Miscellany*. At the end of each academic year public examinations and literary and oratorical exhibitions attracted great interest. Many graduates, who organized the Alumni Association in 1861, returned to the campus on these occasions and the presence of leading state officials added to the prestige of the celebration.

THE legislative "organic act" of 1866, which reorganized the University, was stimulated by the necessity of implementing the Morrill Land Grant of 1862, which allocated to Wisconsin 240,000 acres of public land. Congress stipulated that institutions receiving land grants offer instruction in agricultural and technical subjects as well as military tactics. The Land Grant Act also provided that all expenses for the administration of the income from the sale of the lands be paid by the state and further forbade the purchase, erection, or repair of buildings from funds derived from the income of the grant. After defeating the bid of Ripon College and Lawrence Institute for the land grant the Legislature, in allocating it to the University, directed the regents to establish a College of Arts, in which instruction was to be offered in mathematics and the physical and natural sciences, with applications to the industrial arts; and a College of Letters, embracing instruction in the liberal studies of language, literature, and philosophy. The organic act also required the regents to provide, without expense to the state or to the University funds, an experimental farm of at least 200 acres near the campus. Eager to have the projected College of Agriculture in Madison, Dane County issued bonds to the amount of $40,000, from which the regents bought land west of the campus.

Nor was this all. The organic act required that all able-bodied male students receive instruction in military tactics and that all departments of the University be open on equal terms to men and women alike. Partisan instruction in religion and politics was forbidden. In place of a chancellor, the reorganization act provided for a president with more limited powers than the chancellors had enjoyed, without a seat or voice in the Board of Regents.

Moreover, the regents henceforth were to be appointed by the governor rather than chosen by the Legislature. That political considerations influenced the selections by Governor Fairchild and his successors was clear, but in general able and experienced men were named, several of whom, whether as members of the Legislature or in their private capacity, found opportunities to confer favors on the institution. Governor Fairchild named two alumni to the board, but a sustained movement to require the appointment of alumni failed. The newly appointed regents adopted bylaws which organized committees and which kept control of internal affairs.

The selection of a new president presented several problems. Much could be said, and was said, for the appointment of a Wisconsin man familiar with the state and its educational problems. When Josiah Pickard, a former regent and superintendent of public instruction, turned down an offer, the regents, convinced of the need of a scientist, looked to Paul A. Chadbourne, professor of natural history at Williams College and incipient president of the newly organized Massachusetts State Agricultural College at Amherst. A man who had come up the hard way, and who had turned from theology to science, Chadbourne had organized exploring expeditions in the Arctic and elsewhere for the collection of scientific data and delivered lectures on natural history at the Smithsonian Institution and on the harmony of science and religious orthodoxy at the Lowell Institute which had been published and were used as a textbook at Harvard and at some of Wisconsin's denominational colleges. Chadbourne's main objection to coming to Wisconsin was the provision in the recent act of the Legislature admitting women to the full privileges of the University. Since he was in a position to bargain, since Wisconsin had not been a pioneer in coeducation, and since the regents set no great store on it, they were willing to recommend to the Legislature an amendment specifying that women were to be allowed to attend the University under conditions specified by the regents. Chadbourne at last accepted the presidency. Years later E. A. Birge enjoyed the irony of fixing Chadbourne's name on Ladies Hall.

Although not a man of profound learning and, indeed, narrowly orthodox in his Calvinist faith, Chadbourne was a gifted administrator and enjoyed unprecedented success in his relations with regents and faculty. He chose not to exercise at once or fully his prerogative in dismissing the faculty. Several of the professors, however, resigned to go elsewhere. By petition from the alumni and others, John Sterling, the virtual father of the University, was reappointed — he was, in fact, the only member of the old faculty to survive the reorganization of 1866. Chadbourne's appointments were sound and wise. This was notably true of William F. Allen, a graduate of Harvard who had continued his studies of the classics and history in Germany, and who was to demonstrate distinction in the first and a good deal of originality in the second; of William W. Daniels, a graduate of and an instructor at Michigan Agicultural College, whose sound scientific training was enhanced by further study at Harvard's Lawrence Scientific School, and who was thoroughly familiar with farm life and its problems; of Addison E. Verrill in comparative anatomy and entomology; of John E. Davies in physics; and of Roland D. Irving in geology.

Aware that the normal schools had come to stay, Chadbourne discontinued the teacher training department or, rather, converted it into the quasi-separate Female College. The ladies pursued their studies in separate quarters under their own preceptress, though they were allowed to attend University classes and, when they fulfilled the requirements for graduation, to receive degrees despite Chadbourne's inclination. Engineering was launched under the auspices of the instructor in military tactics. The College of Law was organized in 1868. Though largely dependent on student fees and staffed by practising Madison lawyers and judges, the college attracted a growing number of students in the one-year course. Chadbourne would have liked to have a medical school, but the indifference of the profession and limited resources convinced him that it was better to strengthen existing courses than to embark on new, costly, and risky ones.

The public responded favorably to Chadbourne's remarkable energy and leadership. In speaking at teachers' institutes and normal schools and at meetings of agricultural and professional societies, he won friends for the University. Under pressure from the regents, especially ex-Governor Edward Salomon, the Legislature, too, at last smiled on the University. Admitting that an injustice had been done when permission was given for the use of the University's capital fund for buildings, the Legislature in 1867 allocated annually the sum of $7,303.76 for a period of ten years, until the injustice was compensated for. After this first step the Legislature, in the year after Chadbourne's departure, made its first direct gift, $50,000, for a building for women students. In making it a legislative committee suggested that the state was obligated directly to support the University since, in the interest of rapid settlement, its land had been sold without waiting for a rise in sale price, with the result that its maximum return had not been realized.

Though Chadbourne was not responsible for this windfall, his popularity was still high when he made severe criticisms of state universities in an article that appeared in *Putnam's Magazine* in 1869. In this he argued that vocational education could best be offered at special institutions and that state universities over-emphasized practical training at the expense of liberal studies. In addition, he thought, such institutions undertook to do more than their resources justified. Whatever his reservations about state universities, Chadbourne gave Wisconsin leadership that, together with the support of leading figures in Wisconsin's public life, did much to lift the University to a new level. When, after a stay of less than four years, he accepted the presidency of Williams College, expressions of regret were both general and sincere.

The faithful John Sterling carried on the executive tasks of the University until the new president, the Reverend John Twombly of Boston, arrived in Madison in time to begin the fall term of 1871. His reputation as a fund-raiser for the educational interests of New England's Methodists testified, in the eyes of the regents, to his practicality. Twombly's outspoken championship of coeducation and his addresses in favor of relating the high schools of the state to the University won favor in some quarters and he seemed to be off to a good start. But the tide quickly turned. The students, who had tolerated his paternalism and evangelical zeal, discovered that he had misrepresented the regents in alleging their opposition to coeducation. No scholar, with his whole teaching experience limited to three years in a Methodist academy in Massachusetts, Twombly failed to arouse any student support for his classroom performance. To the faculty he was a man of little tact or culture. Nor did he do well with the regents. He had stated in the University's catalog that complete coeducation had been achieved, and in a way to offend some of the board. Nor did the regents relish his repeated insistence that they persuade the Legislature to seat the president on the board. Offering no cooperation or support, the regents decided that they had made a mistake in calling Twombly and that he must go.

The chairman of the executive committee, General Charles Hamilton, writing to Twombly two weeks before a meeting of the board in early June, urged him to resign. Indignant at criticisms he claimed he had never before heard, the president defended his record and took Hamilton to task for what seemed to him high-handed and unfair action. Some regents felt that the matter should be quietly and smoothly handled. But despite an arrangement to keep the board's decision private, the news quickly spread. More than 4,000 Methodists petitioned the Legislature to keep Twombly. At a meeting of the board on January 21, 1874, General Hamilton offered a resolution to the effect "that in view of the incompetence of J. W. [*sic*] Twombly, he possessing neither the learning to teach, the capacity to govern, or the wisdom to direct, he be, and is hereby removed from his position of President, and from all connection with the University."[6] A substitute motion to the effect that the president was removed from his office carried, and that evening the regents received Twombly's resignation. It was clear that in a real contest between regents and a president, a president had little chance to survive.

ON the very day that the regents forced Twombly to resign they announced the election of Professor John Bascom of Williams College as his successor. "Though possessed of independent and uncompromising moral convictions," wrote Bascom toward the end of his life, "I have always been exceedingly shy and have suffered deeply from every form of personal collision."[7] This self-judgment explains in part the impression of austere coldness or at least detachment that the new president conveyed to all but his close intimates. Brought up in the upstate New York home of a widow of a Congregational minister, Bascom had, during his studies at Williams and the Auburn Theological Seminary, come openly to reject strict religious orthodoxy. At the same time, in studying modern science, he had come to see no incompatibility between it and basic Christian truths. Before coming to Wisconsin he had expressed in speeches and writings a social and political liberalism which he made more explicit in Madison by championing the obligation of government to serve the interests of farmers and workers, the right of laborers to organize and strike, and of women's rights, including the suffrage. A vigorous moral idealist, Bascom had the Puritan sense of obligation to lift the community to higher ethical levels. This was expressed, among other ways, in supporting the Prohibition party and in campaigning to force Madison taverns to obey legislation against selling liquor to students under twenty-one. With all these convictions it was inevitable that Bascom would become a controversial figure.

Bascom's scholarship, which was in no sense superficial and indeed often original, embraced theology and law, both of which he had studied, and a wide range among the humanities, social sciences, and even natural sciences, at least in their historical and philosophical bearings. He wrote, both before and after coming to Madison, on literature and esthetics, political economy, philosophy, theology, and psychology, all of which reflected a thoughtful if eclectic mind and an open sympathy toward both many traditional values and toward much that marked contemporary thought. Moreover, Bascom was a stimulating, even a great teacher, not only in his classes, but in his ability to lift the intellectual and moral level of students and to imbue a great many with lasting social values; Robert M. La Follette was only one of many to so testify.

When President Bascom arrived in Madison in 1874 to teach in the spring term and to take responsibility for the immediate direction of the internal affairs of the University he was warmly received. The regents had been very eager to have him, and the thirteen years he was to spend at Wisconsin began auspiciously. He firmly and skillfully guided the last phase of the transition to complete coeducation and later gave compelling refutation of the claim that women missed more classes than men and were, by reason of lesser physical strength, unable to equal men in academic performance. President Bascom also gave needed support to the movement, already pioneered by Michigan, for admitting without entrance examinations or tuition graduates from high schools accredited by the University, and a little later, securing teachers' certificates for graduates. Besides helping to realize the dream of a complete system of state-supported free education, coordinated at the several levels, this raised standards in both high schools and the University. It was no longer necessary to keep the Preparatory School, and the general preparation of entering students was considerably improved.

In the year that President Bascom came to Wisconsin the income of the University was about $60,000. This was derived from the land grant funds, from student fees, and from the legislative appropriations of 1867 and 1872. The latter, $10,000 annually, formally recognized the obligation of the state to support the University by reason of the fact that the state had allowed the deterioration of the endowment. Bascom at once urged the need for increasing the University's income. Additional funds were required, he insisted, not only for a library and science building but, in particular, for the increase of professorships in the interest of greater efficiency and much needed specialization. While Bascom's efforts to augment the University's income were telling, the role of the regents and of friends in public life was, of course, indispensable. Everyone concerned harked back to the positions earlier taken: the state was responsible for an increased and regularized support of the University because mismanagement of the funds and the too rapid sale of land endowment required, in justice, compensation. Increasingly emphasis was also put on the much larger annual income of Michigan despite the fact its original land grant was smaller and less valuable than Wisconsin's. As a result of much effort the Legislature was persuaded in 1875 to appropriate $80,000 for the first Science Hall and, the next year, to follow Michigan's example in granting a mill tax, one-tenth of a mill on each dollar of the property evaluation of the state. In 1883 the proportion was raised to one-eighth mill. After the disastrous fire that destroyed Science Hall in 1884, the Legislature voted, in all, almost $400,000 for the new Science Hall and its related buildings. The year before Bascom's presidency ended a committee of the Legislature, in a comparative study of western state universities, reported that only Michigan, with a student enrollment twice that of Wisconsin's 387, enjoyed a larger annual income; thus the state had, since the reorganization of 1866, moved slowly, and somewhat deviously, toward assuming financial responsibility for the University.

In President Bascom's time faculty freedom continued to be limited. The president handled admission requirements, credits, and the grading system as well as student discipline. Professors were seldom consulted about new appointments and in many instances were without knowledge of the recommendations the president made to the regents. In one instance, however, the faculty itself took the initiative in recommending the establishment of a chair of Norse studies. Sometimes the board turned down Bascom's recommendations for new professors or for promotions; in at least one case the refusal rested on the man's commitment to Prohibition. Permission to leave the campus, even for such an errand as an official inspection of a nearby normal school, had to be secured from the executive committee of the regents. Nor were faculty permitted, without the board's permission, to supplement what they regarded as inadequate salaries by outside earnings. The regents also continued to approve courses, textbooks, and degrees. Against President Bascom's protests, the regents had the last word in cases of discipline of individual students. It was also risky for a professor to venture opinions on controversial matters: John Freeman, a popular professor of English, was reprimanded by the regents for expressing, on a postcard, a critical opinion of a decision of the Michigan Supreme Court. Yet despite the many restrictions on faculty freedom, they never protested. Only on the matter of salaries did they express criticisim of the regents, and here they were in complete accord with President Bascom.

Carl Schurz's opinion, expressed in 1858, that the University could be compared with a German gymnasium, certainly had no validity in the 1870s and 1880s. In answering criticisms President Bascom was on sound ground in holding that in the humanities the University had no rival among Wisconsin's denominational colleges, and that in the sciences it was well ahead of them. By 1887, when Bascom resigned, the faculty included several men of scholarly and scientific distinction. This was largely the consequence of the appointments Bascom recommended and of his insistence on the need for specialization in order that each professor might be a master of his subject. If John Sterling represented the passing order in scholarship, the new men were well trained and thoroughly abreast of recent developments in their fields. Bascom himself would have lent distinction to instruction in philosophy and psychology in any institution. Several men in the humanities contributed papers, edited texts, and produced books that brought them national recognition. William F. Allen, whom Chadbourne appointed, was a man of broad culture, as his reviews of several hundreds of books for *The Nation* prove, and of first-rate scholarship in Latin and Roman history. John B. Feuling was one of the country's ablest scholars in German and comparative philology. Alexander Kerr was favorably known for his translations of the *Bacchae* of Euripides and, late in life, of Plato's *Republic*. Stephen H. Carpenter's *English in the Fourteenth Century* went through several editions. While not the modern type of linguistic scholar, Rasmus B. Anderson, founder of the first American department of Scandinavian studies, won praise from Longfellow and other authorities for his *Norse Mythology*. While unknown for any publications, other men were thorough scholars and in some cases great teachers.

In the sciences excellent men supplemented the outstanding appointments of Chadbourne — William W. Daniels in chemistry and agriculture, John Davies in physics, and Roland Irving in geology. The new men included Charles A. Van Velzer, a good example of the new approach in mathematics, Frederick Power in the new School of Pharmacy, James Watson, a leading astronomer who headed the Observatory given by C. C. Washburn, the first notable private gift to the University, and his successor, Edward Holden. The Observatory and the new Science Hall provided facilities for scientific work that compared well with those in any Middle Western university.

It was inevitable that Bascom's intellectual position, so much in advance of his Wisconsin constituency as far as modern thought went, would invite conflict with orthodox religion, the business community, and professional politicians. Convinced that the Board of Regents was dominated by businessmen and politicians with little understanding of University problems, Bascom on more than one occasion tried to persuade governors to change the composition of the governing body. He thus ran into trouble with two of the most powerful regents, Napoleon Van Slyk, a leading banker and businessman, and Elisha Keyes, a former colonel, postmaster, mayor of Madison, and "boss" of Wisconsin's Republican party. To Bascom, Keyes was the epitome of pretense and sham, "unscrupulous in small things, prodigal in large things, and negligent and dilatory in all things."[8] Keyes, on his side, could not tolerate Bascom's open activities in the Prohibition party and efforts to purge politics of corruption. Though Keyes was entrusted by the regents with what was virtually the business management of the University, the "Boss" and the president were barely on speaking terms.

But the conflict between President Bascom and the regents was also related to the differing views each held about the functions and rights of regents and presidents. While admitting the ultimate legal authority of the board, Bascom felt that the president, as a specialist in education intimately familiar with the day-by-day events and problems on the campus, should have the upper hand both in the appointment, promotion, and dismissal of faculty and in student discipline, and, under some circumstances, even in the business affairs of the institution. Convinced that Keyes was managing things inefficiently, at times dishonestly, and without regard for economy, Bascom insisted on his own obligation to see that in this sphere the interest of the University was fully protected.

Keyes fairly early decided that Bascom must be replaced by someone more amenable to the authority of the regents, someone, too, who did not try to purify politics, take part in partisan causes, and endeavor to elevate the moral tone of the community. While appreciating Bascom's scholarship and contributions to the University, other regents disapproved of his role in the Prohibition party. Somewhat weary of the struggle Bascom decided to resign, but not at the time and under the terms Keyes tried to impose. Luckily for him his successor was unable to take up the presidency immediately. When Bascom left in 1887 students, alumni, and many citizens expressed deep regret. On his part, the president, in a farewell message to the people of Wisconsin, bluntly declared, "I leave the University of Wisconsin simply because I have had no sufficient liberty in doing my work." In another vein, he beseeched for the University "a generous method and a large spirit, on the part of the faculty who order it, on the part of its governing board, and on the part of the people of the state."[9]

THE increasing economic development of the state, the growing need for specialized training and skills related to this development, new educational currents and tendencies in the nation itself, and the remarkable leadership of President Thomas Chamberlin and President Charles Kendall Adams largely explain the fact that at no time was change as rapid and far-reaching as in the years between the end of Bascom's administration and the inauguration of Charles Van Hise in 1903. From what in 1887 was essentially a small liberal arts college with deviations from the traditional model and with somewhat feeble gestures toward professional education, the institution had taken its place as one of the two or three leading state universities; it was, moreover, well on the way to being recognized as one of the nation's most important universities.

The change was evident in many spheres. The old unity of the institution that had survived many trials gave way to the establishment of separate faculties of Letters and Science, to the continuing importance of which the new presidents and, above all, Dean Edward Birge contributed; Law; Engineering, with increasing specialization and larger enrollments; and Agriculture, in which development was perhaps most striking of all. Each college had not only its own faculty but its own dean. The period also saw the development of the special departments of Pharmacy, Education, Extension, and the premedical course. The scope and importance of the overall change was also evident in the expansion of the physical plant, with new buildings for Law, Engineering, and Agriculture and with an armory and gymnasium and a new home for the library. The scope and meaning of the changes were also documented in the increase in financial resources and the related expansion of a faculty of 35, not counting part-time Law School staff, to a total of all levels of instructional staff of 125 in 1903.

Enrollment of students grew from 539 in 1886-1887 to 2,422 in the academic year 1899-1900 and to approximately 3,000 when Van Hise took office. The geographical spread of students was wider than ever before. While many students were in part, and a few entirely, self-supporting, a considerable proportion of the 56 percent whose fathers were business or professional men were able to indulge in what critics regarded as extravagant, formal, and even exclusive social affairs. After 1885 the dormitory system, except for Ladies Hall, was discontinued, and students lived in the increasing number of fraternity houses or in boarding and rooming houses relatively free from University supervision. The effort made in the late 1880s to outlaw hazing succeeded only in part. Raucous student pranks sometimes occasioned tilts with the police and even encounters with the courts, and critics believed that drinking and even worse misdemeanors characterized the conduct of too many male students. If the more serious moral and social tone President Bascom encouraged was somewhat relaxed as social life became more sophisticated and organized athletics more pronounced, serious students found opportunities for intellectual growth in the somewhat languishing literary and debating societies, in student journalism — represented by the *Daily Cardinal,* which was established in 1892 — and in literary publications, as well as in the classes of popular and stimulating teachers. Besides, the new importance of the professional schools and the presence of an increasing number of graduate students heightened a university atmosphere.

By 1887 the state had come to accept responsibility for contributing financial support to the institution; the annual receipts of the University, derived from the University Fund, the Land Grant Agricultural Fund, the federal government's allocations, student fees, and the state added up to almost $227,000. The state's contribution represented more than half of the total. In the years that followed two additional mill taxes, fees from railroad licenses, the sale of the University's farm and dairy products, and private gifts increased the resources of the University. In 1903 its income reached $675,000, with the contributions of the state well over 70 percent. As a result, the regents and state officials could claim that the University was being more generously supported than any of the comparable institutions in nearby states. Several factors explain its mounting prosperity. The activities of several regents, the development of a University lobby, and the persuasiveness of President Chamberlin and President Adams in presenting the needs and the services of the institution, were all influential. The increased support of the state, however, was accompaied by the Legislature's appropriations of specific sums for the several parts of the University and for particular purposes. The institution of a centralized state system of accounting further restricted the freedom of the regents.

In the interest of lessening the burdens of the faculty several innovations marked further changes. New administrative offices, deans, a registrar, and a secretary of the faculty were functioning in the 1890s. Even more important was the rapid growth of the committee system — committees on each general course, on rules for admission and advanced standing, on the accreditation of high schools, and many others.

In some respects the role of the faculty was an assenting rather than a policy-creating one. The regents determined the salary for each professorship, and President Adams held that a faculty member was not entitled to criticize the regents or president in matters affecting his status. Nor was there any clear understanding about the number of hours a professor was expected to teach.

Yet the tradition of faculty freedom, which Bascom encouraged, at least in words, was not lost. To maintain a good measure of faculty control over instruction in the face of too large a faculty to permit meaningful discussion, Adams proposed in 1898 that in addition to a general University faculty, special faculties be organized for the several colleges. After deliberation, the faculty accepted the plan. On another occasion, when the Legislature was considering a bill to remove the president from the Board of Regents, the faculty vigorously dissented. Moreover, when President Adams failed to enforce faculty rules for the eligibility of athletics, the faculty protested and had its way.

Nor did the regents interfere with the internal affairs of the University as often as they had once done. When President Adams was asked to look into student complaints about the teaching of Professor Rosenstengel, the regents accepted his report that the professor's methods were well suited to bright and diligent students.

The only serious threat to academic freedom took place in 1894 when State School Superintendent, Oliver E. Wells, an ex-officio member of the board, publicly charged Professor Richard Ely, a nationally known economist and leading member of the faculty, with believing in strikes and boycotts, in justifying the one while employing the other, and in teaching, both in his books and classroom, pernicious socialist and anarchist doctrines. Though President Adams assured him of his support, Ely understandably, in view of the atmosphere of the day, feared for his position. He decided, however, against a libel suit. A committee of the regents undertook to investigate the truth of the charges, which Ely denied in stating that he had become more conservative than he had been when, at the Johns Hopkins University, he had written *Socialism and Reform* and that his position was explicitly antianarchist. Thus Ely did not take his stand on his right to teach whatever kind of economics he believed, in his special competence, to be true. The committee found Ely not guilty of aiding in a local printers' strike or in boycotting the firm for using nonunion labor.

The affair attracted nation-wide attention. John M. Olin, who had been denied promotion and tenure in the Law School because of his Prohibionist activities, suggested to the committee that it might well go beyond exonerating Ely and indicate support for an instructor's right to teach what he believed to be the truth about the great living issues of the day. The committee agreed. President Adams probably wrote the part of the report dealing with academic freedom. This stated that the regents could not presume to recommend the dismissal or the criticism of a professor even if, in some quarters, his views were regarded as visionary. Such a course would be equal to saying that no professor should teach anything that is not accepted by everybody as true. "In all lines of academic investigation it is of the utmost importance that the investigator should be absolutely free to follow the indications of truth wherever they may lead. Whatever may be the limitations which trammel inquiry elsewhere we believe that the great state University of Wisconsin should ever encourage that continual and fearless sifting and winnowing by which alone the truth can be found."[10] The regents censured Wells and adopted the committee's report in full. This bold and eloquent defense of academic freedom was an important event not only in the process by which Wisconsin became a great university but in the general history of academic freedom in America.

The two presidents who served the University from 1887 to 1903 had a good deal to do with guiding and in some cases instituting all these changes. Thomas Chamberlin (1887-1892), a graduate of Beloit College and well known as the chief of the Wisconsin Geological Survey, was, in his forty-fifth year, a distinguished scientist and, as director of the glacial division of the United States Geological Survey, one of the nation's leading geologists. He also was a man of originality and force, catholic in his intellectual interests and a major force in creating the modern University. When he left to head the Geology Department at Chicago, the regents chose Charles Kendall Adams as president (1892-1902). A leading historian who had introduced the seminar method at the University of Michigan, Adams had a rich if not entirely happy administrative experience as president of Cornell. The regents, good businessmen and politicians able to get appropriations from both the Republican and Democratic parties in the Legislature, had confidence in and worked well with both presidents. A contributing factor was Chamberlin's insistence, before taking the office, in having clarified the functions of both regents and president, in the hope of avoiding the troubles that had plagued Bascom.

Chamberlin's main contributions were to emphasize the University's obligation to encourage the advancement of knowledge through research and to demonstrate its value to the people of the state. A pragmatist in judging principles and policies by their results, Chamberlin insisted that a state university must train students not merely for their own satisfaction and profit but for the community's good. Here at last was the "practical" man for whom the governors of the University had so often searched. But he was no narrow utilitarian. His broad interest in the whole range of knowledge was soundly anchored to the proposition that education must provide the data for the study of civilization in all its aspects.

To implement his conception of the role and function of the University, Chamberlin, in addition to reorganizing the institution into the College of Letters and Science, Law, Agriculture, and Engineering, introduced something like general education in the first two years of the undergraduate curriculum and a specialized major and related minor field in the last two years. What had been a loose ad hoc compromise with the elective system that Harvard had initiated was now systematized and made explicit. Moreover, undergraduate instruction on its upper level was to instill competence in the techniques of investigation in each field and thus prepare students for graduate work. To encourage graduate study and research Chamberlin persuaded the regents to establish eight fellowships — a step that none of the state universities had yet taken. He also insisted on the Ph.D. as the necessary qualification for promotion of the younger faculty. Drawing heavily from the Johns Hopkins University, the country's leading graduate institution, the twenty-two professors Chamberlin appointed or promoted included Frederick Jackson Turner, who succeeded his Wisconsin teacher, William F. Allen, on his death in 1889, Charles Homer Haskins, a promising young medievalist, Joseph Jastrow, who established in Madison one of the first psychological laboratories in the middle west, and Richard T. Ely, a leading economist who headed the newly organized School of Economics, Political Science, and History. William A. Scott and others augmented the staff of the school. It attracted able students, many of whom were to become leaders in their field. It became the leading center in the Midwest and one of the two such leading centers in the whole country for training men for public service and for illuminating social, economic, and political problems by ad hoc research, the results of which were published in bulletins.

President Chamberlin also gave strong support to professional education in other fields, the time for which was now ripe. Under his auspices the premedical course, based on solid instruction, was established. In 1889 the Law Department was renamed the College of Law, with a lengthened and more substantial curriculum, a full-time dean, and more adequate funds. The Agricultural College had survived efforts to remove it from the University and to make it a separate institution. Under the able, energetic, and devoted William A. Henry, named to a professorship in 1880, it began to profit from the farmers' institutes and the Short Course, the first experiment of its kind. The establishment of the Experiment Station, supported with federal funds, stimulated a research program. Though the foundation was thus laid for developing a farm constituency and for fruitful research, the Agricultural College enrolled only an occasional full-time student and had by no means won full support from the agricultural interests of the state. Chamberlin contributed to the broadening of research, established a pioneer Department of Soil Physics, and helped to set up the dairy course, the first of its kind in the country. In 1890 Stephen Babcock, professor of agricultural chemistry, announced the invention of a swift and accurate device to determine the butterfat content of milk. His refusal to patent the device, immensely useful to dairy farmers, paid off in the increased fame of the college. In 1893 Regent John Johnston summed up the achievements of the College of Agriculture and the Experiment Station:

"There is not a county in Wisconsin which is not richer because of the university. The cheese of Sheboygan, the butter of Rock, the tobacco of Dane, the sheep of Walworth, the horses and cattle of Racine and Kenosha, and the potatoes of Waupaca are all better because of our University."

For the College of Engineering Chamberlin also won better support. Departments of Electrical and Railroad Engineering were established, research was encouraged, and a short-term course for mechanics was launched. Though this did not turn out well, the gesture indicated the sincerity of the University in proclaiming the idea of service to all walks of life. And, to quote Regent Johnston again, "the existence of those men who dig in the sunless mines of Gogebic has been made comparatively comfortable and safe through the discoveries of science."[11]

All these things did a good deal to actualize the long talked about idea that the University was of practical service to the people of the state. In addition, Chamberlin inaugurated the summer school for teachers and University Extension, which sponsored lectures in both practical and cultural subjects in various parts of the state.

President Charles Kendall Adams, who succeeded Chamberlin when he left to head the Geology Department at Chicago in 1892, differed in many ways from his predecessor, notably in the greater popularity he enjoyed with students and in his championship of organized, competitive athletics. Yet he also built on the foundations Chamberlin had laid for a great university. This was evident in his success in getting funds for increasing salaries of the faculty, in suggesting ways for raising academic standards for students — including the requirement of a thesis for candidates for the bachelor's degree — in establishing the School of Music in 1894 and the School of Commerce in 1900, and, above all, in keeping distinguished scholars when attractive invitations came to them from elsewhere and in appointing a number of research scholars well abreast of new developments in their fields. Any list of these scholars, however abbreviated, would have to include the men Adams brought to strengthen the faltering interest in the classics—Charles Forster Smith, whose translation of Thuycidides was accurate and readable and who was later elected president of the American Philological Association; Arthur Laird in Greek and comparative philology; Moses Slaughter; and, for unfortunately brief stays, Charles E. Bennett and Herbert Tollman. Modern languages were also strengthened by the appointment of Julius Olson in the Scandinavian field, William Giese in Romance studies, and, notably, Alexander R. Hohlfeld and his lieutenants, who gave Wisconsin leadership in German philological and literary scholarship. John Freeman, who had become a professor in Bascom's time, pioneered in the study of American literature, and what was probably the first doctorate in this field was awarded to William Cairns. The journalism course made Wisconsin one of the pioneers in this branch of English. Philosophy, though brilliantly taught by John Stearns, who was also professor of pedagogy, did not hold the place that it had when Bascom taught it, but the appointment of German-trained Frank Sharp in 1894 marked a trend toward the American emphasis on a down-to-earth philosophy.

President Adams gave full support to the School of Economics, Political Science, and History. Its staff undertook studies closely related to Wisconsin problems and, without approaching the leadership Columbia and Chicago had in sociology, it was well in advance of many institutions in recognizing its importance and in bringing as special lecturers leaders in the field and its applications. History, with Turner as its leader, and, after Haskins left for Harvard, with Dana Munro and George Sellery as medievalists, and, later still, Carl Russell Fish and Ulrich B. Phillips, was thought by many to be the leading center in the country. Many of its graduate students were to become nationally known scholars.

The strength of the social sciences and the humanities depended on library resources as well as on men. In comparison not only with eastern institutions but even with neighboring states, Wisconsin was lamentably deficient in both books and periodicals and in facilities for their use. President Adams determined to remedy this situation insofar as possible. He solicited increased appropriations and gifts. The most notable achievement was the construction of the handsome classical-style building which housed both the University Library and the splendid collections of the State Historical Society.

Though favoring the social sciences and humanities, President Adams also recognized the importance of maintaining Wisconsin's reputation in the natural sciences. Charles Van Hise, with an enviable record as chief of the Wisconsin section of the United States Geological Survey, was the first professor to hold a Wisconsin doctorate. Charles Slichter began his long career as a distinguished mathematician and, later, dean of the Graduate School. Benjamin Snow, an unusually gifted lecturer, brought prestige to physics as Charles R. Barnes and Robert A. Harper did to botany and William S. Marshall to entomology. William Snow Miller supplemented Birge's work in the premedical course.

When another effort was made in 1895-1897 to sever the Agricultural College and convert it into a separate entity, President Adams and Dean Henry defeated the move. New men and new researches added to the prestige of the college. With Harry C. Russell in charge, Agricultural Bacteriology was established at the end of Adams' first year, while the famous Wisconsin Curd Test for bacterial count was publicized in 1896. Professorships in Horticulture, Animal Husbandry, and Practical Dairying were established. Knowledge of important work in soils, fertilizers, pest and blight control, and improved varieties of grains and grass was disseminated in the bulletins that now reached large numbers of farmers.

In the autumn of 1901 President and Mrs. Adams, seeking health, left Wisconsin for California, with Dean Birge taking charge of the University. The devotion of the Adamses to the institution was again proved when they willed their library and entire estate to it for the establishment of fellowships in English, Greek, and modern history. There could be no question that, in the decade in which Adams was president, he had contributed, through his gift for public relations, for promoting scholarship, and for institutionalizing academic freedom, much that was important and necessary for the future course of the University.

IN choosing the fiftieth anniversary of the graduation of Wisconsin's first class for the five-day celebration of the University's Jubilee, the faculty, which organized the affair and solicited voluntary contributions for its support, seemed determined to rectify Bascom's judgment that no institution of its grade was so little known to the people of the state and to the outside world. Seventy-nine universities in the United States, Canada, and Europe sent representatives, as did more than a dozen learned societies. Though President Bascom was unable to attend the Jubilee, his address was read; President Chamberlin gave his in person; these and other addresses by leaders from the University world made the Jubilee a major event in the history of American higher education. Receptions, banquets, academic processions, and other festivities lent color to the occasion, which was well publicized in the state and the nation.

The inaugural address of the new president, Charles Van Hise, was of special significance, both because he was a product of the University and the first alumnus to become its head. Already widely recognized for his pioneer work in microscopic minerology and in structural and historical geology, Van Hise knew at first hand the wilderness of northern Wisconsin and Michigan, which he deeply revered and loved. This was reflected in the freshness and vigor of his address and in its commitment to the democratic principle, to the idea of progress through education and the utilitarian application of science to the widening benefits of civilization. In all this he was a true son of pioneer and post-pioneer Wisconsin, and a pioneer himself in his appreciation of the contributions of the many ethnic groups that made so considerable a part of the state's population. His address boldly built on the leading ideas of his predecessors, on Bascom's belief in the obligations of a state university to serve the social and spiritual well being of all citizens, on Chamberlin's dogged faith in the duty of the University to increase knowledge through original research and to strengthen the professional schools, and in Adams' conviction of a great future for the University as a leader in both higher education and in service to the people. Nor was it a new idea when Van Hise declared "I am unwilling to admit that a state university under a democracy shall be of a lower grade than a state university under a monarchy."[12] The University, as he conceived it, was one and indivisible with the state. The hope for democracy and for the University was inextricably bound up with the mutual and reciprocal contributions of each to the other. In these terms Van Hise projected the progress and well-being of each. To insure this future the people must understand the functions of the University and it in turn must understand and serve the true interests of the people of the state, and, indeed, of the nation and the world itself. It was no accident that the motto on the seal of the Jubilee, the most important event thus far in publicizing these interrelations, was "service to the commonwealth." Nor did Van Hise share the fears of those who felt that the emphasis on the utilitarian and practical applications of research endangered the liberal arts tradition: new constituencies were being added to the University; its boundaries were to become those of the state itself.

In the tasks thus set forth Van Hise was to be aided by able and efficient co-workers in the faculty, in the Board of Regents, and among the public officials of the state. He was of course also to derive support from the steady economic growth and prosperity of the state's agriculture, commerce, and industry. But he was also to meet opposition. His allies and his critics drew strength from the distinctive characteristics that colored the life of the state and, in some degree, the nation itself in the early decades of the twentieth century.

This development was, of course, the rise and fortunes of the so-called Progressive movement. The interplay of this with the state's prosperity, with Van Hise as the mediator and, in a true sense, as far as the University went, the leader, explains in large part the material progress of the institution in these years. The area of landed property was doubled; the new buildings, with equipment, represented an outlay of almost $3,000,000; the total income, derived in considerable part from the mill tax which was restored in 1906 and by legislative appropriations, quadrupled: in 1903 it totaled $427,000, in 1918, $1,600,000. In 1910 the state's contribution amounted to three-quarters of the total University budget; by 1920 it was little more than half. In other words, the proportion of the University's budget met by state taxes decreased. In the regular college year, student enrollment doubled; the faculty jumped from 184 in 1902-1903 to 751 when the United States entered the First World War in 1917; and in this span, 219 higher degrees were granted. The College of Agriculture and the revived Extension flourished. The premedical course came into its own. Existing departments were strengthened and new ones added. In the words of Dean Edward A. Birge of the College of Letters and Science, this was, indeed, a "noteworthy record of rapid progress." Moreover, all this expansion, Birge added, was accompanied by "the development into fact of the University spirit and of University method."

It is by no means certain that the mere economic growth and prosperity of the state would in itself have insured such developments within the University. It is, however, certain that the character and reputation of the University would not have been what it was without the Progressive movement which, while provoking much opposition, nevertheless put the state and its Progressive leader, Robert M. La Follette, in the vanguard of the national Progressive movement.

The Progressive movement in Wisconsin was a revolt against the alliance of corporate wealth with machine politics in an effort to spread more widely the material benefits of modern civilization. The progressive aimed to develop the powers of the state government sufficiently to control great business organizations in the public interest, to preserve the remaining natural resources of the state subject to an orderly and nondestructive development by private enterprise, and to distribute the burden of taxation in such a way that corporate wealth would have to support both the state agencies which controlled it and, in good measure, the expanded social services designed to bring a larger measure of advantages to the public. This program greatly influenced the University. Since the Progressive program favored greater support for public institutions, the University could expect to profit from such largesse. Moreover, since fact-finding, legislative blueprints, and the regulatory commissions established to achieve the Progressive objectives needed trained experts, it was

natural to turn to the University for such services. President Van Hise and
Dean Birge served on several such agencies, and by 1908 forty-one professors were giving some of their time to the Railway Rate Commission, the
Tax Commission, the Industrial Commission, and other agencies. In
addition to such services and the administration of the University, President Van Hise also, in writing *The Conservation of Natural Resources*
(1910) and *Concentration and Control* (1912), won the praise of national
authorities and public leaders, including President Theodore Roosevelt.

The association of the University with the Progressive movement owed
much to the role of Robert La Follette, a friend and classmate of Van
Hise, and to Frederick Jackson Turner, a neighbor and close associate.
Van Hise, to be sure, had been impressed by Bascom's doctrine of the
obligation of the University to improve the moral and civic tone of the
community, but La Follette and Turner helped him to understand more
clearly the economic basis of politics and the need for positive measures
and action to implement Bascom's ideal. But Van Hise's leadership in
developing the internal relation between the University and the Progressive movement also owed a great deal to his own insight and characteristics, which Professor J. F. A. Pyre identified as largeness, energy, and
definiteness. Largeness enabled him to have faith in boundless progress,
to see the whole; energy enabled him to accomplish what must have
seemed to many superhuman tasks and to expect on the part of others
untiring and efficient effort; definiteness proved to be a useful tool in
presenting facts and figures in persuading regents and legislatures to meet
the needs of the University. All these traits in turn were related to his
practical idealism, that is, to his faith that if the people were enlightened,
they would see the identity between their own and the public interest,
including the needs and services of the University. Practical idealism also
meant that if compromises were now and then necessary in the interest of
expediency, the larger vision would re-emerge without permanent detri-
ment and even, perhaps, stronger than ever. All these characteristics
stood Van Hise in good stead in the mission he had undertaken.

The role of the University in the Progressive movement was widely,
perhaps too widely, publicized, since Stalwarts, as Republican opponents
of the Progressives were called, had a great deal of influence among
regents, in the legislatures, and in the general population. A news
bulletin brought the activities of the University to the state and even the
national press. The agricultural exhibits at the St. Louis Exposition in
1903 won applause. Delegations from many cities, states, and foreign
countries came to see the University at first hand to take home such
lessons as seemed applicable. Especially impressive was the way in which
the renewed and expanded University Extension was actualizing President

Van Hise's belief in the discovery and conservation of human talent, exemplified in his statement, "I shall never rest content until the beneficient influences of the University are made available to every home in the state. . . . A university supported by the state for all its people, for all its sons and daughters, with their tastes and aptitudes as varied as mankind, can place no bounds upon the lines of its endeavor, else the state is the irreparable loser."[13] Articles in widely read periodicals extended the reputation of the University beyond the reports of its visitors. Lincoln Steffens, prince of the "muckrakers," celebrated the University as an implement of democracy and social welfare. Frederick C. Howe's *Wisconsin, An Experiment in Democracy* and Dr. Charles McCarthy's *The Wisconsin Idea,* with an introduction by Theodore Roosevelt, stressed the role of the University in disseminating useful knowledge and in providing the state with experts in effecting reform legislation. Some of the publicity was extravagant in its praise and misleading in failing to note opposition to the Progressive measures and the part of the University in them. President Van Hise, however, generally welcomed the publicity which pictured Wisconsin as the leading state university if not even the most important institution of higher education in the whole country.

Opposition within the state, particularly in conservative business circles and in many newspapers, charged that the University was deep in politics rather than in service, that professors were neglecting their duties as teachers, that too many out-of-state students were not paying sufficient tuition to cover the cost of their education, and that University expenditures were extravagant. Nor did everyone accept President Van Hise's facts and figures designed to show that the University yielded more in economic benefit to the state than the expenditures bestowed on it. Undaunted, Van Hise sought to strengthen the University among legislators, newspaper editors, and alumni. In the belief that people would support his conception of the University if they understood the facts, he refuted critics by pointing out that expenditures by no means all came from tax money. He welcomed legislative investigations, which for the most part gave a fairly clean bill of health. He even felt that the harshly critical report of Dr. William H. Allen, instituted by the Board of Public Affairs, and convincingly refuted by Dean Birge and Professor Sellery, could not do the institution any real harm in the long run.

Even with the defeat of the Progressives in 1914 and the conservative state government that came into power, known to be critical of the University, Van Hise did not despair. Though appropriations tapered off in relation to what they had been, Governor Emanuel Philipp in the end was converted to a favorable view of the University.

Van Hise was severely tested in his relations with the splintered Progressives and the divided opinion in the state when the First World War broke out in 1914. He was sensitive to the deep rooted isolationism in the Middle West and to the pro-German sentiments of a considerable section of the state's German-American population. Following President Woodrow Wilson's initial appeal for neutrality, Van Hise asked the faculty not to discuss controversial issues relating to the war either in class or in public. Regent James Trottman reminded him that such an admonition was a violation of academic freedom. As the country veered toward "preparedness" and entry into the struggle, Van Hise supported faculty and students in expressing their patriotism in words and deeds and vigorously refuted the allegations that the University was derelict in its national obligations. Moreover, he joined the great majority of the faculty in taking Senator La Follette to task for his opposition to the war—an action that deeply wounded his old friend. Van Hise's conviction that America must take a leading role in an international organization for peace-keeping still further separated the two men.

Sensitive to the fact that power rested in the regents, Van Hise sought to educate the board in his conception of higher education. Though he was sometimes stymied, he succeeded on the whole fairly well as new men, less familiar with the institution, replaced such staunch and generous regents as William Vilas. At the same time Van Hise's awareness of the occasional need of expediency sometimes affected his relations with those members of the faculty who had incurred the disfavor of influential members of the board.

In his relations with the faculty Van Hise, though sometimes socially inept, succeeded on the whole in realizing his conception of his role as a leader among equals, a leader obligated to improve scholarly standards, productive research, and close ties with the people of the state. He invited discussions of educational policy and recognized the importance of faculty committees, however inefficient these seemed to him. On one occasion, when he felt his lack of sympathy with a faculty report might militate against a fair presentation to the regents, he asked a faculty member to make the presentation. He accepted department recommendations for promotions and for new appointments. Van Hise also mediated in quarrels between professors. When a bitter controversy developed between students and alumni on the one hand and a majority of the faculty on the other over regulations affecting interuniversity athletics, his mediating role, which in fact was partly delegated, was accompanied by a measure of expediency. In defending academic standards and the interest of the faculty, President Van Hise was, if not always completely dedicated to the democratic principle, courageous and sincere. Thus he used his influence to defeat a movement to consolidate the University and the normal schools on the ground that this would militate against academic standards on the Madison campus. He also urged the importance of larger faculty salaries both in the interest of meeting rising living costs and attracting and keeping outstanding scholars. When the Carnegie Pension Fund was established Van Hise persuaded its directors to include state universities and the regents to meet the criteria necessary for admitting the University to this important plan for the economic security of professors.

If in some minds Van Hise set a higher value on productive research than on teaching, he insisted that the best teaching was done by scholars actively engaged in enlarging the boundaries of their fields. If others felt that he stressed the sciences and vocational and professional subjects at the expense of liberal culture, Van Hise maintained that each could enrich the other. He regretted, moreover, the failure to establish a Department of Fine Arts. He tried, without success, to convince the regents and legislatures of the need for reestablishing men's dormitories and of instituting a commons and a Union, as adjuncts to the more graceful aspects of life.

Van Hise's record on academic freedom reflected a sincere belief in its importance as a means of extending the boundaries of knowledge. When Max Otto was attacked by conservative religious groups for the naturalistic principles that informed his course, "Man and Nature," Van Hise, in his Commencement address of 1912, declared that a university as an institution would be destroyed if those who believed that "existing conventions, morals, and political and religious faiths are fixed" were able to keep professors from presenting opinions with humility and "the realization that ultimate truth has nowhere been reached, that the advance of tomorrow may modify the statement of today."[14] But as a practical idealist, Van Hise also believed in the expediency of compromise and in circumspection on the part of "controversial" members of the faculty. This seemed to him necessary at times of public clamor about the "radicalism" of the University unless its financial support be curtailed. Thus he lent himself in support of the regents' censure of Edward A. Ross for two so-called indiscretions. One was the announcement in class of a public lecture by the anarchist, Emma Goldman, and in showing her about the campus when she called on him at his office. The other involved having a Progressive educator from Chicago address his class without first receiving permission from the lecture committee. Van Hise also played a somewhat less than forthright role in mediating between the regents and the Class of 1912 when it sought to present, as its class gift, a plaque on which was inscribed the great statement of the regents at the time of Ely's trial in 1894. The president also rejected out of hand the proposal of the newly organized American Association of University Professors for handling cases of dismissal or threatened dismissal of a professor. In 1917 Van Hise also forbade the use of a University hall for a lecture on socialism by Max Eastman, on the ground that such a refusal was made in the case of suffragettes and Christian Scientists.

If liberals, Progressives, and Socialists felt that, after the Stalwart victory in 1914, Van Hise veered too often in a conservative direction, it should not have been forgotten that even before this he followed a somewhat cautious course when he felt the large interests of the University were at stake. In 1910 a good deal of dissatisfaction was expressed in the faculty about the interference by the regents in the educational procedures of the University. These included making promotions and salary adjustments without the recommendations of the departments or the president; an undue concern over the teaching hours of the staff; the belittling of research in all subjects except those clearly practical; uncertainty about tenure; a tendency to interfere with academic freedom; and continued criticism of an agreed-upon arrangement by which Professor Turner had been given every other semester for research. The decision of Turner to accept an invitation from Harvard was the immediate occasion for an airing of these complaints at a meeting of regents, selected faculty members, the several deans, and Van Hise. Though the president said little, his moral influence was on the side of the faculty. The regents specified that the acts complained about were clearly within their legal rights, but indicated that they had no intention of interfering with customary methods of educational administration by the faculty, that they would continue to allow the faculty the initiative in formulating educational policies, and that they desired appointments to be made through the regular channels as developed by the University. Just where the victory lay was an open question; but the caution of the president in the matters relating to academic freedom, already referred to, suggest that in his mind the ideals of academic democracy and academic freedom were not without limitations.

Committed to the practical and professional functions of the University, Van Hise supported the deans of the Engineering, Law, and Agricultural colleges in their efforts to expand and improve their offerings and to reach the people of the state in as effective ways as possible.

The College of Engineering, which depended on Letters and Science for instruction of its students in mathematics and the basic sciences, had, by the beginning of Van Hise's administration, established a reputation for original research in several fields, contributions being reported, in the main, in the *Wisconsin Engineer*. To be sure, its chief task was to provide instruction for a constantly growing enrollment. John B. Johnson, the first dean, began his administration in 1899 and proved to be energetic and ambitious, with an interest in the bearings of the new technology on his profession. After his untimely death three years later, Professor Frederick Turneaure took over the deanship. Neither the plan to conduct summer courses for artisans nor President Van Hise's hope that two years of liberal study might become the prerequisite for admission to the college, materialized. Nor was a program of research worked out comparable to that in agriculture. Important work was done, however, in electrical and chemical engineering and in mining and metallurgy. In providing information, technical advice to state agencies, and services to the public, the college exemplified the idea of usefulness to the state.

The Law School, of which Henry S. Richard, who had been trained at Harvard, became dean in 1903, moved toward complete integration with the rest of the University. The full-time faculty proved hard to keep intact as able men accepted calls to better paying institutions. In adopting the Harvard case system of instruction Wisconsin was a pioneer among Middle Western law schools, as it was in requiring two years of college work for entrance. In 1914 Wisconsin again set a new course in requiring a six-month apprenticeship in a law office as a requirement for the degree. Though the primary work of the Law School was instruction, some members of the staff contributed original articles to the professional press. There was also a response on the part of some of the faculty to the Wisconsin Idea. Professor Eugene Gilmore prepared a report on riparian law and the preservation of Wisconsin's water sites, a report which, undertaken at the request of the Wisconsin Conservation Commission, aroused a good deal of hostility in the business community. The Law School, in undertaking work in comparative law and in the relation of law to modern social and industrial problems, also demonstrated a responsiveness to the doctrine that the University must serve the public interest.

Under the energetic leadership of Dean Henry the gospel of scientific farming was carried, through the short course and Extension, to every corner of Wisconsin. Considerable success met the skillful lobbying for legislative support, particularly when it was evident that the compromise between empirical observation and fundamental research yielded fruitful results. This was notably true of the work in feeding and dairying, including the application of bacterial operations to cheese-making, milk pasteurization, and tubercular testing. When Harry Russell became dean in 1907, the older disciplines, agricultural chemistry, physics, and agronomy were well established as academic disciplines, and the newer fields, soil bacteriology, plant pathology, agricultural genetics, and nutritional studies were proving to be significant. Building on the nutritional studies that Stephen Babcock had begun in the 1890s, E. V. McCullom, Harry Steenbock, Edwin B. Hart, and other young men launched experimental work which, with that being done in other institutions, proved to be revolutionary. Steenbock's discovery of a process for recovering vitamin A in its pure form and the creation of vitamin D in foods by irradiation with ultraviolet light raised many problems. In the end, Steenbock's proposal for the establishment of a trust to take over the patent led to the organization, in 1925, of the Wisconsin Alumni Research Foundation. By far the largest part of revenues went to the foundation, which allocated them to a research committee in the University for the further support of basic research.

The development within the College of Agriculture of the home economics course, of agricultural economics, agricultural sociology, and agricultural journalism reflected the trend toward increasing specialization and professionalization. Though Van Hise, some regents, and Dean Birge at first favored keeping within the College of Letters and Science the basic sciences from which the College of Agriculture was to build, Dean Russell in the main succeeded in retaining and expanding these in his own college. Thus the College of Agriculture contributed substantially to proving Van Hise's thesis that fundamental research and application each enriched the other and served effectively to improve qualitatively and quantitatively the University's service to the people.

The solid beginnings of premedical work were expanded and enriched before the First World War. President Van Hise at once re-recommended the appointment of a professor of anatomy and in 1904 Dr. Charles R. Bardeen began his work. Due to him, more than to anyone else, the steady development of the medical sciences was pushed forward. Preclinical work was begun in 1907 when Dr. Harold Bradley initiated instruction to physiology and physiological chemistry, to be joined a bit later by Charles Bunting in pathology, Mazyik Ravennel, director of the State Hygienic Laboratory, in bacteriology, and, in 1914, Paul F. Clark in the same field. Wisconsin was the second institution to start a student health program which, despite opposition on the part of several Madison physicians, flourished under the direction of Dr. Joseph Evans. The Wisconsin Psychiatric Institute, associated with Mendota State Hospital, began its program in 1915. Finally, in 1924, the State of Wisconsin General Hospital opened its doors and the next year a full medical course was at last instituted.

IT was of interest that Dean Birge, who had begun the first premedical work in the 1880s, was the president of the University when the Medical School at last became an actuality. Appointed at the death of Van Hise in 1918, he regarded his role, in view of his age, as that of a caretaker. Thus he was reluctant to launch programs the execution of which would necessarily fall to his successor. Spartan in his tastes, keen, witty, precise, balanced in judgment, Dr. Birge had in general shared Van Hise's views about the functions of the University. Nevertheless, he felt that the most important task of a university was to develop among its students "a certain temper of mind" related to the larger aspects of learning on which prosperity and happiness in the end depended. To some he seemed an admirable choice, a conservative force for stability in the troubled post-Van Hise and post-World War I atmosphere. To others, his caution and reluctance to push vigorously for much-needed funds for buildings for a greatly expanded student population, and for larger salaries to meet inflation and competition for staff from other institutions, seemed unfortunate. Nor did everyone like his downgrading of University publicity and seeming deference to the conservatism of some of the regents. In many quarters the atmosphere was hysterically antiradical, and Birge circumspectly permitted students to choose controversial public speakers only if the "other" side were also presented. But few doubted his steadfast devotion to the University or the importance of the services he had generously given for over a half-century. In any historical account of the University, Edward A. Birge must be counted among its most distinguished and influential leaders.

NOTES

1 John H. Lathrop's inaugural address, January 16, 1850, is included in *The Inauguration of the Chancellor of the University of Wisconsin* (Milwaukee, 1850).

2 Records of the Board of Regents, November 21, 1848, vol. B, p. 9.

3 *Regents' Annual Report*, December 31, 1853, pp. 14-15.

4 *Regents' Annual Report*, 1858-59, pp. 9-17.

5 *Regents' Annual Report*, 1864-65, p. 23.

6 Records of the Board of Regents, January 21, 1874, vol. C, p. 196.

7 John Bascom, *Things Learned by Living* (New York, 1913), pp. 42-43.

8 John Bascom, "To the Good People of Wisconsin," *Wisconsin Prohibitionist*, June 23, 1887, p. 1.

9 *Wisconsin Prohibitionist*, June 23, 1887, p. 1.

10 Report of the Investigating Committee, in Papers of the Board of Regents, September 18, 1894.

11 John Johnston, "Address on Behalf of the Regents," *The Addresses at the Inauguration of Charles Kendall Adams . . . January 17, 1893* (Madison, 1893), pp. 42-43.

12 Charles R. Van Hise's inaugural address in *The Jubilee of the University of Wisconsin* (Madison, 1905), p. 125.

13 Charles R. Van Hise's address to the Wisconsin Press Association, February 1905, in the President's Papers.

14 Charles R. Van Hise, *The Spirit of a University*, commencement address (Madison, 1912), pp. 6, 10.

CHAPTER 2

The University of Wisconsin, 1925-1950

MARK H. INGRAHAM

THE history of any period starts with chaos preceding creation and ends only with the last trump. However, we shall confine ourselves chiefly to the events and developments occurring between August 5, 1925, when the regents of the University refused to accept gifts from private foundations, and July 24, 1950, when ground was broken for the Memorial Library. This period embraces President Glenn Frank's administration, that of Clarence Dykstra, and the first five years when E. B. Fred was president. Another way of characterizing it is that these years include a boom, a depression, a war, and the start of recovery from all three. Though many people will be mentioned, few evaluative statements will be made — at least about the living. I not only fear for others' toes, but I dread omissions.

This study, although checked as far as possible by records, is largely guided by memory. Whether, after more time has passed, historians will agree with my judgments is, of course, open to doubt as is also the question as to who would be more apt to be correct. I hope that it is written with the conscience of a scholar, yet inevitably it is written also with the bias of a participant and the devotion of a lover.

Mark Hoyt Ingraham was born in Brooklyn, New York, March 19, 1896. He came to the University of Wisconsin in the fall of 1919 and, with the exception of three years, has been associated with it ever since. At the University he was instructor in mathematics, 1919-1921; fellow, 1921-1922; assistant professor, 1924-1926; professor, 1927-1966. He was dean of the College of Letters and Science 1942-1961. During the period covered by his essay he twice served on the University Committee, in particular, in 1933 when it brought in the report concerning financial retrenchment, and was chairman when it recommended the organization of the faculty divisions. He was chairman of the Committee on the Quality of Instruction and Scholarship and also of the Committee on University Functions and Policies. In sending his manuscript to the editors he stated: "If an essay were allowed a dedication, this one would be in memory of Edward Burr Van Vleck, the distinguished scholar for whom the mathematics building was named, who thrice brought me to Wisconsin, and had the greatest influence upon me of any teacher at the University."

Most of the changes in the curriculum come from alterations that instructors make in individual courses, the additions and subtractions of courses instituted by departments, and the creation of new departments. Usually these developments are caused by the increase in knowledge, but some occur in response to new needs or changing philosophies of education. These influences call at times for major reviews undertaken by college faculties through standing or especially appointed committees. It is also possible that some courses were added because many members of a staff, enlarged to meet the demands of an increased student body, wished to give some advanced work. Although we know that the standard story of a student following a lecture in his father's notes with the instructions "laugh here" is a canard, there is no way to document how individual courses have changed from year to year; my belief is that this is the most important single method of curriculum change.

Between 1925 and 1950 the Department of Geology and Geography had become two. Psychology was no longer bracketed with Philosophy; Sociology was not, as formerly, a subheading of Economics. Junior grows up and leaves home and sometimes divorces occur. The departments of Art History and the History of Science had been created *de novo*. Courses in Polish were decreed by the Legislature, and the Irish were not far behind. The first led to the development of the Department of Slavic Languages.

The net result was that in 1950, in spite of Education, Commerce, and Pharmacy having been given independent status, the College of Letters and Science (which they had left) had eight more departments at the end of the twenty-five-year period than at the beginning. Agriculture and Home Economics had added five; Medicine had developed a divisional system but, counting subdepartments, the number had tripled; while Engineering had succeeded in grouping twenty departments into seven.

During the 1925-1950 period there were three general reviews of the Letters and Science curriculum made by special committees headed by Carl Russell Fish, History, report submitted 1930; Farrington Daniels, Chemistry, 1940; and Frederic Ogg, Political Science, 1946. The last grew out of a controversy concerning the special position of history among the freshman requirements. Each of these reviews led to important changes and also made a number of abortive recommendations. The "Fish Report" stimulated the use of proficiency examinations and made possible more flexibility for the better students. Some of its recommendations ran into difficulties through the costs that would be entailed to put them into effect as the depression dragged down budgets. Other provisions were thwarted by departmental autonomy, and still others by the lessening of the euphoria which comes after the excitement when the meeting is over. Dean Sellery said: "it was a great report ahead — too far ahead — of its time."[1] I would agree that it was a great and important report, but I believe that its faults lay in nostalgia rather than in foresight. It probably also suffered from faculty resistance to innovation born of their attitude towards the Experimental College.

In 1925 Alexander Meiklejohn, who had recently been president of Amherst College, outlined his ideas on a new curriculum for liberal education in the *Century Magazine* of which Glenn Frank was editor. Soon after Frank became president of the University he brought Meiklejohn to Wisconsin, and not long thereafter the Experimental College was established within the College of Letters and Science with Meiklejohn as director. The first class entered in 1927. The students, all male, lived together in a dormitory and followed a unified curriculum for two years, taught largely through the tutorial method. The students were bright, devoted to the program, and often offensively scornful of the rest of the University. The faculty, a number of whom were Amherst graduates, were chiefly brought in from outside by Meiklejohn. They were an idealistic, brilliant, and conscientious group. After four classes had passed through the two-year program the experiment was terminated, having provided an exhilarating and successful experience for many of the students but, as a model, having small effect upon the future program of the University or, as had been hoped by Frank, on American education in general. The faculty members who remained in the University were a great asset throughout their whole service, in some cases of many years, being exceptionally good teachers and forming a salutary liberal element in the faculty. A segregated, noncoeducational, imported program, administratively sponsored and approved only as an experiment by the faculty, should not have been expected to survive.

One of the basic difficulties in securing a liberal education is the fragmentation of the program. We trust students to recognize the interrelations of splendid courses in various fields, taught by able specialists many of whom are not aware of the connections themselves. Even if the Experimental College was not viable, it faced the right problems. Many institutions tried their hands at solutions, one of the most successful being the program at Columbia University under Jacques Barzun. The "Ogg Committee," along with recommending major improvements in the traditional program, also recommended the offering of an alternative integrated program for the first two years which, after it was worked out by a special committee under the chairmanship of Robert Pooley, was inaugurated in 1948 under the name of "Integrated Liberal Studies" (ILS) with Pooley as chairman. It has been a marked success and is still thriving. Its success was due partly to its intelligent organization

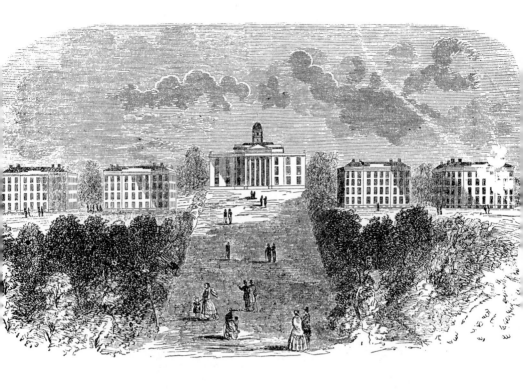

Projected "View of the University of Wisconsin" from Gleason's Pictorial Drawing Room
Companion, September 6, 1851. The two outside structures were never built. The magazine's description:

UNIVERSITY OF WISCONSIN.

'he Institution is founded on a grant, by
gress. of seventy-two sections of land for the
port of a State University. The Institution
chartered in 1845. The Corporation is a
rd of Regents, with general university pow-

It is already accumulating the means of
arting knowledge, by the formation of a li-
y, the collection of cabinets, &c., &c., and
, the manifestations of proper liberality on
part of the public, will confer immeasurable
fit on the present, and future generations.

In addition to the undergraduate department,
the Charter provides for departments of Law,
Medicine, and Normal instruction. The site is
a beautiful eminence, in the town of Madison,
one mile west of the Capitol, commanding a
view of the valley of the Four Lakes—a scene
of unrivalled interest and promise, embracing
the flourishing town of Madison. with a broad
and lovely margin of agricultural lands. Considering the advantages of its position, and the
probable value of its public endowment, it bids to
become the leading Institution of the Northwest.

The University's first century of leadership (left to right, top to bottom): John Hiram Lathrop, 1849-1858; Henry Barnard, 1859-1860; Paul A. Chadbourne, 1867-1870; John H. Twombly, 1871-1874; John Bascom, 1874-1887; Thomas C. Chamberlin, 1887-1892; Charles K. Adams, 1892-1901; Charles R. Van Hise, 1903-1918; Edward A. Birge, 1918-1925; Glenn Frank, 1925-1937; Clarence A. Dykstra, 1937-1945; Edwin Broun Fred, 1945-1958.

The University was guided by three presidents in the past two decades: Conrad A. Elvehjem, 1958-1962 (top, right), saw graduate education as a national resource and the University as an instrument for world development. Fred Harvey Harrington, 1962-1970 (middle, left), is shown here with the chancellors of the expanded university, left to right: Harrington; Lorentz H. Adofson, U.W.-Center System; J. Martin Klotsche, U.W.-Milwaukee; Donald R. McNeil, U.W.-Extension; Irvin G. Wyllie, U.W.-Parkside; Edward Weidner, U.W.-Green Bay; Edwin Young, U.W.-Madison; and Vice President Robert L. Clodius. John C. Weaver, 1971—(bottom, left), presided over the merger of the University of Wisconsin and the Wisconsin State Universities. He is shown here with Emeritus President E. B. Fred (1945-1958) and Chancellor Young in dedication of North Hall as an historic site on the opening of the University's 125th Anniversary celebration.

Madison campus leadership in the past decade was provided by three chancellors who had known it well as faculty members: Robben W. Fleming, 1964-1967 (left); William H. Sewell, 1967-1968 (right); and H. Edwin Young, 1968 — (above), who is pictured talking to campus demonstrators in 1969.

but even more to the fact that its faculty was composed of top-flight scholars already at Wisconsin who were also among the best teachers in the University.

The "Daniels Committee," appointed by Dean Sellery, reported in 1940 with less eloquence than the "Fish Committee" but with a somewhat surer touch of what was possible. It made a number of recommendations that led to successful developments largely after World War II was over. The following three were among these:

1. The development of an introductory course for freshmen to give them a broad idea of the nature and subject matter, but of course not the content, of various fields of knowledge which form a liberal education. This course, "Freshman Forum," varied from year to year and for some while was carried on the air by WHA.

2. A senior survey course, "Contemporary Trends," on the impact of science and technology on society. Professor Daniels initially organized this course but the lectures were given by nearly twenty faculty members.

3. A course on the history of science which became the basis for the development of the distinguished department in that field.

The "Ogg Committee" did a masterly job of analyzing the curriculum of the College of Letters and Science, but used restraint in making recommendations. They did resolve the problem of the freshman history requirements in such a way as to minimize hard feelings and enlarge, perhaps improve, the opportunities of the freshmen.

THE space necessary to describe the results of the University's research during this period would be measured in volumes—not pages. Only specialists in the same subspecialty can judge directly the work of a colleague. It is possible to make some estimate of the short-term effects of a discovery on health or wealth, but not the long-term ones. Newton did not have astronauts in mind. But to compare the importance and the quality of investigations of the solutions of differential equations, German influences on American literature, the statemanship of Gladstone, the treatment of syphilis, the welding of metals or the blood-types of pigeons, is impossible; yet, distinguished work on each of these subjects was done at the University of Wisconsin between 1925 and 1950.

Some idea of the recognition that was accorded research at Wisconsin can be obtained from ratings of the graduate work in individual departments made in 1925 and 1957 and reported for comparison purposes by the American Council on Education in 1966. Eighteen subjects were considered for both years, listing in rank order the fifteen leading departments in each subject. Wisconsin was on all eighteen lists in 1925, and on seventeen of them in 1957. It was first in German in 1925 and in Geography in 1957. Some rankings went up and some went down. In describing the ten major universities in 1957, Chesly Manly, writing for the *Chicago Tribune,* placed Wisconsin ninth and pointed out that it was second only to Columbia in the number of Ph.D.s granted on a single campus. Other objective yardsticks, not wholly devoid of subjective elements, can be cited. For instance, Raymond T. Birge (nephew of President E. A. Birge) tabulated the location of members of the National Academy of Sciences. In 1933, the first year he used, Wisconsin had nine and ranked ninth. In 1949 it had ten and was tied for tenth; and — to carry forward a bit — in 1965 it had twenty-four and was tied for ninth. In all these years it was first in the "Big Ten."

One Nobel prize winner in physics (1956) was an undergraduate at the beginning of our period; and another, in genetics (1958), was a member of the faculty at the end of it.

If we have to speak in generalities — even if valid generalities — about the quality of research, we can be more specific concerning its support and the allocation of research funds.

In 1925, the year when the University started to refuse grants from foundations, there was a sizable income for that time from federal funds, as well as some state appropriations, to support the research of the Agricultural Experimental Station; and about twenty-five thousand dollars from the state for research under the Graduate School. These funds were for "organized research," but outside of the College of Agriculture most of the research was carried on by professors paid from instructional funds — an allocation fully justified by the fact that the best university instruction at all levels, but especially in graduate work, is given by scholars. This important but nebulous area was listed as "research related to instruction" or, sometimes misguidedly called, "incidental research" (which I suppose is better than calling it "disorganized research").

This situation remained true throughout the period, yet the part played by "organized research" grew rapidly. In 1930 the University was again receptive to gifts from foundations. The financial report of the University for 1949-1950 showed a total of some $3,700,000 for organized research, i.e., 13¢ out of each University dollar. The state appropriated more than a million dollars of tax money for "organized research," and the federal government supplied more than half-a-million dollars. Earnings from fees and sales were both substantial, and over $1,300,000 of gifts went to research. The Wisconsin Alumni Research Foundation (WARF), which had made its first grants-in-aid amounting to $1,200 in 1928-1929, in 1949-1950 provided more than half a million dollars.

As important as the size of these funds was their distribution. In the case of Agriculture this was largely determined by the director of the Experiment Station, who also was the dean of the College of Agriculture, and by objectives specified in the appropriations. During this period the deans of Agriculture were: Harry A. Russell, 1907-1931 (he became director of the Wisconsin Alumni Research Foundation in 1931); Chris L. Christensen, 1931-1943; E. B. Fred, 1943-1945; Ira L. Baldwin, 1945-1948; Rudolph K. Froker, 1948-1964. The funds of the Graduate School were allocated by the faculty Research Committee, whose chairman was the dean of the school—Charles S. Slichter, 1920-1934; E. B. Fred, 1934-1943; Ira L. Baldwin, 1943-1945; and Conrad A. Elvehjem, 1946-1958—all of them scientists. It will be noted that Fred and Baldwin served in each capacity, and that Fred and Elvehjem became presidents of the University. To a large extent the patterns were set by Slichter and Russell; and, although Slichter was technically in these matters merely the chairman of the Research Committee, the scholar who knew he had Slichter's support for a project could have stopped worrying—even if some of them did not.

The development of research was properly influenced by the needs of the state, but it is noteworthy that throughout these twenty-five years the University had control of its research program through faculty committees and through administrators who were themselves research scholars. The University must share credit for this with the state and with the federal government, with the great foundations, and particularly with WARF, which showed admirable restraint. It must be admitted that all these sources of support gave funds more readily for the natural sciences than for the social studies or for the humanities, which fact, although it took nothing away from the latter two and even made possible the diverting of some funds for their use, did lead to a certain imbalance.

The primary functions of the University are instruction and investigation. Yet its resources of knowledge and trained intelligence would not be used to the full if these were its only services.

As types of public service I shall consider two examples (not chosen at random): the first, the expert borrowed from the University working on a particular project for the state or, increasingly, for the federal government; the second, the dissemination through Extension of the practical results of discovery.

1. Professor Edwin E. Witte, trained in labor economics under John R. Commons (who had influenced state legislation in the Van Hise-La Follette era), was chosen in the mid-1930s by Frances Perkins, secretary of labor under Franklin Roosevelt, to head the commission drafting the original social security legislation. This he did with great skill and with as much sound economics as the process of political compromise would admit. The crucial job of making the plan work was carried out under the leadership of another of Commons' students, Arthur J. Altmeyer, who gave form to the Social Security Act by his early direction of the program.

2. The second example is the adoption throughout the dairy industry of the state of artificial insemination of cattle. The first work on the subject was not at Wisconsin. However, technological problems were solved around 1940 in the University's Department of Biochemistry. The promotional effort was spearheaded by Edwin E. Heizer of the Dairy Industry Department, working through the Agricultural Extension Division and its county agents. The division's long record of giving sound advice on such matters as milk-tests, canning, and disease-resistant strains of oats made the task easier. This program was a major factor in increasing the yield of milk per cow by 50 percent.

More University people were engaged in public service during the war period than at any other time in these twenty-five years. World War II united rather than divided the nation.

Of course, first recognition goes to the students and the young faculty members who left the University to serve in the armed forces, and also to those other young people who served instead of entering the University but many of whom afterwards came to it with the aid of the G.I. Bill.

The University carried on many special programs, largely in the sciences, including mathematics, and in the languages. In addition, the United States Armed Forces Institute was established in Madison and at the start used primarily correspondence courses of the University's Extension Division, a fact that helped their being credited by other major institutions.

Many faculty members went on leave to play major roles in war-related work, and some who stayed in Madison devoted much time to it; as examples, President Dykstra, as mentioned elsewhere, headed the draft; Farrington Daniels of Chemistry was scientific administrator of the investigations in Chicago on the controlled use of atomic energy; and new and more prolific strains of penicillin were developed on the campus by bacteriologists and botonists. Wisconsin-trained economists were so numerous in the War Labor Board that it was reported that you could empty its offices by yelling down the hall, "To Hell with Wisconsin."

I have had a chance to read Dean F. C. Young's excellent essay (Chapter 7) on students during the years after 1950 and find no reason to describe the students before that date as different from those of the fifties. However, some attention is given below to the handling of certain situations by the faculty. As so often is true, changing but frequently cyclicly varying attacks were made on perennial problems.

Between 1925 and 1950, as before and since, the handling of cases of student misconduct was constantly discussed and the responsibility shifted from time to time. During the whole of the period there seemed to be general consensus, shared by the public, the regents, the faculty, and I believe by most students, that some form of supervision of student conduct was required. No one really wanted the burden. In 1925 it was carried primarily by the dean of men and the dean of women. They also did much of the advising on student activities and the supervision, including financial, of these activities. It was the dean of men who warned of the delusions if not the snares involved in drink, gambling, and profanity, and tried to do something about the first two. These two deans personally tracked down those who offended against the moral code of society or who broke the social regulations of the University. President Frank was certain that the role of the advisor to students and to student organizations and that of the disciplinarian were incompatible; and Deans Scott H. Goodnight and F. Louise Nardin expressed pleasure at the idea of limiting themselves to the former functions. Some persons in the state evidently feared that the University was becoming too permissive and, on November 22, 1930, President Frank made a statement to the regents: "The University should not, in my judgment, even consider the irresponsible attitude of the Continental universities. It is the improvement and humanization of our processes that is our concern."[2]

Even before this date the faculty, under stimulation from the president, had created a Committee on Student Conduct: five members appointed along with the deans of the colleges and the dean of men and the dean of women. The committee could delegate authority to sub-committees, always including the dean of men in the cases concerning men and the dean of women in cases concerning women.

It was not long before the president pointed out that the dean of men and the dean of women in their advisory work were compromised by their continued disciplinary function, and the faculty again authorized a committee to study the matter. When its report was amended beyond acceptability to this committee, a second committee was appointed whose report the faculty finally passed. It recommended "that the Dean of Men and the Dean of Women have no connection with the punitive aspects of discipline cases," but they were still to report cases to the committee for consideration.[3] Two or three other recommendations were included in the report, and the committee said that it was "not under the impression that it has found a final solution for the problem."[4] This was the most sapient remark in a wise report. After this, the structure of the disciplinary process stayed without major alteration for a long time.

From the point of view of the administration *The Cardinal,* the student newspaper, was a constant problem. The editors were brash, testing the patience of their elders. One way or another the University subsidized it, and it carried official notices. This made it difficult to disown. More than once it was proposed to place some kind of control over it. Clearly, complete censorship was undesirable, and partial censorship left the University powerless but responsible. Little was done. One could always hope that next year's editor would be better—and they sometimes were.

The period 1925-1950 was one of reasonable athletic success and even more of controversy.

The basketball teams coached by Walter Meanwell had, just prior to 1925, won three Big Ten championships and been second once in five years. Around 1925 was a period of low scores. Wisconsin defeated Illinois in 1931 twelve to nine, the year before, fourteen to nine. H. E. ("Bud") Foster became coach in 1935, and in 1941 Wisconsin won not only the Big Ten but also the NCAA title.

At the end of the period the boxing teams were making a phenomenal record of victories but some of the faculty were beginning to question its suitability as a college sport.

The cross-country team won the Big Ten title eleven times—eight of these under the beloved Tom Jones, whose track teams were also doing well.

The football team was usually somewhere in the middle of the pack. Although the 1942 team was recognized as number one in the country, it was technically rated second in the Big Ten.

In 1932 Clarence Spears came as football coach, and it was not long before he and "Doc" Meanwell were unhappy with each other to such an extent that both the Athletic Board and the regents felt impelled to take action. These two bodies did not see eye to eye; and although the regents had final authority, Wisconsin would be dropped from the Western

Conference if it were determined that the faculty did not have control of athletics. The Athletic Board recommended the dismissal of Spears and the retention of Meanwell as athletic director, but early in 1936 the regents dismissed both. The faculty and student members of the Athletic Board, led by Professor Andrew T. Weaver, father of President John C. Weaver, resigned in a body. After considerable negotiations, the regents made a statement on the control of athletics by the Athletic Board (subject to review by the regents) which was accepted by the faculty on recommendation of the faculty members of the Regent-Faculty Conference Committee. The Athletic Board was restructured at this time.

Although the story of the struggle against racial discrimination in the University community belongs largely to a later period, it had much of its background in the twenty-five years considered in this essay. Three special episodes are mentioned below.

On January 15, 1930, at a meeting of the Board of Regents Mrs. Meta Berger, the widow of Victor Berger (a Socialist congressman from Milwaukee), introduced the following resolution: "BE IT RESOLVED that it is the sense of the Board of Regents, that the authority with the power to place rooming houses or halls housing girl students of this University on the accredited list, shall not place on the accredited list any rooming house or hall which in any way discriminates against any student on account of race, creed, or nationality."[5] This was referred to the Executive Committee to study and report. I have not discovered what happened to it, but it certainly did not become law.

The second significant episode was when the chairman of the House Committee of the University (Faculty) Club directed the manager to refuse a room to a Negro. As soon as the membership found out, a meeting was called and the precedent was promptly reversed.

The credit for starting the most effective drive against racial discrimination goes to the Student Board, in particular to its Committee against Discrimination. Their report was sent by the Student Board to the faculty Committee on Student Life and Interests on May 9, 1949, and asked for a much stronger stand on the part of the University than they believed it was taking. Perhaps the chief problem tackled concerned housing, and the Student Board made a number of recommendations on the matter, the first and fifth being: "(1) We recommend that houses to be retained on the University Approved List be required to follow a policy of non-discrimination at all times." "(5) We recommend that a permanent committee consisting of an equal number of students and faculty be established to investigate and to report on all cases of discrimination brought to its attention. A committee of this sort would have authority and would be respected by the public and the house owners."[6]

The majority of the Student Life and Interests Committee were somewhat defensive and toned down the recommendations of the Student Board. A student, Lyle Miller, and Professor Henry Ladd Smith of Journalism made a minority report in full support of the Student Board and, in particular, raised the question of discrimination in the national charters of some fraternities and sororities. The faculty, after discussing the matter, referred it to the University Committee for study and report. The University Committee came nearer agreeing with the minority than with the majority of the Committee on Student Life and Interests, and recommended the establishment of the Committee on Human Relations (later called the Committee on Human Rights) to work chiefly through persuasion and education, but put more teeth into its recommendations concerning fraternities and sororities. The faculty in adopting the report added a molar or two of its own.

This marks the start of continuous effort for improvement in the recognition and the observance of human rights. The record of the Committee on Human Rights has been outstanding for sense and courage and sometimes for compromise between those who sought the ideal and those who believed in the art of the possible.

I end this section on students with two quotations, the first a reminder to the faculty and the second a reminder to the students; both have frequently been used by others.

In 1931, after forty-five years of teaching at the University of Wisconsin, Charles S. Slichter said: "But actually I did not teach freshmen. I taught attorneys, bankers, big business men, physicians, surgeons, judges, congressmen, governors, writers, editors, poets, inventors, great engineers, corporation presidents, railroad presidents, scientists, professors, deans, regents, and university presidents. For that is what those freshmen are now, and of course they were the same persons then."[7] Those who now look back on the students of the second quarter of this century realize that many of them are now leaders in American life.

In 1949 the Committee on Functions and Policies concluded its chapter on the quality of instruction with "When all is said and done the student must recognize that the shortcomings of the University, no matter how unfortunate, should never obscure the fact that here the hard-working intelligent individual has magnificent educational opportunities, and that if these are missed, it will be chiefly through his own negligence."[8]

A university's effectiveness is primarily determined by the quality of its faculty. This quality can only be appraised as an aggregate of individual judgments as to the distinction and adequacy of the persons of which the faculty is composed. Neither the space allowed nor my ability will permit this.

What may be said in the large? First of all, the size of the faculty kept appoximate pace with the growth of the student body. In the fall of 1925-1926 the faculty consisted of 136 professors, 85 associate professors, 84 assistant professors, 198 instructors, a total of 503. There was also a large number of teaching assistants. The student enrollment at Madison was 7,760. Four years later the enrollment had increased by more than 20 percent and the full-time faculty by 15 percent. In another four years, as the depression deepened, the student enrollment reached a low of 7,374, and the full-time faculty was back to 507. From then on, until World War II, there was a steady rise in enrollment as well as in the number of faculty members. For a short hectic period during the war, the enrollment at the University and, to a somewhat lesser degree, the size of the staff fluctuated violently from month to month. By the fall of 1950 the student body, still including many of the returned veterans but down about three thousand from the 1947 peak, was up to 15,766, and the figures for roughly comparable staff were 356 professors, 203 associate professors, 273 assistant professors, and 263 instructors. The student body had increased 103 percent from 1925, and the full-time staff 118 percent. In light of increased research activities and a growth in graduate enrollment of 287 percent, the staff had increased less than could have been expected. The proportion of instructors was already decreasing.

No faculty could keep pace with the specialties created by the growth of knowledge. However, this growth is reflected in many additions to the programs and hence to the faculty of the University. In 1925 there was no one specializing in computer science, but in 1950 the program, which has grown amazingly since, was already underway. In 1933 Aldo Leopold started work in wildlife management. The Enzyme Institute was initiated about 1946.

For a long time surveys which pretend to gauge the distinction of universities have listed Wisconsin in the first dozen. Such judgments must be taken with a handful of salt, for they frequently reflect opinions formed earlier and adhered to tenaciously. Yet Wisconsin consistently maintained its position.

I believe that some measures which may be moderately objective, but may also be shrewdly selected, were not as important as the realization of those who have represented Wisconsin in many groups that the University was greatly respected outside, and also were not as important as the faculty's own sense of worth and distinction. The above can be written in the present as well as the past tense. A word about faculty turnover and faculty stability is perhaps worthwhile. The annual turnover among full-time members of the faculty often exceeds 10 percent. However, about 20 percent of those on the faculty in 1925 were still serving in 1950. Those who come and go make important contributions, but the stability and character of the faculty were determined by the core who were at the University for a long period.

A discussion of the academic administration of the University should start with the chairmen of the departments and the departmental secretaries. It was probably true that in the early days of the University the chairmen were more nearly "heads" than chairmen and were sometimes called so; but, when most of the large departments contained a number of mature and often distinguished scholars, this was no longer appropriate. During the administration of Van Hise the method of annual appointment of chairmen by the deans, after determining the desires of the departments, was formulated; but in 1925, although on the books, this method was often ignored and chairmen frequently continued in office for considerable periods without recommendations for reappointments from the departments. President Dykstra, however, soon discovered the official rule and made the deans aware of it, perhaps in a hope that this would result in some younger leadership at the departmental level. Most colleges observed the "new rule," although I believe the Medical School retained a somewhat more authoritarian structure. Annual appointments did not lead at once to the rapid turnover of chairmen which is now usual. At least four departments had the same chairmen in 1950 as in 1925: namely, James G. Halpin of Poultry; John A. James of Agricultural Education; J. Howard Matthews of Chemistry; and Herbert D. Orth of Drawing. At present I believe there is no one now chairman who was chairman in 1950.

The work of the departmental secretary was growing increasingly important and complex. In the early days the secretaries largely served the chairmen. By 1950 they helped a whole cadre of scholars, not only in administrative matters but in typing (and often editing) scholarly manuscripts. Some were bilingual. The larger departments no longer depended upon one person, and some had a considerable staff. With frequent changes of chairmen and the flow of personnel during World War II, the secretaries often provided valuable continuity in the functioning of the departments.

During this period, as mentioned earlier, three new independent schools were created: Education, Commerce, and Pharmacy. The nucleus of each had been in the College of Letters and Science. In all three cases the independent status was in accord with the wishes of almost all of the faculty budgeted in the new schools, and also with the expressed desire of professional groups in the state. One feature worth noting is that all members of the faculties of other colleges who taught upper-level courses normally elected by majors in the School of Education belonged to the faculty of that school. This led to good feelings between members of the professional departments of Education and other members of the faculty and has, in my judgment, resulted in their having greater influence in the University faculty than is usually the case elsewhere.

During the period 1925-1950 there was no Senate, and often faculty action was taken by a relatively small number of its members. These were usually members who made it a habit to attend meetings, to study the agenda, and to discuss the topics informally with others. In a certain sense they formed a self-selected senate—an interested, well-informed, and intelligent one. No topic not on the calendar could be taken up without unanimous consent. The system worked well. It is true that some faculty meetings had over-representation of those whose interests were threatened, some coming to vote rather than to consider a subject; but these occasions were relatively rare. About half of the meetings during these twenty-five years had attendance under one hundred. There were twenty-eight meetings, slightly over one in ten, where the attendance was two hundred or more. The chief attraction of ten of these meetings was to hear an address by the president: once, E. B. Fred; once, Clarence Dykstra; once, acting-president Sellery; and seven times, Glenn Frank. Not only did Glenn Frank speak well, but the faculty was often uneasy about what he might say. The *piece de resistance* at three meetings concerned athletics. Student discipline (sometimes called social control) was the subject of two. Committee reports—functions and policies, divisional organization, revision of the calendar, and the future of the University Club—drew good attendance. The two meetings on the McMurray case (see below), two concerning the building of a new library, and several on athletics were more emotional than most. It would seem that curiosity about presidential thoughts and the real importance of the subject drew larger attendance during this period than threats to vested interests. This is in part due to the fact that most curriculum matters were primarily the concern of college faculties, not of the University faculty.

Any even quasi-legislative body, with more members than the House of Representatives, must do much of its work through committees. Faculty members bewail the time spent on committees but resent being left off of them.

The 1925 catalogue listed twenty-two standing committees of the faculty but, in spite of several of them being discontinued, the number had increased about 50 percent before 1950.

There were two committees which throughout the whole period were elective: the Nominations Committee, elected by nominations from the floor, which in turn nominated candidates for other elected or partially elected committees; and the University Committee. Most of the members of the Library Committee and the faculty members of the Regent-Faculty Conference Committee were elected. Before 1950 two new elective committees were added, that on the Kemper K. Knapp Bequest (elected, as the donor had desired) and that on courses. The executive committees of the faculty divisions also were elected but by the memberships of their respective divisions. From the small numbers of elective committees it is clear that the faculty chose, after specifying special ex-officio members (the Administrative Committee was entirely ex-officio), to leave the selection of most committee members to the president, in a few cases "in conjunction with the University Committee."

The University Committee was the chief faculty committee for considering University policy. It consisted of six members; two were elected each year for three-year terms, with provisions guaranteeing the spread of membership among the colleges. Some of its most notable reports during this period include:

1. A report in 1926 recommending a system of sabbatical leaves. This was aborted by the depression. The growth of research assignments, usually called "research leaves," met many of the same needs more generously for research scholars and less generously for those with modest or nonexistent research records than the sabbatical leaves would have done.

2. The report in 1933 on budget cuts.

3. A report in 1939, modified in 1940, on tenure. Although there were some differences, it followed in general the 1940 Statement of Principles of Academic Freedom and Tenure adopted by the American Association of University Professors and by the Association of American Colleges. The adopted recommendations went promptly to the administration and were followed, but did not go to the regents at the time, and indeed it was some years before the regents approved a set of rules on the question of tenure. The preamble of the report said, as could have been said at any time during these twenty-five years: "It is the considered judgement of the Committee that in respect to academic freedom, and in respect to tenure for those holding permanent appointments, the situation here at Wisconsin presents no immediate problem. The academic freedom and the tenure that we have rest on a tradition that has its source and support in the enlightenment and good faith of the Regents, the Administration, and the Faculty. No action on the part of any or all of

these groups can secure for these privileges any legal guarantee, nor does there seem to be need of such protection."[9]

4. The report of 1942 recommending the faculty divisional organization.

5. The report in 1950, on human relations (rights).

The University Committee was consulted in 1937 in connection with the selection of President Frank's successor, and in 1945 represented the faculty in picking Dean Fred to succeed President Dykstra.

In 1950, on recommendation of the Committee on Functions and Policies, the faculty added to the duties of the University Committee the advising of the administration, if requested, on educational questions but with the right to refer such matters to the faculty.

During the last decade of the forties the Library Committee did yeoman service in pushing for a new library and, through its representatives, in helping to plan the building.

Of course the faculties not only of the colleges but that of the University worked through special committees as well as standing committees. Some of these have been cited elsewhere. Two large all-university committees merit a word at this point.

The Committee on the Quality of Instruction and Scholarship was created in 1940 "to study the nature of the adjustments [mostly budgetary] that have been made, their effects upon the quality of instruction and scholarship, and possible alternatives, and to submit its findings for the consideration of the Faculty and Administration." Although the University Committee had recommended that this special committee be elected, the faculty decided that it should be "appointed by the president acting in conjunction with the University Committee."[10] It is not surprising that the committee concluded that the University could do a better job if it had more money, but the chief accomplishment of the committee was giving to the faculty a detailed analysis of the sources of income and of the expenditures, especially for salary, of the University. Furnishing such information to a faculty was at the time unusual among American universities and colleges.

The Committee on Functions and Policies was appointed in 1947 by President Fred with the blessing of both the faculty and the regents and with the advice of the University Committee. In 1948 it reported on the University's role in the state's educational system and recommended the merger of the University with the state's colleges, but only under certain conditions. If this were not done, it recommended that the Milwaukee State Teachers College be transferred to the University and developed along with the Extension Division into a broader four-year institution.

(The committee did not foresee the later happy development of a full-fledged university in Milwaukee.) The merger proposal made soon after by Governor Kohler did not satisfy the conditions laid down by the committee — which reconvened and opposed the governor's recommendations. Nor did the regents desire a merger. The second report of the committee was an internal survey, issued later in 1949, and was dubbed by the press the University's "report card." There were some poor grades (e.g., library facilities and cheating on examinations), some average grades, but the record as a whole was one of which any university could be proud.

During the whole of this period there was no serious question as to the faculty, mostly working through the colleges and departments, being primarily in charge of the curriculum, both in determining what courses would be offered and in setting degree requirements. There were numerous attempts, partially successful, through committees of one sort or another to moderate the undue proliferation of courses. But rarely did this keep an enthusiastic scholar from giving work in his specialty. One professor, in requesting authority to give a course in human parasitology, expected others to share his shock that "there are students who graduate from this University without even knowing what a bedbug looks like." I have been in dormitories of other universities which precluded such a dire situation.

The role of the departmental faculties has been the major one in the recruiting and the promotion of their fellow members. This, however, has always been controlled by limitation of funds and by the reviews of the administrative officers, chiefly the deans, and after 1942 by the reviews made in cases of tenure by the divisional committees.

The faculty divisions were created by the faculty in 1942. Two features different from those often found elsewhere were: (1) there was no initial attempt to assure that every faculty member be in some division; however with time, the coverage has been expanded until it is nearly complete; and (2) many faculty members, including the memberships of whole departments, belonged to more than one division; sadly, this is no longer true. From the start each division had an executive committee elected by its members which, along with some general duties and some minor special ones, had two major obligations: first, to study the course offerings of the division, especially interdepartmental courses; and second, to advise the deans of the colleges concerning appointments to positions of tenure recommended by the departments. In practice, the divisional committees have not frequently advised contrary to the nominations of the departments, but the necessity of submitting names to one's colleagues has had a salutary effect on the actions of the departments. I believe the divisional committees have tended to place too great emphasis on published research.

The creation of the faculty divisions was a controversial matter and was passed subject to review by the faculty at the end of three years, when it was renewed for another three years, and then made permanent. The original passage was perhaps helped by Professor William H. Twenhofel's statement, in opposing the measure, that he came from a department that had not made a mistake in fifty years. Few things need as careful scrutiny as infallibility.

One of the elements of strength at the University has been the fact that promotions of able people have not been slowed by a system that allocated just so many of each rank to a department. It would be easy, but unwise, to name pairs of people who—if only one could have been promoted—might have been bitterly competitive, yet, in fact, cooperated generously when the road ahead was open to both.

In general, before the appointment of President Dykstra the faculty had no formal influence on the selection of the president, although it is certain that individual regents consulted with individual faculty members of their acquaintance. In fact, the "Frances Street Gang" has been credited, presumably incorrectly, with a major role in selecting their neighbor Van Hise.

The regents in 1924-1925 first tried to get Roscoe Pound, dean of the Harvard Law School, to accept the position and, when he refused, made (with no faculty consultation) an offer to Glenn Frank—which led to witticisms as to the relative value of a pound and a franc.

When the regents looked for Frank's successor they invited the University Committee to review the list under consideration and to comment upon it. The committee called in others for consultation and in the end asked that certain names be deleted. As far as I can determine, the regents gave no further consideration to such names. There was an implied veto but little input by faculty representatives.

When Dykstra resigned, the regents went a good deal further and invited the faculty and deans to elect committees (which mostly worked as one) to consult with the regents regarding the selection of a new president. There was real discussion both within the committee and with the regents, and I had the duty of asking E. B. Fred to no longer attend meetings of the committee since he clearly was a leading candidate. (Some years later I made the same request, for the same reason, of Conrad Elvehjem.) The question was completely settled when Sumner Slichter and Warren Weaver, alumni of the University, either one of whom would have made a distinguished president, refused to be considered since each informed the regents that Fred was the right person. In this case the first choice of the committee was selected by the regents, and those who were in on the selection of Fred never regretted their choice.

It may well be that the happy result of this method of selection was one reason for it being used again when President Fred retired.

Histories of universities do not generally discuss clubs, yet the governance of the University of Wisconsin was, during the second quarter of this century, almost a soviet of dining clubs. Breaking bread with others does not always lead to agreement but is perhaps the best road to understanding and develops close friendships.

In this period the University Club was the place where faculty decisions were often arrived at and later recorded at formal meetings. The faculty considered the Club important enough so that, in 1933, when it was proposed to give the building to the University in order to save certain costs, the faculty expressed its willingness to have membership a condition of employment if voluntary membership would not cover the remaining expenses.

But the best discussion of University affairs, as well as much else, went on in small dining clubs. Perhaps the oldest and the one with the most prestige was "Town and Gown," founded in 1878. Its membership has included almost all of the University's presidents, starting with Charles Kendall Adams, some of the state's governors, a number of justices of the state Supreme Court, a covey of deans, and a bevy of lawyers. It was here that Senator Vilas discussed the need for special research professorships without giving away the secret that he was providing for them in his will. Another club had during this period almost constant representation on either the University Committee or the Library Committee, the elective committees of the faculty. Another furnished both the University of Wisconsin and the University of Chicago with presidents.

Most of these clubs provided for a large interdepartmental spread among their members and many drew from outside the University. The typical meeting consisted of a dinner often—in many clubs usually—in the home of a member, followed by general conversation and a discussion led by a member on some topic in which the others and sometimes he, himself, had no special knowledge. No formal faculty structure assured that individuals would have interests and acquaintances beyond their departments to the extent that these social groups did.

Serving the dinners was a contribution of the wives to the University community—putting up with professors was even a greater one.

The faculty's role in determining educational policy was promoted by its restraint and by the responsibility of its actions. It was also promoted by the respect shown the faculty by Presidents Dykstra and Fred and by a group of deans who, although some of them could be arbitrary in individual matters, relied on the collective wisdom of the faculties.

There was seldom a period when the deans had more influence than during Frank's presidency. In the first place, they were a group of very able men with striking personalities, among them Charles S. Slichter of the Graduate School, Harry L. Russell of the College of Agriculture, George C. Sellery of the College of Letters and Science, and Charles R. Bardeen of the Medical School. All had been selected by Van Hise or Birge from the faculty of the University. All had strong research interests, and perhaps all represented at least a passive resistance to the president's efforts to remake the university before he was acquainted with it. In this I believe they represented most of the senior faculty. Although the faculty may at times have felt a "they and us" attitude towards the administration, the deans in general belonged to the "us." Each of these men had some enemies, more friends, and even more admiring — though sometimes grudging — supporters.

When Dean Sellery became acting president the minutes of the meeting of January 11, 1937, contained the following:

The Acting President addressed the Faculty briefly, saying that it was neither his duty nor his desire to pass judgment on the rights and wrongs of the recent upheaval by which the Board of Regents gave an immediate leave of absence to President Glenn Frank. In his plea for the confidence and support of the Faculty, he gave his profession of faith as follows:

"First, I am a faculty man, bred in the faculty points of view and convinced of the superior wisdom of faculty conclusions in the matters entrusted to the faculty by the laws of the University. I shall regard it as my duty during the few months of my tenure to represent the faculty decisions and desires in matters confided to the faculty before the Board of Regents.

"Secondly, I believe in faculty tenure, not so much for the protection of those who are now on the faculty as for the guarantee it affords that we shall be able to attract to our faculty young men of promise and capacity.

"Thirdly, I believe in straightening out certain salary inequalities as fast as our means permit.

"Finally, I believe in the greatness and worth of the University of Wisconsin and of the State of Wisconsin, which created and nurtures it. We are still a great university and we shall continue to advance in greatness and worth with the State. We are both, state and university, sound in heart and head. Do not, I beg of you, sell the University or the State of Wisconsin short! Sursum corda! (Lift up your hearts!)"[11]

This was clearly an implied criticism of Glenn Frank and a sermon for his yet unselected successor.

THE public places too great emphasis on the roles of the regents and of the administration in comparison with that of the faculty. However, it would be a supercilious faculty member who would not recognize the vital position a president has in the life of any university. An essay on the University in the years 1925 to 1950 must try to assess its three presidents—Glenn Frank, 1925-1937; Clarence Dykstra, 1937-1945; and Edwin Fred, 1945-1958.

Frank succeeded Charles E. Van Hise, 1903-1918, and Edward A. Birge, 1918-1925, both of whom had been chosen after long service on the faculty.

Van Hise had been a member of the faculty for some time before becoming the first person to receive the Ph.D. degree, in 1892, from the University of Wisconsin. He was one of the notable university presidents that America has produced, leading the University in the direction of greater public service and making explicit duties it had already started to perform. He emphasized the role of the faculty. He has been given much well-deserved recognition.

Birge deserves more credit as president than he has received, although all who know of the period recognized his stature as dean and as limnologist. He had come to the University in 1875 and had been dean of the College of Letters and Science from 1891 until, in 1918, at the age of sixty-seven, he became president upon the death of Van Hise. He was seventy-four when he retired. In 1918 he faced a difficult situation—the maladjustments that always come with war and the bitterness of feelings in a state with a big German population. A large group of the faculty had made public a sharp letter of criticism of Senator La Follette's antiwar stand. This had been signed by both Van Hise and Birge. Wounds had to be healed and the position of the University consolidated. Birge was effective in doing both. He clearly remained the leader in the faculty; but to a large extent the regents, with his skillful help, presented the case of the University to the public.

I believe the University of Wisconsin is unique in that it has had four presidents who belonged to the National Academy of Sciences: Thomas Chrowder Chamberlin (1887-1892) elected to the academy after he had returned to work in Geology; Van Hise, also a geologist; Fred, a bacteriologist; and his successor, Conrad A. Elvehjem (1958-1962), a biochemist and dean of the Graduate School at the end of our period.

Glenn Frank (1925-1937) was editor of the *Century Magazine* and not quite thirty-eight years of age when he was appointed president of the University. He had had little background in educational work, but a good deal as a writer and a speaker. Like many other able, intellectual young men he had come under the spell of Alexander Meiklejohn, an inspiring teacher and a rather casual administrator. Frank seems to have assumed that Meiklejohn's criticisms of American education were valid and applied to Wisconsin. He had a greater urge to change than to study the institution he had come to head.

Frank was a polished speaker with a penchant for alliteration. In fact, his speaking was oratorical enough to make some forget the substance or doubt there was a substance — an unfair conclusion for he had something to say, even if he said it too well. I believe it was H. L. Mencken who called him "the great gliberal."

Frank soon acquired the hearty dislike of George Sellery, dean of the College of Letters and Science, and of many of the senior members of the faculty, especially those in that college, for his desire was to remold liberal rather than professional education. The latter he supported but left alone. Frank also disliked Sellery and had decided to replace him as dean. He told Warren Weaver, professor of Mathematics and later vice president of the Rockefeller Foundation, that he wished him to succeed Sellery. Weaver, who "liked and admired" Sellery, was willing to be dean but not to be part of getting rid of Sellery, and insisted on being free to talk to him. The episode is described in Sellery's *Some Ferments at Wisconsin* (1960) without identifying Weaver. Weaver, who had told me this in confidence at the time, has recently given me permission to disclose his name. Frank did not go through with the plan.

Frank was a truly tolerant man, remarkably lacking in rancor even after his dismissal, and willing to let everyone have his say although perhaps rather unwilling to change positions he had taken in haste. I believe he was somewhat ineffective as an administrator partly because he devoted so much time to speaking and to writing a syndicated column. Saying was a substitute for doing.

One of the regents who clashed with him during the early days of the depression was Harold Wilkie, a Madison lawyer, then often in the minority on the board. He was particularly critical of Frank's desire to protect the higher salaries, including his own, from as large a cut as Wilkie rightly believed should be taken in light of the general policy which had been recommended by the faculty. Not long thereafter Wilkie was joined by a number of other La Follette appointees to the board and became its chairman. Governor La Follette had become convinced that Frank should leave. In a closed Board of Regents session Frank was asked to resign but refused. The subsequent hearings and dismissal were so ruthless and such a travesty on due process that the academic world was shocked. The faculty said little. Some of its members, active in faculty affairs and disgusted with the procedure, consulted together to consider making a public statement to the press but decided not to do so because they felt the protest would be hollow unless they could also say that they would like to have Frank continue as president. They could not.

Clarence Addison Dykstra (1937-1945) came to Wisconsin at the age of fifty-four from being city manager of Cincinnati, where he had earned a fine reputation enhanced by the way he had handled the problems created by the then-recent flood. Although most of his career had not been academic he had been educated as a political scientist, had taught at Ohio State University and UCLA, and had been a member of the faculty of the University of Kansas.

Like Frank, he was particularly interested in undergraduate liberal education and was troubled by the lack of unity or pattern in the educational experiences which the students were having. He kept raising questions — important ones. He, however, clearly believed in faculty control of educational policy and, although he would like to influence, he did not wish to subvert it. It was largely at his instigation that the faculty divisional organization was formed. He was an excellent administrator, getting things done on time, and a man whose word was to be trusted.

He was at the University during a time of great confusion, arriving after the trauma of Frank's dismissal, and seeing the University through World War II which he did effectively in spite of being the civilian head of the draft and serving on the National Defense Mediation Board.

Lillian Dykstra was immensely liked, energetic, and vivacious. She had a particularly difficult position because of her husband's prolonged absences in Washington, and she filled it magnificently.

Dykstra was a fine president who did not have a chance to get close to the faculty, in large part because of his absence and the absence of many of them during the war. Certain irritations, especially in connection with the start of the School of Business Administration, built up between him and the regents; and I think that both he and they were relieved when he resigned to become chancellor of UCLA.

As president, Edwin Broun Fred was the right man in the right place. He had also been the right man as professor, as graduate dean, and as dean of the College of Agriculture, as well as on the back of a horse or amidst his tomato plants. Let us list a few of the reasons why he did so well. He was an indefatigable worker, being at his laboratory or office long before most others had come and still there when others had left. He had been on the faculty of the University since 1914 and knew its history and its ramifications in the state as few others did. He also knew the details, where to find available funds, and even which faculty member was squabbling with which other one — not unimportant information. He was uniformly courteous. There were other traits, usually advantageous, but on occasion not so. For instance, he had a passion for consensus and would go to great lengths and spent much time to secure it. This avoided scars and led to cooperation, but sometimes delayed action. He desired to discover the opinions of others before he revealed his own. There has been many an able university administrator who could persuade governing boards and faculties to go along with his clearly taken positions. Fred had the rarer art of being hesitantly persuaded by these bodies to do what he had intended to do all along. He was a pleasant person to work with but not always an easy one, for he would give the same job to more than one person and could talk about many things before taking up what one had come to discuss; for example, a cow barn instead of a history appointment, or vice versa.

As a fellow faculty member with an established record as a scholar who had worked in many ways with his colleagues, there was never a question of faculty confidence in him. What was probably less certain was how he and the regents would get along. Here his record was superb. Perhaps a case history can illustrate this paragraph.

Howard McMurray, a political scientist and a liberal Democrat, was recommended for an appointment as associate professor, starting in the second semester of 1946-1947. He had been a faculty member in Extension but had resigned in 1942 to run for Congress and had served one term. For one year he had been a lecturer in the College of Letters and Science. He resigned and ran for the U.S. Senate in 1946 and was defeated. The regents delayed action on the appointment, and some believed that it was because they did not like McMurray's liberal opinions. Before the regents had voted formally, a vigorous letter to Fred from the Department of Political Science had reached the press, implying that there had been a breach of academic courtesy. President Fred recommended McMurray's appointment, stating: "I believe that upon questions of academic qualifications the judgment of the department concerned and of the Dean of the respective College should be given the greatest of weight and should be followed unless proved to be clearly wrong."[12] At the meeting of January 19, 1947, the regents, on a four to two vote with one abstaining, turned down the recommendation, and most of them made statements for the record denying that political bias had entered in but stating that they were troubled that McMurray's academic work seemed ancillary to his political career. Fortunately, Fred did not turn the question into one of "confidence," but said, prior to the decision, "As a matter of public record the President of the University wishes to make it clear that in his opinion the Regents of the University are intelligently, seriously, and conscientiously discharging their responsibility."[13] It would have been possible, if the president had been distrusted, for both the faculty and the regents to be incensed at him.

However, the faculty endorsed his statement on the weight that should be given departmental judgment and asked that in the future the Regent-Faculty Conference Committee be brought in on such matters. The next month, at the end of Fred's second year in office, the regents passed a resolution of praise for the work he had done and was doing. President Fred had traversed a malodorous academic morass and had come out smelling of roses.

I mention here, as typical, a few events of his administration before 1950 in which he played a leading role, not always a visibly conspicuous one, in distinction from the majority of actions that occur at a university neither greatly forwarded nor seriously impeded by the administration.

1. He led in the starting of a new building program, in the development of the Campus Planning Commission, and in securing funds for the library. These are described in Chapter 4.

2. In June 1948 he secured the appointments of Ira L. Baldwin and A. W. Peterson as vice presidents of academic affairs and of business and finance respectively. Each of them, in the very best sense, could run a tight ship, thereby complementing President Fred's talents as a navigator.

3. He skillfully developed relations with the Wisconsin Alumni Research Foundation and the University of Wisconsin Foundation. The program of grants-in-aid was enlarged during both Fred's deanship of the Graduate School and his presidency. The University Houses were built with funds from WARF, and it was made clear to certain of the foundation's trustees that rental provisions should be established by the University rather than by the foundation. The program of special professorships was inaugurated with those named after Frederick Jackson Turner (UWF) and Slichter (WARF).

I would also place as an accomplishment the demonstration that if a president devotes all his time to the University he need not squander too much of it on social occasions. He signalized this by refusing to have an inaugural ceremony and by never wearing formal garb. Perhaps his success in this regard is chiefly due to the intelligent and attractive way Mrs. Fred represented him.

At Fred's last meeting with the regents as president, in June 1958, Mrs. Fred was invited to be present; and A. Matt. Werner, as the senior regent, delivered an encomium and, for the regents, gave Fred a watch inscribed "In appreciation of wise and gracious leadership, 1945-1958." The regents then, after many whereases, passed the following richly merited resolution: "THEREFORE BE IT RESOLVED: that The University of Wisconsin Board of Regents extend to Edwin Broun Fred deepest gratitude for his long devotions and exceptional contributions to Wisconsin, wish him the greatest of satisfactions in his years ahead, and express the hope that his friendship for the members of this body will be continued into the far future."[14]

DURING the second quarter of this century, as at other times, the regents were, in Fred's words quoted elsewhere, "intelligently, seriously, and conscientiously discharging their responsibility."[15] They made many wise decisions, usually, as should be the case, on the recommendation of administrative or faculty bodies which had studied the matters. I think they made one or two bad blunders—at least this is what their successors sometimes believed.

The most unfortunate action of the board is the one used as the starting point of this essay: the passing of Regent Daniel Grady's resolution "that no gifts, donations, or subsidies shall in the future be accepted by or in behalf of the University of Wisconsin from any incorporated Educational endowments or organizations of like character."[16] In March 1930 the regents rescinded this action but not before serious harm had been done, both because of actual grants that were lost and because of deterioration of relationships with the great foundations.

In 1925 there were seventeen regents, one from each of eleven congressional districts, four at large, and the president of the University and the superintendent of public instruction, ex-officio. In 1939 the number was changed to ten, nine at large, and the superintendent of public instruction, ex-officio. This change made for less localism, a more compact board, and an almost total change of personnel. The new board made it clear in their resolution on the death of Glenn Frank that they did not agree with the board which had dismissed him.

As mentioned elsewhere, the regents twice came close to an open conflict with the faculty, once in regard to the control of athletics and once in connection with the McMurray case; but both times the genuine desire on the part of each group to remain amicable and to play its appropriate role led to a reasonable *modus vivendi,* if not to complete understanding.

Most regents were careful not to misuse their positions, but a few would urge a favorable decision in a question related to discipline or to the academic record of some student. Dean C. J. Anderson of the School of Education once told a regent, who came in to urge an action favorable to a student, to "get out of my office"; and, in reply to "Can't a citizen of

Wisconsin come to see you about a student?," said, "Not if he is a Regent." To the credit of the regent, he left without showing anger. Most regents, as well as most legislators for that matter, would merely ask for a report which could be passed on to the individual or the parents.

As in many groups, the tone of the Board of Regents is set by a few persons. I shall mention several.

Theodore Kronshage, Jr., was chairman of the board in 1925 and had been a tower of strength to Birge.

Daniel Grady of Portage came on the board in 1923 and served until 1930, being chairman for the last four years, and then, after a year off, was again regent from 1931 to 1938. Although he carried the board with him in the ill-starred refusal of foundation funds, he was in later years the great dissenter. He dissented when the regents expressed their willingness to again accept gifts. He dissented when Frank was fired. He dissented when the University joined the Mid-West Library Center; and he voted to approve the appointment of Howard McMurray. However, the advocate of the unpopular is not always the advocate of the devil. He had a gift for writing memorials, was picturesque in both looks and speech, and even his opponents enjoyed his skill as a raconteur.

As Grady had passed from being chairman to being the spokesman of the minority, so Harold Wilkie changed from being a minority member to being chairman of the board from 1935 to 1940. During this period he was its dominant member, having the advantage from the point of view of influence of being on the scene as a Madison attorney. He seems to be remembered chiefly for his role in the dismissal of President Frank. This is an inadequate picture, for he did much else. He represented the lower-paid groups in the faculty and in the classified personnel. He respected faculty judgment (for example, he wanted to have the University Committee appear before the regents in connection with salary reductions), and it was a board over which he presided that asked for the advice of the University Committee on the selection of Frank's successor — an innovation at the time. Without the Frank episode he would be remembered as a strong and useful leader, which is probably a juster estimate.

After Wilkie left the board there were at the same time as regents, Michael J. Cleary and Herman L. Ekern, a thoughtful conservative and a thoughtful liberal. Cleary was president of the Northwestern Mutual Life Insurance Company and Ekern had been speaker of the assembly, commissioner of insurance, attorney general, lieutenant governor of the state and co-author of the State Teachers Retirement Act.

I will mention only one regent of this period who is still living, A. Matt. Werner, notable for both the quality and the length of his service. He came first to the board in 1940 and served until 1969. He was a man of principle but also one of compassion and human understanding, as well as a calming element among the regents.

Now and then there have been some regent appointments as political rewards. It is said that when one of the La Follette family, who was defending Governor Blaine's appointments as representative of many elements among the Wisconsin citizens, was asked concerning one who acknowledgedly was a mistake, she replied blithely, "Oh, he is the representative of ignorance." However, the boards were a credit to the state; and not only were their leaders able and public-spirited but, equally important, their leadership was recognized so that the actions of the board bore the stamp of its best minds.

THE governors of the state have much to do with the welfare of the University. They appoint and often influence actions of the regents. They make budget recommendations to the Legislature; and they help set the tone of the state's attitude toward the University. During the twenty-five years we are considering, the state had nine governors—none of them inimical to the University when in office through some were critical while campaigning. Two of them were also regents; Walter J. Kohler had been a leading regent before he was governor, and Oscar Rennebohm became one after he left office. Rennebohm was not only the University's friend in state affairs but its generous benefactor through private giving. Perhaps I should mention as a friend of the University, the octogenarian, Governor Walter Goodland, especially, some said, after it had won his respect by dealing strictly with a close relative.

In 1925-1926 the income of the University was nearly seven million dollars, of which three million seven hundred thousand came from state appropriations—something over half of the total. By 1950, with a much larger student body, greater responsibilities especially in research, and a substantial increase in prices, the total income of the University was about thirty-one million dollars; and, although the state's wise and generous appropriations had increased to eleven million dollars, these represented only about one-third of the total University income. Students were paying a larger share of the cost of their education. The programs of federal support for University research were getting underway. One of the most significant changes was in "gifts and grants," which in 1925 represented 2.4 percent of the University income, but in 1950 was about 6 percent of the total, nearly an elevenfold increase in actual amounts. The period 1925 to 1950 was one of great growth in private giving to the University.

The first major bequest, doubling its trust fund, was the residue amounting to more than $300,000 of the estate of J. Stephens Tripp, of Sauk City and Prairie du Sac. Tripp had died in 1915, and the trust fund from his bequest was established by the regents in 1921.

Senator William S. Vilas, who had been a strong regent of the University, died in 1908 and left his estate to a permanent board of trustees: first, for the protection of his wife and daughter, and then for the use of the University under specified conditions. Income from this estate did not become available to the University until 1961. The will was remarkable in many ways, especially in the protection of the academic freedom of the Vilas Professors whose positions were provided for and in the fact that it created a special board of trustees to handle the investments and to grant funds to the University to be used in accordance with the conditions of the bequest. It also required adding part of the income to the capital until the trust should amount to thirty million dollars.

Howard L. Smith, professor of law at the University, who died in 1941, left his estate—after certain provisions to protect his widow—to the University for its humanistic program. He was a true wit and one of his earliest and most notorious feats was the reply to the redoubtable Senator Vilas which "set Madison agog," and which is said to have concluded with the assurance that "even the Vilas sinner may return." It is interesting that both Vilas and Smith left the bulk of their estates for the use of the University.

Another notable bequest was that of Kemper K. Knapp, of the class of 1879, who died in 1944, leaving the major portion of his estate, valued at about two million dollars, to the University. During his lifetime Knapp had formed the habit of giving generously to his alma mater.

The most productive gift for the benefit of the University, which came on the very heels of the regents' refusal to accept grants from private foundations, was a patent given by Professor Harry Steenbock of Biochemistry to the Wisconsin Alumni Research Foundation (WARF), which was incorporated in 1925 to accept this patent and others and to devote the income to the promotion of scientific research at the University. Through June 1950 the foundation had given $4,430,000 to the University. Since then, its gifts have rapidly increased until now they are almost that amount annually. In general, income from the patents was invested, and the grants to the University made from investment income. We should not forget that, although the University is grateful to Steenbock for his generous support of research, the public may well remember him chiefly as one who made a major contribution to the conquest of rickets—and, as a side-effect, eliminated the staining of many a baby bib by cod-liver oil. It seemed to Steenbock and to his advisers, Slichter and Russell, that a private foundation would be better able than the University to invest income productively, to defend health-related patents, and to prevent their misuse by quacks. In this they were following, I suppose unconsciously, the precedent set by Senator Vilas.

In 1945 the University of Wisconsin Foundation (UWF) was established with the full approval of the regents to solicit gifts for the University. Such an arrangement provided desirable flexibility and good management; and, besides, some businessmen who wanted to help the University liked giving to an independent foundation rather than to an arm of the state. One of its first major grants was for the establishment of the Frederick Jackson Turner Professorship of History, matching the Charles Sumner Slichter Professorship financed by WARF. These chairs were filled with distinction by Merle Curti, one of Turner's students who was already at the University, and by Clinton N. Woolsey, a neurophysiologist. By the summer of 1950 the foundation's campaign, which led to the construction of the Wisconsin Center building, was well underway.

A gift that deserves special mention was made in 1943 by "two friends of the University" with the expressed desire that it "be used to strengthen and enlarge the cultural and artistic undertakings of the University," since "even in the midst of war it is well that we remember the total experience of the race."[17] However, no formal restrictions were placed upon either the principal or the income from this gift except that the "gift remain completely and forever anonymous." It is still known as "The Anonymous Fund."

Although the quarter-century, 1925-1950, opened in a period of prosperity, adversity was "just around the corner." The fact that the University weathered it better than most similar institutions is because of many factors, two of which will be discussed below.

By the fall of 1932 it was clear that the relatively minor cuts in the University budget which had resulted from the start of the depression would be followed by much larger ones. There already were general salary reductions which someone believed would be more palatable if called "waivers," a word which led a few to think mistakenly that the University would repay them. These first cuts ran from 0 percent to 13 percent of salary and were decided upon when there was not time to fully consider alternatives.

At the November 1932 meeting of the University faculty, Professor Michael F. Guyer of Zoology moved that the faculty request the University Committee "to undertake as its chief project during the current year, an approximate appraisal of and report upon the respective University activities, in terms of essentiality and relative costs, in order that the members of the Faculty may gain a better understanding of the whole budgetary situation and thus be enabled to assist the Administrative Officers more intelligently than is now possible in meeting emergencies and effecting economies."[18] I was told that this motion was hatched in a dining club by persons alarmed at what they believed was Frank's tendency to by-pass the faculties — especially that of the College of Letters and Science.

The report of the University Committee was finished in May of 1933 and acted upon at the June meeting of the faculty. There were twelve recommendations, a number of which dealt with how to make savings with the least adverse effect upon the University's programs. Two recommendations, dealing with maintenance of staff and with salary cuts, will be considered in some detail. The first of these stressed the importance of maintaining tenure (some seven years before the 1940 Statement of the AAUP and the AAC which described what was then considered good practice). In discussing nontenured staff, the report said:

Every appointment should be held valid for its duration. We recommend that deserving assistant professors whose terms expire should be reappointed.

In dealing with staff members in the lower ranks, the University should act with a full realization of the gravity of the social problem involved, and with the utmost consideration for the welfare of the individual and the future of the teaching profession. These younger men and women may be divided into three classes: (1) Those exhibiting qualities of character and intellect which would justify their holding ultimately a permanent place in a university of the first rank; (2) those doing meritorious work, but not that of the highest type; (3) those whose capabilities are doubtful. We recommend that the first group be retained; the second be retained as far as their services can be used; the third be not reappointed at this time.

Wherever it appears necessary to make reductions in staff beyond that produced by resignations, such reductions should be made with the imposition of the minimun of hardship. We recommend that every effort be made to give the men or women involved some form of employment until they are able to secure better positions.

On the matter of salary reductions, the committee said in part: "We recommend that (1) In determining the scale of salary waivers, sufficient allowance be made to permit promotions in rank and normal salaries of particularly meritorious members of the staff, and as far as possible to meet competition from outside of the University; (2) The waivers be based on a sliding scale of the type used for income taxation; (3) The lowest bracket receive a waiver commensurate with the decrease in the cost of living."[19] The committee also worked out tables from which estimates of the savings produced by any particular waiver scale could be readily computed. This made the proposals more acceptable to the business office.

The faculty passed all these recommendations by voice vote—that is, nearly unanimously. It is clear that these actions enhanced the respect that the regents had for the faculty. The administration and the regents in general followed these recommendations. In 1933-1934, and for three subsequent years, the waivers ranged from 12 percent on the first $500 of salary to 25 percent on the amount between $9,000 and $10,000. The waiver for those few with salaries above $10,000 was a flat 20 percent. Also in accordance with the recommendations of the University Committee, promotions and raises in salaries continued to be made. In 1937-1938 salaries in the budget were "net"; some were still below the 1933 unwaivered salaries but many were higher than their earlier prewaivered levels.

Maintenance of staff was greatly aided by grants from WARF to provide research appointments—some of these to a number of promising scientists who had just received their doctorates from the University and some to members of the staff. In this manner the University kept the services and increased the loyalty of its faculty, especially of the younger members, in a way that many other institutions failed to do. It also rescued the careers of some very good scholars. These emergency grants had been urged by Harry Steenbock, Harry L. Russell, and Charles S. Slichter. In addition to helping to meet a crisis, these actions established a program of research leaves which was continued with increasing funds from WARF, research appropriations from the state and other sources, but never again dipping into the principal of WARF.

The period under consideration has often been described as one of "nonbuilding." This is not accurate. It is true that the amount built from state tax funds was small, although twice a program that seemed about to get underway was halted—once by the depression and once by World War II. Of course priorities had changed after each of these emergencies had passed. However, in the area of student services this was a time of considerable construction. The Memorial Union was started in 1926 and opened in 1928 and had an addition, including the theater, finished in 1939. Early in this period a series of much-needed men's dormitories was put up along Lake Mendota, unfortunately destroying a beautiful grove of weeping willows. The Field House, as well as much of the Stadium, was constructed during this time. The Union was built from gifts, and additions were made with money from gifts and from student fees. The dormitories were in part self-liquidating from rental charges, though favorable conditions were made possible by an internal loan from the bequest of J. Stephens Tripp and through grants from the PWA program of the federal government. The athletic facilities also had help from this program but were largely financed from sales of tickets.

Before 1950 WARF had started enriching the University's building program through grants to cover part of the cost of structures used in scientific research—notably, an addition to the Biochemistry Building—and by erecting near the base of Picnic Point a set of apartments known as University Houses in order to aid in recruiting staff who were finding it difficult to get suitable places to live within the limitations of academic salaries. This project was at first considered an investment by WARF but later, partly due to some differences of opinion on rental policies (the University placed the application of a black professor ahead of his regular position because of the difficulty he was having in securing other housing) these apartments were given to the University, the net income, however, to be used for the same purposes as those furthered by the foundation.

In connection with the physical facilities of the University, the acquisition of the present Arboretum through gifts, and the purchase of Picnic Point belong to this era.

During this whole period the need for academic buildings was becoming more and more desperate. This was in part caused by the growing student body but it was, in addition, a reflection of the increasing number and complexities of research programs and also, in the case of the library, of the ever increasing size of the book collection.

In 1945 the Campus Planning Commission was created to advise the president and regents concerning priorities, the location of buildings, and the acceptance of plans at various stages. It was broadly representative, with membership from the administration, the faculty, state government personnel, and alumni. A large share of the work was carried on by a much smaller steering committee. During the first year the burden of leadership rested on its executive secretary, Professor James G. Woodburn of Hydraulic Engineering, and then passed to Ira L. Baldwin, who represented President Fred as chairman of the steering committee.

At the very start an analysis of the University's future requirements convinced the commission that the University would need to use much land not then owned by it (south of University Avenue to Regent Street and east of Park Street to Lake Street), making it possible to locate many buildings in convenient walking distance of each other—which would not be the case if the new structures were strung out on land the University owned along Lake Mendota and farther west. The Regents accepted this analysis and notified the public of a program of gradual acquisition of land. Now, 1975, a score or so of major University buildings and many lesser ones are in this area.

Three important buildings, chiefly financed by the state, were being constructed by the end of 1950. Babcock Hall, the dairy industry building, was started in 1949 and opened in 1952. The stories of the Engineering

Building and of the Memorial Library are closely associated with each other.

Even in 1925 the State Historical Society Building, which also served as the University library, was overcrowded. On December 7, 1936, the faculty voted to "request the Regents to place first on any building program of the next biennium, the enlargement and improvement of our university library facilities."[20] By the fall of 1948 it was clearly first on the lists of all general University bodies dealing with the building program. The University had received seven and a half million dollars to use toward a list of the top priority needs, which would cost thirteen million dollars. However, the plans for the library were far from complete, whereas those for several other buildings, especially the Engineering Building and the dairy industry building, were ready or nearly so. At a special faculty meeting on October 5, 1948, President Fred said, "It is my judgment that if plans for the Library were complete, this building would be placed as first choice in our building program by the Steering Committee, the Campus Planning Commission, and the Regents. It would certainly be my first choice."[21] However, all these groups recommended going ahead with other buildings, the most expensive being the plan for Engineering, rather than to hold up the whole program until the finishing of the plans for the library, probably in the next biennium. With many expressions of disappointment the faculty concurred. Bids were opened for the Engineering Building in November 1948, and it was occupied in 1950.

The 1949 session of the Legislature was crucial. The faculty on May 23, 1949, stated unanimously:

The faculty of the University of Wisconsin reaffirms its resolutions placing first in the building needs of the University a Library building. These were adopted by unanimous vote on December 7, 1936 and on May 2, 1949.

During the last 20 years the University of Wisconsin Library has dropped behind those of institutions of similar rank in the Middle West and in the Nation, both in its collections and in facilities for using existing collections. This situation has reached a critical stage with the increased enrollment of upperclass undergraduate and graduate students—a large number of whom are greatly dependent upon Library facilities and equipment for their work.

At the present time the University of Wisconsin cannot provide these students with the high quality of instruction to which they are entitled and a majority of faculty members are, because of inadequate Library facilities, unable to render the most efficient services to the students and the people of the State.

The faculty of the University of Wisconsin is pleased to note that the Governor appreciates the needs of the University for a Library and respectfully urges the Legislature to approve his recommendation of an appropriation providing for the building of a Library at the University of Wisconsin.[22]

President Fred called on many persons for help, but himself worked the hardest. Governor Rennebohm not only recommended the necessary appropriations but supported his recommendation by the many effective means at his command. A few days before the end of the session the Legislature passed the appropriation, a welcome climax to Wisconsin's Centennial year.

It was a gala occasion when finally the ground was broken for the library on July 24, 1950. Shovels were provided for all who wished to turn a spadeful and sign the scroll; over 700 did so. Some very small tots furnished their own toy shovels, and later one of these children, then a freshman, introduced himself to Fred as having been a participant.

One should not forget temporary buildings. In 1925 there were still a number of wooden shacks from World War I in use on the campus. The termination of World War II provided surplus structures. A very large Quonset hut was placed on the lower campus for use as a reading room and, nestling up to it, several small ones used as classrooms. The group was sometimes referred to as "the sow and little pigs." A number of temporary buildings went up for classrooms, offices, and laboratories, especially on the agricultural portion of the campus. There was a storage warehouse for lesser-used books. Much of Camp Randall was covered by trailers for married veterans. In addition to all of these, living quarters — including eating and limited recreational facilities along with some classrooms — were made available at Truax Field on the east side of Madison and at the Badger Ordnance Works somewhat beyond Sauk City. The fact that most of these buildings were eyesores and only marginally satisfactory does not take away from the fact that they were indispensable. One story illustrates: Mrs. Fred commented to a veteran's wife how sorry she was that the row-housing was so flimsy. Reply: "Oh, no! Any one of us can baby-sit for three families."

It is fair to say that during the quarter-century, 1925-1950, with the growth in the size of the student body and of the faculty, as well as the increase in research programs, the physical facilities of the University had become less and less adequate. However, progress had been made in living and social facilities for the students, and at the very end of the period the great building program of the next decades was underway. Yet those who graduated in 1925 could still feel at home on the campus in 1950. The University had changed the looks of the countryside through the introduction of hybrid corn more than it had altered its own appearance.

NOTE ON SOURCES

The Archives of the University of Wisconsin contain a vast amount of material on the history of the University. Some of it, such as the records of the regents and the financial reports, are in excellent order. Materials from members of the faculty are sometimes in the same order, or disorder, in which the professors kept them.

I have used the Minutes of the Board of Regents and its Executive Committee, the financial reports of the business officers, the Minutes of the University Faculty with their accompanying documents, and the University catalogues, announcements, and staff directories more than any other sources.

There are a number of biographies published by the University of Wisconsin Press: G. C. Sellery, *E. A. Birge,* a memoir (1956); Edward H. Beardsley, *Harry L. Russell and Agricultural Science in Wisconsin* (1969); Sylvia Wallace McGrath, *Charles Kenneth Leith, Scientific Adviser* (1971); Mark H. Ingraham, *Charles Sumner Slichter: The Golden Vector* (1972); Diane Johnson, *Edwin Broun Fred: Scientist, Administrator, Gentleman* (1974). In addition, there is a very readable, semi-autobiographical volume, George C. Sellery, *Some Ferments at Wisconsin 1901-1947, Memories and Reflections* (1960). This describes a number of interesting and controversial events at the University. It is not without prejudices, but ones that to a large degree I share.

NOTES

1 George C. Sellery, *Some Ferments at Wisconsin* (Madison, 1960), p. 44.

2 Frank's statement to the regents, November 22, 1930, Records of the Board of Regents, vol. M, p. 337.

3 The Report of the Special Committee on the Organization of the University's System of Student Counsel and Discipline, in Faculty Document 385, p. 2. The Report was discussed at the Faculty Meeting of June 1, 1931.

4 Faculty Document 385, p. 3.

5 Meta Berger's Resolution, January 15, 1930, in Records of the Board of Regents, vol. M, p. 193.

6 The Report of the Student Board Committee against Discrimination, in Faculty Document 914, part 3, pp. 6-7. Faculty Meeting, October 3, 1949.

7 Charles S. Slichter, *Science in a Tavern* (Madison, 1938), pp. 177-178.

8 Committee on University Functions and Policies, *Second Report, Internal Survey* (Madison, November 1949) (as revised, July 1951), chap. 4, pp. 42-43.

9 University Committee, Special Report on Tenure, in Faculty Document 584, p. 1.

10 Faculty Meeting Calendar, January 8, 1940, p. 2, and Faculty Minutes, p. 3; The General Report of the Committee on the Quality of Instruction and Scholarship, in Faculty Document 165b, November 1942, part 2, p. 1.

11 Sellery's Address to the Faculty, in Faculty Minutes, January 11, 1937, p. 1.

12 E. B. Fred's statement to the regents, in Records of the Board of Regents, January 17, 1947, vol. 8, exhibit F; Faculty Meeting Calendar, February 3, 1947, p. 1, Agenda Item 6.

13 Sellery, *Some Ferments,* p. 115.

14 Board of Regents Minutes, June 17, 1958, pp. 19, 21.

15 Sellery, *Some Ferments,* p. 115.

16 Regent Grady's Resolution, August 5, 1925, in Records of the Board of Regents, vol. L, p. 190.

17 "Two Friends . . ." to the regents of the University of Wisconsin, September 23, 1943. Letter copy filed in Papers of the Board of Regents, October 16, 1943.

18 University Committee, Report in Response to Faculty Committee Action of November 7, 1932, May 9, 1933, in Faculty Document 432, p. 1.

19 Faculty Document 432, pp. 16-17, 19.

20 Faculty Minutes, December 7, 1936, p. 4; Faculty Document 518.

21 Faculty Minutes, Special Meeting, October 5, 1948, p. 2.

22 Faculty Minutes, May 23, 1949, p. 2.

CHAPTER 3

The University's Supporting Resources, 1949-1974

WILLIAM H. YOUNG

THE past twenty-five years and particularly the decade of the 1960s witnessed the most phenomenal growth in the history of the University. The period opened with the Madison campus crowded with 20,000 students, of which 11,000 were veterans of World War II. Eleven two-year centers in key cities about the state, developed in the postwar era to handle the rush of veterans, took care of 2,500 more. Student fee income at the opening of this period was artificially high due to the payment by the United States of full nonresident tuition for the veterans of World War II. Enrollment then declined until 1952-1953, from which point it rose gradually and then very rapidly as the flood-tide of postwar babies reached the campuses and the proportion of high school graduates attending college sharply increased. By 1973 enrollment had climbed above 73,000 and the University System included not only the central campus at Madison but a growing metropolitan campus in Milwaukee, two developing four-year institutions at Green Bay and Parkside, and seven two-year centers around the state. Tuition payments pushed higher by rising costs, by shifts in the proportion of students in graduate and professional schools, and by rises in the proportion of costs borne by the student, had climbed to more than $37,000,000 by 1972 (the last full year of separate accounting in the merged system). Enrollment had risen more than 300 percent; tuition more than 800 percent.

William H. Young holds the Ph.D. in political science from the University of Wisconsin and joined the Political Science Department at Wisconsin in 1947 after service at the University of Pennsylvania and in the Office of the U.S. Adjutant General. He has been director of the Division of Department Research, State of Wisconsin, and executive secretary to the governor. Within the University he has served as chairman of the Department of Political Science, as assistant to the president and to the chancellor of the Madison campus, as director of the Center for Development, and as acting director of the Center for Public Policy and Administration. He has published books and articles on the nature of American national and state government.

As extraordinary as was this growth in instructional responsibilities, the growth in budgeted research was even more astonishing. The period opened with a total annual research expenditure of $3,700,000, of which $1,500,000 came from gifts and grants—a third, $500,000, from the Wisconsin Alumni Research Foundation. The federally supported nonagricultural research was only about $260,000. The remaining $2,000,000 came from federal and state agricultural appropriations and related operational receipts. By the close of 1972, the annual expenditures for budgeted research had reached $69,000,000, of which the nonagricultural, federal share had climbed to $40,000,000.

As Table 3.1 reveals, the federal government had been expanding its contribution to the University for agricultural education, extension, and experimentation but federally funded grants and contracts for research had grown to more than ten times the old land grant agricultural support. New federal financing also included funds for instruction, work-study, and extension activities. Total federal support, with the indirect cost reimbursement associated with federal grants and contracts now a substantial $10,000,000, was by 1972 more than $71,000,000 (excluding student-aid, auxiliaries, and hospital plant additions).

Table 3.1. University of Wisconsin Income, 1949-1972

Source of income	1949	1959	1969	1972
Student fees	$ 4,732,508	$ 5,550,625	$ 25,524,129	$ 37,142,058
Adult extension	780,158	912,657	2,947,225	4,120,920
State appropriations	9,001,329*	21,318,479	96,006,739**	143,956,698***
Federal aid	1,124,577	2,290,197	4,153,650	5,813,244
Federal grants	262,597	5,326,625	39,647,078	56,115,426
Federal work-study	—	—	542,201	237,270
Gifts, grants	1,444,995	4,835,669	11,058,812	12,465,280
Endowment	42,165	347,094	454,956	1,015,948
Sales—departments	1,146,800	1,338,565	2,320,398	2,468,453
Other (overhead)	337,403	1,264,856	10,935,630	15,733,323
Subtotal	*$18,872,532*	*$43,184,767*	*$193,590,818*	*$279,068,624*
Hospitals	$ 2,711,730	$ 5,197,329	$ 17,198,249	$ 22,621,782
Auxiliaries	5,499,530	7,429,765	18,591,312	24,694,088
Other	715,774	—	7,484,526	—
Total	*$27,799,566*	*$55,811,861*	*$236,864,905*	*$326,384,495*

Source: All figures from annual financial reports of the University.
 *Excludes $1,000,000 for hospital wing.
 **Including fringe benefits for staff—separately appropriated before.
***Including $16,881,717 for amortization of loans for educational buildings—separately appropriated before.

This phenomenal expansion of federal support far overshadows in size and perhaps also in consequence any other development in the past twenty-five years in the sources of income for the University. Most of the increase, it should be noted, has been in grants and contracts for specific projects and programs. The indirect cost reimbursement represents the major federal increase in resources available for general institutional support. Of course the University community has benefited through enriched instruction, high-quality faculty, and superb additions to available equipment and apparatus, but the bulk of federal grants are not available to the administration for disposition in accordance with an annual determination of priority needs. Federal grants are awarded to specific faculty members for approved programs.

The great upsurge in federal support also tended to obscure the steadily growing support from the Wisconsin Alumni Research Foundation (See Table 3.2). The annual WARF grant for research

Table 3.2. A Summary of the Wisconsin Alumni Research Foundation Grants to the University of Wisconsin — Madison and Milwaukee Graduate Schools, 1949-1974

Year	Total funds
1948-1949	$ 492,000
1949-1950	536,428
1950-1951	633,008
1951-1952	688,118
1952-1953	773,012
1953-1954	798,012
1954-1955	860,340
1955-1956	950,340
1956-1957	1,030,340
1957-1958	1,323,340
1958-1959	1,448,340
1959-1960	1,790,352
1960-1961	1,737,418
1961-1962	1,794,723
1962-1963	1,678,559
1963-1964	1,628,275
1964-1965	1,808,552
1965-1966	1,808,552
1966-1967	1,897,127
1967-1968	2,851,121
1968-1969	2,844,000
1969-1970	3,155,800
1970-1971	3,359,000
1971-1972	3,520,000
1972-1973	3,755,000
1973-1974	4,000,000

Source: Figures obtained from "Reports from the Graduate School to the Wisconsin Alumni Research Foundation Trustees and University Administration."

projects of many types grew from $492,000 in 1948-1949 to $4,000,000 in 1973-1974. Added to amounts appropriated by the state and to some general grants from the federal government, the WARF funds provided through the Graduate School and its Research Committee the discretionary research funds each year awarded to the faculty on application. By this means research funding in the humanities and the social sciences, largely unsupported by specific federal funding, has been provided to the University faculty. The escalation of WARF annual research grants has been accompanied throughout the period by substantial additional contributions by that foundation for buildings (See Table 3.3). More than $16,500,000 has been given during 1949-1974 for this purpose — an average of more than $660,000 per year. The Chemistry Research Building, Molecular Biology, Primate Laboratory, Genetics Laboratory, Elvehjem Art Center, and many other campus landmarks, bear witness to the incomparable help provided by the foundation.

The great rise in federal support did not substantially weaken the

Table 3.3. Wisconsin Alumni Research Foundation Grants for
Buildings and Major Equipment

Buildings and equipment	Total grant	Year of grant
Chemistry addition (Charter Street)	$ 66,000	1938
Biochemistry — two additions	137,500	1938
	1,300,000	1954
Chemical Engineering	500,000	1950
University Houses (Faculty housing — 150 units)	2,710,839	1951
Astronomy Observatory (Pine Bluff)	200,000	1955
Birge Hall (Biology)	250,000	1955
Sterling Hall addition (Mathematics Center)	1,200,000	1955
Service Memorial Institutes (Medical School)	750,000	1956
Enzyme Institute	350,000	1948
	300,000	1957
Primate Laboratory and addition	160,462	1953
	300,000	1957
Chemistry Research	1,454,000	1959
Computer equipment	500,000	1960
Genetics Laboratory	850,000	1960
Van Vleck Hall (Mathematics)	150,000	1961
Zoology Research	750,000	1961
Veterinary Science Research	475,000	1961
Molecular Biology and Biophysics	1,100,000	1963
Elvehjem Art Center	400,000	1965
Engineering Research	185,000	1966
University Bay Drive property	110,624	1966
Agriculture Life Sciences Library	1,207,900	1967
Electron microscope housing	265,000	1974

Source: All figures supplied by the Wisconsin Alumni Research Foundation.

dedication of the people of Wisconsin to their University as measured by the growing allocations from state tax funds. The state's contribution throughout the period has been close to 50 percent of the total operational costs, declining in the last decade to about 45 percent (excluding the substantial annual grants for buildings). It has risen from $9,000,000 to $127,000,000.

During the period there also has been a strong upswing in support from private foundations, associations, corporations, and individuals. With Ford and Rockefeller foundations leading the way, gifts and grant income has risen from $1,500,000 in 1949 to almost $12,500,000 in 1972. The Ford Foundation, in particular, has helped stretch the contribution of the campus beyond the state and nation to the Third World, sponsoring projects in Indonesia, the Philippines, and Singapore and promoting graduate training in national economic development and in

Table 3.4. University of Wisconsin Foundation: Payments to or for University of Wisconsin

Year	Amount
1946	$ 9,437
1947	25,500
1948	22,050
1949	28,990
1950	61,997
1951	141,351
1952	165,128
1953	65,246
1954	66,222
1955	185,130
1956	145,400
1957	1,389,821
1958	731,116
1959	173,072
1960	245,231
1961	266,654
1962	206,714
1963	590,151
1964	366,587
1965	152,746
1966	772,120
1967	618,667
1968	405,943
1969	2,219,896
1970	640,146
1971	1,045,949
1972	1,068,363
1973	1,938,779
Total	$13,748,406

Source: All figures supplied by the University of Wisconsin Foundation.

university administration, and greatly expanding the curriculum to include the history, culture, language, politics, economics, and agricultural experience of the new nations of Africa, the Near and Far East, and Latin America. The Rockefeller Foundation has supported efforts to assist the strengthening of universities in the developing nations. Strong support through the period also has been provided by the American Cancer Society, the American Heart Association, the Polio Foundation, and other medical establishments. The University of Wisconsin Foundation, organized in 1946 to channel gifts from alumni and friends to the benefit of the institution, has collected more than $26,000,000 since 1949, and has transferred more than half of this sum to such impressive campus features as the Wisconsin Center building and the Elvehjem Art Center. While more than half of that foundation's returns have been used for capital expansion, much has also gone for fellowships, scholarships, professorships, library collections, and other types of campus enrichment.[1]

The state, on its part, has not only provided money to underwrite the public share of the instructional expenditures for the rapidly expanding student body, it also has provided new classrooms and laboratories on an unprecedented scale. From the development during World War II of a Post-war Construction Fund to meet the long-postponed needs for state facilities, out of which came funds for the beginning of the building boom, through the development of a special construction fund and building commission which financed the Memorial Library and the first part of the Engineering Building, to the revolutionary, legalized State Building Corporation, with the power to borrow for state capital needs, the state has virtually rebuilt the Madison campus and more than tripled the physical plant.

Now the great period of growth seems to be over. Enrollments are stabilizing where they are not declining. The birth rate has dropped so strongly that a few years hence there will be many fewer young people to seek college entrance, although changes in the proportion of young men and women applying for college admission could brighten the picture. The building boom, however, is coming to a halt, although many campus needs remain unfilled. Now the capacious federal treasury is pouring out its support in smaller and more stringent measures. But WARF and the University of Wisconsin Foundation continue to flourish.

NOTE

1 As part of the campus 125th Anniversary celebration, the *Wisconsin Alumnus*, vol. 75, no. 6 (September 1974), was devoted to a review of private gifts to the campus, "The Bounty of the Years," by Hazel F. McGrath.

The Madison campus from the west. In 1878 (top) there was a solar observatory among the corn shocks. In 1974 (middle) the view from Camp Randall was a hodge-podge of buildings, but from Picnic Point (bottom), some of the natural beauty still was evident.

Students helped fight the fire when Bascom Hall's dome burned in 1916.

CHAPTER 4

The Growth of the University's Physical Resources, 1949-1974

KURT F. WENDT

THE physical growth of the University at Madison during the last quarter of a century was phenomenal by any standard of measurement. During these years more than 70 percent of the present total building space was constructed, reflecting roughly a trebling of student and faculty populations for the same period. This is graphically illustrated in Figures 4.1, 4.2, and 4.3. Figure 4.1 shows the change in both graduate and total enrollments. Special note should be taken of the relative increase in the proportion of graduate students since space requirements for graduate students are several times as great as for undergraduates. The data of 1940-1941 are included for comparison purposes because the data for the years 1942-1952 are grossly distorted due to World War II and its aftermath. Figure 4.2 shows the growth and change in composition of the academic staff. Note that group positions supported by gift, grant, and contract funds were not included. These were relatively small in the first years of this period, but gradually grew until in 1973-1974 some 1,500 were so employed as assistants, specialists, and other nonfaculty academic staff. Figure 4.3 shows the tremendous growth in space, especially during the last twenty years, required to accommodate the increasing students, staff, and programs.

Given the policy of the state to provide opportunity for higher education to all qualified students who desired it, such growth was to a substantial degree predictable. By 1949 most of the children who would

Kurt F. Wendt, emeritus dean and emeritus professor of mechanics has been a member of the faculty of the University of Wisconsin since 1927. For eighteen years prior to his retirement in 1971 he served as dean of the College of Engineering. His teaching and research in the field of materials and stress analysis have been widely recognized and his effectiveness has been noted by many awards from state and national organizations. He has served as a member of the Campus Planning Committee since 1953 and as the chairman or deputy chairman during the last seventeen years.

be attending the University in the 1960s already had been born; the percentage of eighteen-year-olds in the population of the state entering public colleges had increased steadily from 6.4 percent in 1900 to 13.8 percent in 1950 (it was ultimately to rise to 40 percent in 1970); and the need for greatly expanded graduate training and research was being recognized.

Planning for the future of the University is, of course, a continuing process. It is necessary to establish policies, develop academic programs, and clearly define objectives. Coupled with projections of student demands, it is then possible to estimate faculty needs and, finally, to determine facility requirements. All of the elements in this sequence are subject to change with time, and the least certain seems to be the projection of future student enrollment, both as to total number and as

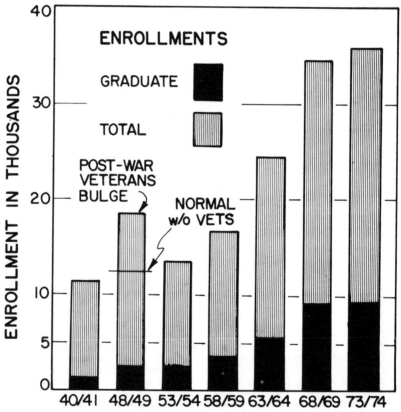

Figure 4.1. First semester enrollments for various years (data from U.W. Registrar's Office).

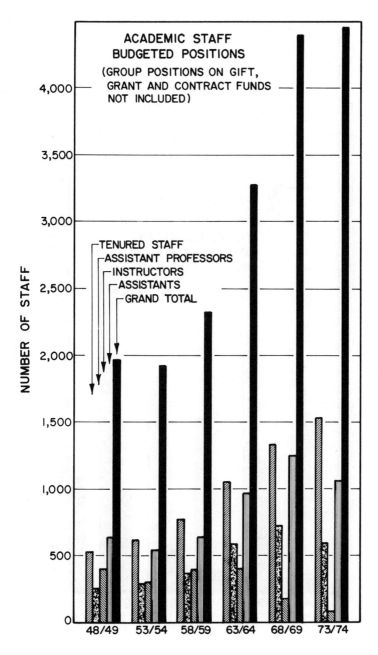

Figure 4.2. Academic staff positions in budget for various academic years (data from U.W. Budget Office).

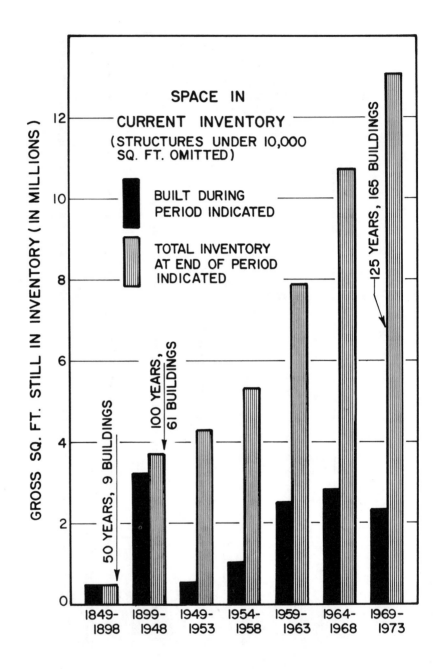

Figure 4.3. Gross square feet of space for buildings still in inventory. Bid dates used throughout (data from Bureau of Facilities Management, State Department of Administration).

to how such students will be distributed by field and specialty.

Any plan for the development of physical resources must therefore embody the maximum flexibility possible for effective present and future land use and for multiple-purpose buildings, in so far as feasible, with due consideration for effectiveness, economy, possible future growth, and aesthetics. Plans for the University at Madison evolved through many periodic studies. Among the most significant of these the following must be included:

1. The first general plan for the University was developed by a Milwaukee architect, John F. Rague, and adopted by the regents of the University with minor modifications in January of 1850. This plan envisioned five buildings including a "Main Edifice," now Bascom Hall, North and South Halls essentially as we know them today except for the addition of modern heating and lighting, and two additional dormitories farther down the hill which were never built. Rague also designed North Hall, the University's first building, completed in 1851 at a cost of $20,000.

2. The 1908 Architectural Commission Plan was "received and placed on file" by the regents on December 16, 1908. The commission consisted of Warren Powers Laird, Paul Phillipe Cret, and Arthur Peabody. Peabody was the University architect for ten years and then served as state architect from 1915 until his retirement in 1938. The 1908 plan was imaginative, ambitious, and bold, and the ideas expressed have had a strong influence on the development of the campus ever since. The lower State Street Mall, now approved for construction, is shown for the first time in this concept. In conjunction with the work of the commission, President Van Hise in his commencement address of 1908 estimated that the student body, then nearly 3,000, might ultimately grow to as high as 10,000!

3. The Wisconsin State Planning Board's "Campus Development Plan" of December 1941 substantially modified several of the basic concepts of the 1908 plan. This was a comprehensive but reasonably flexible plan designed "to facilitate the integration of related activities by colleges." It also envisioned a growth of the University from the then 11,300 to "possibly 20,000." A most important recommendation of the report, which was adopted by the regents on February 15, 1945, was to create a permanent University Campus Planning Commission. This commission, still charged with most of the same duties prescribed in 1945, persists today, though in modified form. The regents did not, however, adopt that portion of the recommendation providing that "the recommendations of the Plan Commission should be amendable only by a very large majority (not less than ¾) vote of all the members of the Board

of Regents."[1] The original commission first met on February 27, 1945, and included the president of the University as chairman, eight deans, six faculty, three regents, and other University and state officials to a total number of thirty-one. It was soon apparent that a compact steering committee was needed to carry on detailed studies and analysis, and on July 24, 1945, a nine-member committee was appointed by President Fred. This arrangement served well until 1959, by which time the expansion problems at the Milwaukee campus were requiring so much time that reorganization became necessary. By resolution of the regents on February 7, 1959, the University Campus Planning Commission and its Steering Committee were dissolved and two Campus Planning Committees, one for Milwaukee and the other for Madison and Extension, were created. The present membership of the Madison Campus Planning Committee consists of the chancellor or his deputy serving as chairman, three deans, four faculty, the director of the Department of Planning and Construction, the state chief engineer, and one student, plus several advisory staff members without vote.

4. The 1958 Sketch Plan, Faculty Document 1365, enunciated a series of development policies which were adopted by the regents on February 7, 1959. These policies provided for the acquisition of some seventy acres of land for expansion of the campus south of University Avenue between Frances Street and Breese Terrace, major increases in housing for faculty and students, the concept of areas of varying densities reflecting frequency and intensity of use, reduction of pedestrian-vehicular conflicts to a minimum, creation of green spaces and general campus beautification, and the creation of a joint city-university planning district surrounding the University. All of these recommendations except the last have been implemented in substantial degree. The majority of the southward expansion, within the limits specified in the Sketch Plan, has been completed. The density concept has resulted in a departure from the old four- or five-story height limitation on academic buildings to provide high-rise facilities such as Van Vleck, housing mathematics; Van Hise, nineteen stories and the University's tallest building, housing languages and central administration; Earth and Space Sciences; Russell Laboratories, housing forestry, wildlife, and entomology; Molecular Biology and Bio-Physics; and the Engineering Research building. The first high-rise on campus was Chadbourne Hall, the eleven-story women's dormitory. The Sketch Plan and its schedule for implementation were designed to accommodate 30,000 students by 1970. Actually they provided enough space to accommodate a growth in the student body to 40,000 plus. In 1959 President Elvehjem reported that

. . . the Regent Committee on the Future of the University agrees that, because of the nature of non-instructional facilities, no limitation on the expansion of such facilities need be considered; and they hesitate to establish, even for long-range purposes, a ceiling on the size of enrollments to be accommodated on the Madison campus. However, to preserve present efficiency in the use of buildings, the Regents agree that no expansion of instructional facilities should be contemplated beyond the point at which the interval between classes would have to be lengthened to allow for travel between distant buildings.

What limits such a rule might place on Madison enrollments would depend largely on how intensively the "close in" areas of the campus are utilized for building. It is felt that the campus, held to the above restrictions, can accommodate between 25,000 and 30,000 students.

It is our feeling that the ultimate size of the enrollment will not be as important a factor in maintaining the kind of quality of University education as will be the rate of growth. The deans have informally agreed that, granted the staff and the facilities, the University can handle over-all enrollment increases as high as 10 percent per year without impairing the quality of University offerings or causing serious administrative problems. [2]

The end of World War II brought a tremendous influx of veterans, many of them married and with families, and jumped student enrollment from 9,000 in 1945-1946 to more than 18,600 in each of the following three years (see Figure 4.1). This bulge obviously was temporary and could only be accommodated by using temporary measures. The Campus Planning Commission created in 1945 had a baptism of fire. Surplus army barracks were secured and transplanted to the campus to provide classrooms and laboratories. Several of these, such as T-23 and T-24, still are in service. Large Quonset huts covered the lower campus, and temporary buildings dotted the west slope of Bascom Hill. Housing was developed by moving in large numbers of surplus military trailers to Camp Randall and other nearby locations, and using surplus military housing at Truax Field and the Badger Ordnance Plant. The latter, being some twenty-five miles from the campus, required establishment of a bus system to transport students back and forth.

In 1949, at the beginning of the last quarter-century, the planning, design, construction, and maintenance of all state facilities except for highways was by statute the responsibility of the state chief engineer. For obvious reasons it was necessary to delegate much of the planning function and most of the maintenance to the larger agencies, including the University. Architectural design was either provided by the staff of the chief engineer, which included the state architect, or was contracted for by him with private architectural firms. Construction was, and continues to be, on a competitive bid basis, with contracts being finally approved by the governor. Construction was supervised jointly by the University and the chief engineer.

The University was fortunate to have as superintendent of physical plant an able planner and architect, Albert F. Gallistel, who served with distinction from 1907 to 1959. With a staff of two or three he carried on the planning and supervision function for the president and subsequently for the Campus Planning Commission in addition to his responsibility for operation and maintenance of the entire physical plant and supervision of the larger staff required for those operations. When the forecasts of growth made during the period 1940-1950 indicated the enormous expansion that would be required to meet future demands for all types of space, it became necessary to reorganize and expand the planning staff. In 1949 a separate Department of Physical Plant Planning was established, and in 1957 this was expanded to a Department of Planning and Construction with three divisions—planning, architecture, and engineering. This department continued to work closely with the state chief engineer and under his delegation prepared general plans for development, detailed programs for each building contemplated based on analysis of needs expressed by the faculty, represented the University in negotiations with the architects during the design process, and supervised construction including the processing of change orders and approval of work vouchers. The state chief engineer continued to appoint contract architects, and was responsible for recommendations to the governor in matters of final plan approval and awarding of contracts. He was kept constantly informed and both he and the director of the Planning and Construction Department served on the Campus Planning Commission. The faculty was kept closely involved by appointment to building committees created for each building early in the planning stage.

In 1959 the Legislature extensively reorganized the state government and created, among others, the Department of Administration. This department, along with many other duties, was charged with the responsibility for supervision of all engineering or architectural services and construction for the state or any institution of the state except for the highway commission and for certain engineering services of specified boards and commissions. Specifically included was every contract involving an expenditure of $2,500 or more. After several changes in departmental structure, the present organization consisting of a Division of Administrative Services and a Division of Operations evolved in 1971. The latter division is further subdivided into five bureaus, one of which, the Bureau of Facilities Management, now supervises all aspects of planning, financing, designing, and construction of physical facilities except highways. Engineering and architectural services are supplied through the state chief engineer. The bureau advises the State Building Commission and serves as its technical and analytical arm.

Despite the substantial services now furnished by the bureau, the University, as one of the largest agencies, must still carry on its traditional function of campus planning and the preparation, with faculty involvement, of the detailed programs for each contemplated building.

In 1955 the Legislature created the Coordinating Committee for Higher Education to coordinate the activities of the University of Wisconsin and the state colleges and institutes and to recommend necessary changes in programs and facilities. To execute its assignment the CCHE joint staff worked closely with all of the public educational institutions in the state and developed enrollment projections, estimates of other expansion pressures, and formulas for space requirements.[3] The latter included uniform space standards for offices, classrooms, instructional laboratories, research, libraries, and physical education. These, while admittedly approximate, have proven useful as guidelines, but must be used with care. A comprehensive study of our system reported by John V. Yurkovich and others sets forth the detailed methodology for determining facilities requirements.[4] The basic requirements include a space classification system, a perpetual space inventory, room utilization studies and records, and a system for projecting staff and students.

The complexity of the political and technical procedures required to translate University needs into effective and efficient facilities is evident. It is a tribute to all concerned — faculty, administration, regents, legislators, and state government personnel — that such a tremendous program of construction was accomplished so expeditiously (see Figure 4.3). Virtually every segment of the University has participated in this spectacular growth, which includes 104 major building contracts. Among the most notable buildings, in addition to the high-rise units already mentioned, are the new facilities for the School of Education and the Law School, Communication Arts, Engineering Units I, II, and III, the unique Biotron, the Wisconsin Center, the Humanities Building, the Elvehjem Art Center, the extensive student dormitories and married student apartments, the eighty-million dollar Medical Center complex under construction, the numerous buildings for the College of Agriculture and Life Sciences, and the completion of the library group, including the Memorial Library and the Undergraduate, Law, Medical, Agricultural and Life Sciences, and the Engineering and Physical Sciences library units. Not included in the inventory is the fourteen-story WARF building valued at six-million dollars; the top two floors house

WARF offices and conference rooms, and the lower twelve floors are rented by the University for use as a "surge" office facility. The current depreciated value of the buildings erected and under construction during this period, not including equipment, utilities, land, or landscaping, is in excess of four hundred million dollars. The total replacement cost of the entire plant cannot be reasonably estimated. Who, for instance, would have the temerity to put a dollar value on the land alone?

Not quite half of the funding for this development has come from state appropriations, one-sixth from grants from federal agencies, just under one-quarter from self-amortizing projects, and the important balance, one-eighth of the total, from the Wisconsin Alumni Research Foundation and from individual gifts directly or through the University of Wisconsin Foundation.

Long-range projections indicate a nearly stable enrollment at Madison at both graduate and undergraduate levels for at least the next decade. This trend is clearly evident in Figure 4.1. One of the important generators of space demand is research, which is closely related to graduate enrollment and size of tenured staff. Figure 4.4 shows annual expenditures for the Madison campus exclusive of plant additions, and dramatically illustrates the rapid increase in research support since 1953. Actually, the picture is somewhat distorted because the cost of "departmental research," which is not funded by direct appropriation or grants, is included in instructional costs and is estimated at 20 to 25 percent thereof. The difference between total expenditures and the sum of instruction plus research represents mainly dormitory, Union, University Hospital, and physical plant maintenance operations. For the twenty-five-year period, expenditures for instruction, research, and in total have grown by factors of 9.7, 20.6, and 9.9 times respectively. Reduced to constant dollars these factors would be roughly 3, 6, and 3, or, except for research, roughly the same as for enrollment growth. With the nearly constant enrollments predicted for the next decade the pressure for additional space, except to accommodate new programs and new areas of knowledge, will diminish, and the current ratios of expenditures are likely to be maintained.

The task ahead was in part defined by the faculty in 1969 in Faculty Document 257 which calls for "a physical and functional unification of the campus and development of an environment conducive to scholarly pursuits," and the creation of "a campus which is at once beautiful, functional and compatible with the needs and responsibilities of the State, the City, and the University."[5] The Madison Campus Planning Committee responded with the proposed 1973 Master Plan, which includes rehabilitation and improvement of the nearly four million

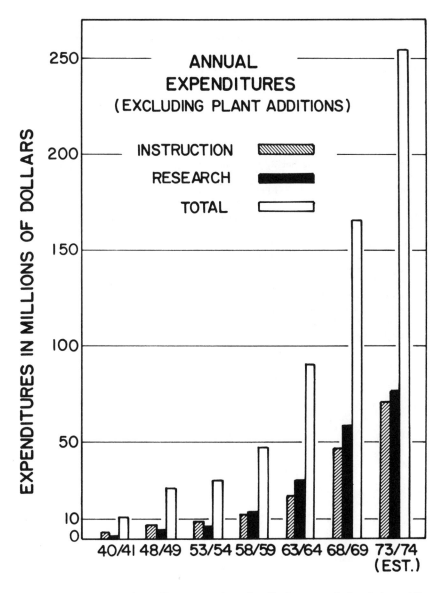

Figure 4.4. Expenditures for Madison campus for various fiscal years, exclusive of plant additions (data from U.W. Office of Financial Planning).

square feet of facilities over twenty-five years old to correct obsolescence and safety code violations, improvements of campus environmental conditions, and completion of additional facilities to replace rental space and accommodate new programs. This plan is now before Central Administration and the regents for consideration.

NOTES

1 Wisconsin State Planning Board, "A Campus Development Plan for the University of Wisconsin," *Bulletin,* no. 14, December 1941, pp. i, 2-3, 18, 11-12.
2 Conrad A. Elvehjem, "Balanced Progress: Key to the Future," *Wisconsin Alumnus,* vol. 61 (February 1960), p. 11.
3 Joint Staff, Coordinating Committee for Higher Education, "Survey of Physical Facilities at Wisconsin State Colleges and the University of Wisconsin," in Recommended Standards, Research Study VI, part 2, June 1958, State Archives, Madison, Wis.
4 John V. Yurkovich et al., "A Methodology for Determining Future Physical Facilities Requirements for Institutions of Higher Education," in Final Report, Project No. 2920, Contract No. OE-5-10-291, December 1966, U.S. Department of Health, Education and Welfare, University of Wisconsin Department of Planning and Construction.
5 "Recommendations by the Madison Campus Planning Faculty Advisory Committee on Long-Range Plan for the Madison Campus," in Faculty Document 257, March 3, 1969 (as modified April 17, 1969), p. 1.

CHAPTER 5

Faculty Governance, 1949-1974

DAVID FELLMAN

W HEN President Fred H. Harrington presided over his first faculty meeting on October 1, 1962, the new president developed a key point in his opening remarks, summarized in the minutes as follows: "Expressing his belief in academic freedom and the democratic approach, he urged the faculty to continue to demand a strong role in laying down policy for the University, stating that this tradition is the most significant feature of this University as compared with other institutions." In referring to the strong role of the faculty in University policy-making, President Harrington was reaffirming a central fact about the institution which dates from its very beginning, and which by 1949 was accepted as a wholly normal and proper feature of the system of University governance.

This concept of faculty self-determination was rooted in the state's formal law as well as in tradition and custom. Thus, the original statute organizing the University of Wisconsin provided that "the immediate government of the several departments shall be entrusted to their respective faculties."[1] With a later change in language from "departments" to "colleges,"[2] this remained the only statutory reference to faculty authority until the enactment by the Legislature of the Merger Act in 1971, which declared, among other things, that "all existing policies, rules and traditional practices of the former university of Wisconsin and the Wisconsin state universities and of the individual institutions shall continue until changed."[3] Finally, the Merger Implementation Act of 1974 spelled out in detail previously unknown to

David Fellman, Vilas Professor of Political Science, has long been active in faculty governance at the University of Wisconsin, having served as chairman of the University Committee, chairman of the Committee on Faculty Rights and Responsibilities, chairman of the Committee on Honorary Degrees, and chairman of the Special Codification Committee, which, over a period of several years, rewrote and modernized the Rules and Regulations of the University. In addition, he has been active in the American Association of University Professors, and served as the national president from 1964 to 1966. At the present time he is a member of the Faculty Senate.

Wisconsin statute law the basic position of the faculty in the policy-making of the institution. It provides: "The faculty of each institution, subject to the responsibilities and powers of the board, the president and the chancellor of such institution, shall be vested with responsibility for the immediate governance of such institution and shall actively participate in institutional policy development. As such, the faculty shall have the primary responsibility for academic and educational activities and faculty personnel matters. The faculty of each institution shall have the right to determine their own faculty organizational structure and to select representatives to participate in institutional governance."[4]

This statutory recognition of the faculty's place in institutional governance did not break new ground; it was largely a codification of practices and traditions which had developed during the first century of the University's history, and which by 1949 were fully understood and accepted by all elements of the University community. By 1949 a well-established pattern of faculty governance included the general faculty, college and departmental faculties, and faculty committees. Members of the faculty holding positions as professors, associate professors, and assistant professors, and nonprofessional members of the academic staff who were given faculty status because their training, experience, and responsibilities were comparable to those in the professorial ranks, were eligible to attend general faculty meetings and to serve on faculty committees.

The central institution of professorial governance was the regular monthly meeting of the general faculty, which was held on the first Monday of each month during the academic year, although the president had the authority to call special faculty meetings, and special meetings could also be called by petition of five faculty members.[5] The presiding officer of the general faculty meeting in 1949, and for some years afterwards, was the president of the University. In his absence, the vice-president for academic affairs presided, and in the absence of both, a dean designated by the president presided. The calendar for each meeting was prepared by the president's Administrative Committee.

Attendance at general faculty meetings was wholly voluntary, and thus some meetings were very well attended, while other consisted of but a handful of the faithful who attended as a matter of duty or habit. Routine business did not attract large numbers, and was disposed of in but a few minutes. For example, the general faculty meeting of December 3, 1951, was attended by only fifty-two faculty members, and meeting at the customary time of 4:30 P.M., it adjourned at 4:42 P.M. The meeting of February 11, 1952, did a little better in attracting seventy-four members, but they concluded their labors in four minutes. The meeting of June 5, 1950, drew sixty-four members and sat for thirteen minutes. The meeting of February 1, 1965, with fifty-two members in attendance, finished its work in six minutes. Curiously enough, the meeting of April 5, 1965, which sat for all of five minutes, attracted 257 members. The only business was a motion to grant the Department of Foods and Nutrition full membership in the faculty division of Biological Sciences.

On the other hand, there were quite a few well-attended general faculty meetings. Thus the meeting of January 4, 1960, which was concerned with ROTC policy, attracted an attendance of 426, and the meeting of May 9, 1960, which abolished boxing as an intercollegiate sport, was attended by 422 persons. The meeting of November 5, 1962, the agenda of which related to discrimination in fraternities, drew 468 people. A decision on Rose Bowl policy was reached at a meeting on May 4, 1953, with 498 in attendance. The largest faculty meetings occurred during the troubled years 1966-1970, when serious issues growing out of the military policies of the United States government led to large-scale turmoil on the campus. Here are some examples: meeting of May 23, 1966, 892 present; meeting of February 23, 1967, 833; meeting of October 19, 1967, 1,350; meeting of October 23, 1967, 1,450; meeting of March 13, 1968, 785; meetings of February 24, 1969, and March 3, 1969, both concerned with the Black Studies problem, 650 and 1,262; meetings of April 6 and 7, 1970, on the teaching assistant problem, 1,072 and 974; meeting of May 8, 1970, and May 26, 1970, both on war problems, 1,200 and 630. Finally the two meetings devoted to the proposal for creating a Faculty Senate, held on January 12, 1970, and January 19, 1970, were well-attended, attracting 578 and 410.

During the years since 1949 the impact of the general faculty upon all aspects of University life was enormous. Thus, in the field of curriculum the faculty gave its approval to the Integrated Liberal Studies Program in 1948, and created the Honors Program in 1960. Other notable developments at this level of decision involved the creation of such significant units as the Institute for Research in the Humanities, the Survey Research Center, the Wisconsin Education Improvement Program, the Institute for World Affairs Education, the Institute for Research on Poverty, the Afro-American Studies Department, and the Institute for Environmental Studies.

In addition to the general monthly faculty meeting, the faculty of each college or school meets occasionally at the call of the dean, who determines the agenda, and this has been true throughout the quarter-century under review. With rare exceptions, attendance at this level is small, and the main business is usually the approval of curricular

decisions made by departments. The revision of general degree requirements, however, has generally attracted more faculty attention.
Throughout the past twenty-five years, and indeed for most of the
University's history, one of the most viable elements of faculty governance has been the department. Subject to both faculty and administrative review, the departments create new courses, modify or abolish old
ones, determine the credit requirements for undergraduate majors
and graduate degrees, and control the recruitment and promotion of
personnel. The principal powers of the department are vested in its executive committee, which consists of all tenured professors and associate
professors, who in turn may by vote delegate to the chairman certain
important functions, such as the preparation of a salary budget for
submission to the dean. A noteworthy feature of the Wisconsin departmental system lies in the fact that all members of the departmental
faculty have a right to indicate by secret ballot their preference for
chairman. While the departmental vote is technically advisory to the
dean, the fact is that the dean almost invariably accepts the majority
decision, particularly if the majority is substantial. Furthermore, chairmen are chosen for a year at a time, and while some departments prefer
to re-elect their chairmen year after year, others rotate the office at fairly
short intervals of three or four years. In short, it is fair to say that this
crucially important office is, in effect, filled by the democratic method of
faculty election. Finally, the importance of the department in the
University community is reflected in the fact that attendance at departmental faculty meetings is almost invariably close to 100 percent. Like
other rational people, professors understand where decisions important to
them are made.

At the request of the Board of Regents, made in August 1947,
President E. B. Fred appointed a Committee on University Functions and
Policies, consisting of twenty-two members of the faculty and chaired by
Dean Mark H. Ingraham. The studies and reports of this committee
constituted a significant inquest into the state of the University and its
problems. A first report appeared in October 1948, the most important
point of which was a recommendation in favor of establishing a single
state university system for all of higher education, to operate under a
single board and a single president. A second report, labeled *Internal
Survey,* appeared in November 1949. The first report made it clear that
however higher education is organized in Wisconsin, "the present central
role of the faculty in determining educational policy [should] be
maintained."[6] The 1949 *Report* of this important committee returned to
this theme with a declaration that "the traditions of academic freedom
and of determination of educational policy by the faculty are great assets

that are not shared in equal degree by many universities. These must be maintained."[7] The committee also reviewed the important place of the department in the governance system, and asserted that it "approves the provisions of the University regulations which locate the responsibility for recommending the appointment of new staff members and the promotion of present staff members in the executive committee of the department."[8] In addition, the committee noted with approval that "the college faculty is the chief administrative body in the making and changing of curricula. With the college faculty rests responsibility for surveying the curricula of the college, of initiating committees to investigate and appraise the work of departments and courses, of forming committees to carry out the curricular recommendations of individuals and departments, and of adjusting curricula to changing conditions in the college and the University."[9]

Finally, the committee noted that "Faculty Committees play a large role in the guidance of University policies and the administration of its functions. . . . The basic objective of heavy dependence upon faculty committees is the preservation of a democratically run University. This entails keeping as much policy-determination as possible in the hands of active faculty members. There is a long and proud tradition that Wisconsin is 'faculty-run, not Administration ridden.' This pride is based on the conception of a university as an autonomous group of scholars, and on the thesis that active teachers and research scholars are most likely to know what is best in the management of most educational affairs."[10]

While there have been, throughout the past twenty-five years, a great variety of faculty committees, dealing with such matters as student conduct and student aids, the library, athletics, the planning process, honorary degrees, human rights, public functions, and research and fellowship grants, two faculty committees have long been especially significant in the Wisconsin system, the University Committee and the divisional committee.

The University Committee, consisting of six faculty members, serving three-year terms, with two elected each year, was well established as the faculty's most important committee long before the beginning of the period under review here. While the *Rules and Regulations* of the University contain a long list of duties and responsibilities pertaining to this key committee, perhaps it suffices to note that it is really authorized to concern itself with any aspect of University life, including faculty grievances. As the chosen instrument of the faculty, it has exercised leadership functions with great effectiveness, and has long enjoyed the confidence of both the faculty and the administration in an extraordinary measure. It is, in short, as it always has been, the general faculty's executive committee. At its meeting of March 20, 1950, the faculty approved a recommendation of the Committee on Functions and Policies that the University Committee should have, as one of its functions, "the making, on its own initiative, of studies and recommendations concerning major matters of University educational policy; and that the University Administration be encouraged to ask the University Committee for advice on such matters."[11] The University Committee was directed to feel free to give advice directly to the administration or to refer matters to the faculty for discussion. In addition, at its meeting of October 3, 1960, the faculty transferred to the University Committee the functions of the faculty section of the former Regent-Faculty Conference Committee. Thus the University Committee became the official link between the faculty and the Board of Regents.

Equally worthy of special note are the four divisional executive committees. These committees were created by the faculty in 1942, one each for the biological sciences, the physical sciences, the humanities, and the social sciences. Each divisional executive committee consists of twelve members elected by the divisional faculty. Originally the chairmen of these committees were selected by the administration, but since 1969, when the *Rules and Regulations* of the University were codified, the chairmen have been elected annually by the members of the respective divisional committees.[12] The most important function of these committees is to advise the deans with respect to appointments to tenured faculty positions. In addition, they must approve of new credit courses, and modification of existing credit courses, again subject to final action by the dean. These committees are also free to give advice to administrative officials regarding educational policy. The chief function of these committees has always been in the field of personnel policy. What the system means is that a department is answerable to elected representatives of cognate departments on the crucial question of suitability for tenured positions on the faculty. It is a very significant part of the University's system of quality control, which makes departments answerable to the judgment of scholars in related departments.

One other aspect of the University's committee system remains to be noted. At its meeting on January 9, 1950, on recommendation of the University Committee, the faculty voted to create a Student-Faculty Conference Committee. Furthermore, on March 20, 1950, the faculty adopted a recommendation of the Committee on Functions and Policies that each standing committee should decide whether student representation is desirable. Finally, a principal objective of the *Rules* codification which took place between 1964 and 1971 was to increase the number of students serving on faculty committees. While by rule a faculty committee must have a faculty majority,[13] and while some faculty committees have no student members at all—for example, the University Committee—still great progress was made in 1966 and in the following years in including more and more students on more and more faculty committees.

IN the light of later developments, the system of faculty governance which existed in 1949 was fairly simple. There was one University of Wisconsin, one faculty, one president, and one group of faculty committees. The University included an Extension Division, which operated, among other things, several two-year centers, the most important of which was in Milwaukee. But during the past quarter-century, various forms of expansion created new problems of faculty organization, and therefore led to changes in the historic pattern which had for so long prevailed at the University. In 1947 the Legislature created a Commission on the Improvement of the Educational System, of which State Senator Foster Porter served as chairman, and which issued a series of reports from November 1948 to March 1949 which recommended, among other things, an integrated system of higher education, with a single Board of Regents, and the merger of the Milwaukee State Teachers College with the Milwaukee Extension Division of the University. The Committee on Functions and Policies made similar recommendations in 1948. In January 1953 Governor Kohler proposed legislation to create a state-wide system of higher education under a single board, and failing to achieve this objective, he renewed his campaign for total integration in January 1955. A Madison Faculty Committee on Integration recommended, in a report dated July 22, 1954, that Milwaukee Extension be made a four-year college, but without merger with the State College. Furthermore, on March 15, 1955, a special Committee on Integration, chaired by Professor Fred Harvey Harrington, called for an expansion of the Milwaukee Extension Center. Finally, the boards of the University and the state colleges got together, and on August 31, 1955, they agreed that while the two-board system should be continued, a fifteen-member Coordinating Committee on Higher Education (consisting of five regents from each board, four citizen members, and the state superintendent of public instruction), should be created. In addition, they agreed to a merger of the two Milwaukee institutions, to be presided over by a provost reporting to the president of the University. All this became law by action of the Legislature in October 1955.[14]

This immediately posed the problem of working out a pattern of relationships between the merged Milwaukee institution and the University.[15] To this end President E. B. Fred appointed a Committee of Thirty (ten from Milwaukee Extension, ten from the Milwaukee State College, and ten from the Madison campus), which held its first meeting on December 1, 1955. Furthermore, in February and March 1956 twenty-five subcommittees were appointed, again with equal representation from Milwaukee Extension, the State College, and the Madison campus, to deal with such matters as admissions, instructional programs, graduate work, and space planning, and President Fred appointed a nine-member Executive Committee to coordinate the activities of these subcommittees. In addition, there were joint conference committees at the departmental, school, and college levels. There was to be a single faculty, which meant that faculty members in Milwaukee were eligible to attend general faculty meetings in Madison and to serve on faculty committees. There was a single Graduate School with an associate dean in Milwaukee. The University Committee and the divisional committees were made University-wide by the inclusion of members of the Milwaukee faculty.[16] Since general faculty meetings were held in Madison, for most practical purposes the Milwaukee professors were without voting power.

The period of Madison tutelage over the Milwaukee institution (UWM) did not last long. The Regents approved major university status for UWM in 1963. In September 1965 the regents authorized a separate graduate school for UWM. Furthermore, at a meeting held on March 14, 1963, on recommendation of the University Committee, all coordinating committees at the departmental, college, and school levels were abolished, separate divisional committees were set up at UWM, and the UWM faculty was given final authority to approve its own curriculum programs. Faculty legislation adopted on May 6, 1963, completed the separation of UWM from Madison. Beginning with the meeting of April 6, 1964, when the Madison campus faculty met as such, the fiction of a system-wide faculty meeting has been abandoned. Robert L. Clodius, serving as acting provost, presided over that April meeting. Then Robben W. Fleming was appointed provost—later to be called chancellor—and he presided over his first meeting of the Madison faculty on October 5, 1964. The ending of Madison tutelage over UWM was foreshadowed by a provision in the Milwaukee Merger Act of 1955, which stipulated that the UWM faculty shall have "the same degree of self-government" as is vested in other units of the University.[17]

The problem of organizing effective faculty institutions became much more complicated as the University expanded into a more and more complex system. In addition to UWM, which was established as a unit of the University in 1955, it is to be noted that in 1964 the University Center

System was separated from the Extension Division and set up as an independent administrative unit which, by 1970, included seven campuses. Furthermore, pursuant to legislative authorization in 1965, new four-year colleges were authorized at Green Bay and at Parkside, a site between Racine and Kenosha. Both of these institutions began operations in September 1969. Thus, by the fall of 1969 the University was presided over by a president who was the administrative superior of six chancellors, those for Madison, Milwaukee, Green Bay, Parkside, the Extension Division, and the Center System.

To provide the faculties of these six units with some sort of institution-wide voice in the affairs of what had rather quickly become a multiversity, two new institutions of governance were created, a University Faculty Council in 1966 and a University Faculty Assembly in 1967. The council, which held its first meeting on May 25, 1966, included seven faculty members, three from Madison, two from Milwaukee, and one each from Extension and the Center System. Later on two members were added, one to represent Green Bay, the other Parkside. The council was designed to serve at the all-University level in roughly the same manner as the traditional University Committees operated at the unit levels. The assembly, which first met on February 3, 1968, was designed to exercise faculty legislative authority in matters which concerned more than one unit, where uniform University policy was necessary. Subject to reapportionment every three years, during its short life it included elected members as follows: Madison, thirty-eight; UWM, ten; Extension, eight; Center System, three; Green Bay, three; Parkside, three. In addition, the members of the council and the president and vice-president of the University were ex-officio members of the assembly. This council-assembly system had a short life, for with the adoption of the Merger Act by the Legislature in 1971, the newly devised system became obsolete. At the same time, the Coordinating Council was abolished. Thus, on September 11, 1972, the Madison Faculty Senate voted that no further elections to the University Faculty Assembly should be held. A noble experiment came to an early end without a whimper. Whether a state-wide system of faculty governance will be created in the future remains to be seen. As of late 1974 the prospects for such a development seemed dim indeed, for the main thrust seemed to be in the direction of maximum campus or unit autonomy.

The rules and regulations of such a dynamic institution as the University of Wisconsin change so much and so often that in the late spring of 1963 President Harrington, on the recommendation of the University Committee, appointed a small committee consisting of five faculty members to codify the *Laws and Regulations* as they had been previously compiled from time to time by the secretary of the faculty. The Codification Committee first concerned itself with restating and modernizing the rules relating to tenure and the dismissal of faculty members. Some preliminary changes in faculty personnel policies were approved by a faculty meeting on May 6, 1963. Finally, the whole body of tenure and dismissal rules, embodied in what was labeled as Chapters 10A and 10B of the *Laws and Regulations,* was adopted by a unanimous vote of the faculty on January 6, 1974. When the Board of Regents gave its formal approval to these tenure rules on January 10, 1964, it adopted the following statement of general policy which may be regarded as an important milestone in the history of academic freedom at the University of Wisconsin:

In adopting this codification of the rules and regulations of the University of Wisconsin relating to academic tenure, the Regents reaffirm their historic commitment to security of professorial tenure and to the academic freedom it is designed to protect. These rules and regulations are promulgated in the conviction that in serving a free society the scholar must himself be free. Only thus can he seek the truth, develop wisdom and contribute to society those expressions of the intellect that ennoble mankind. The security of the scholar protects him not only against those who would enslave the mind but also against anxieties which divert him from his role as scholar and teacher. The concept of intellectual freedom is based upon confidence in man's capacity for growth in comprehending the universe and on faith in unshackled intelligence. The University is not partisan to any party or ideology, but it is devoted to the discovery of truth and to understanding the world in which we live. The Regents take this opportunity to rededicate themselves to maintaining in this University those conditions which are indispensable for the flowering of the human mind. [18]

The essence of Chapters 10A and 10B is that no member of the faculty may be dismissed without adequate cause, and without full due process rights which include notice of specific charges and a hearing before an elected faculty committee. The legal security of this system of tenure is reflected in the fact that the Merger Implementation Act of 1974 stipulates that "any person having tenure may be dismissed only for just cause and only after due notice and hearing."[19] A similar provision applies to the dismissal of persons on probationary status, and the maximum duration of the probationary period is limited to seven years. Thus, so far as the University of Wisconsin-Madison is concerned, prior to 1964 tenure rules existed merely on sufferance of the board; after 1964 the Madison faculty acquired legal tenure through formal action of the board; since the spring of 1974 it has had the protection of statutory tenure.

There had been a long debate in the Madison faculty regarding the desirability of abandoning the general faculty meeting and putting in its place an elective, representative Senate. In 1949 the Committee on Functions and Policies recommended against the establishment of a Faculty Senate, and instead urged the strengthening of the University Committee as a means of improving the faculty's position. But there were persuasive objections to the traditional faculty town-meeting open to all who cared to come. The small meetings were too small to be fairly representative. The very large meetings were often much too large to serve as efficient deliberative bodies. Above all, there was a tendency to "pack" a particular meeting on the part of those who wanted approval for some proposition they favored. In any event, after prolonged consideration in several well-attended special faculty meetings, final approval was given by the faculty to the creation of a faculty senate on January 19, 1970. The Board of Regents registered its approval on March 6, 1970. The first meeting of the Senate was held on October 5, 1970. The Senate meets on the first Monday of each month during the academic year, at 3:30 P.M., and is presided over by the chancellor. The vice-chancellor presides in the absence of the chancellor. Senators are elected for two-year terms, half of them each year, from the departments, with one senator allowed for each ten voting faculty members. Small departments are grouped together for electoral purposes by the University Committee.

The agenda for each Senate meeting is prepared by the chancellor in conjunction with the University Committee, which serves as the Executive Committee of the Senate. A by-law of the Senate provides for a question period at the beginning of each meeting, at which time the chancellor, and then the chairman of the University Committee, respond to questions put by senators. The Senate includes 226 elected members, plus the members of the University Committee, who sit ex-officio. Attendance has been excellent; although a majority of the total membership constitutes a quorum, there was only one meeting, that of May 8, 1973, which failed to make a quorum; at that meeting only 107 senators were in attendance. Generally speaking, the experience with the Senate indicates that when faculty members are formally designated by their departmental colleagues to represent them at Senate meetings, most of them accept the responsibility seriously. Of course, the Senate exercises all the powers previously vested in the faculty as a whole.

The original legislation creating the Senate provided that after a three-year trial period, a meeting of the whole faculty shall be called by the chancellor to review its record, and to decide upon its future. A Committee to Study the Senate, appointed by the University Committee, and chaired by Professor James B. Bower, submitted a report to the faculty on May 7, 1973, reviewing the record made by the Senate and recommending that it be made a permanent body.[20] On the basis of comments from 655 faculty members, forty departmental chairmen, and testimony given at an open hearing, the committee made a few suggestions for procedural changes, but on the whole it reported that an overwhelming majority of the members of the faculty (over 90 percent) were in favor of continuing the senate form of faculty governance on a permanent basis.

Three significant actions of the Senate relating to faculty governance remain to be noted. At its meeting of January 4, 1971, it approved the creation of a new standing, elected, seven-member Committee on Faculty Rights and Responsibilities to deal with problems of faculty discipline involving a sanction less than dismissal. At the same time the Senate reaffirmed the faculty's traditional rights and responsibilities, declaring: "The authority and rights of the faculty relate, by way of illustration, to the following: the tenure system; academic freedom; a major voice in the selection and professional development of faculty personnel; a major voice in the determination of faculty merit increases and faculty promotion; a large degree of autonomy with respect to teaching, research, and public service obligations."[21] Furthermore, the legislation creating the Committee on Faculty Rights and Responsibilities was rewritten and after discussion on November 5, 1973, was approved by the Senate on December 3, 1973. Among other things, this committee was designated to sit as the hearing committee in faculty dismissal cases, as well as in cases involving lesser sanctions, but in no case except on specific charges brought by the chancellor.

A second noteworthy development occurred on April 2, 1973, when the Senate created an elective, nine-member Commission on Faculty Compensation and Economic Benefits. There has been a lively debate throughout the American higher education community as to the wisdom of collective bargaining for professors, and this issue was debated by the Senate during the winter of 1972-1973. Finally, on February 5, 1973, the Senate adopted a resolution proposed by the University Committee which declared "that the existing faculty government structure at the department, college, division, Senate and committee levels shall continue to deal with matters of concern to the faculty of the Madison campus."[22] In other words, the Senate registered its continuing confidence in the traditional organs of faculty governance, and rejected the alternatives of some sort of faculty association or collective bargaining trade unionism. The Compensation Commission was conceived in terms of the familiar use of faculty committees to deal with faculty problems. On April 2, 1973, however, the Senate adopted a resolution proposed by the

University Committee which took the position that if the Legislature adopts collective bargaining legislation, every effort must be made to ensure the independence of the Madison faculty as a separate and distinct group, and to protect its ability to make its own choices concerning the desirability of collective bargaining and the make-up of the bargaining unit. At the same time, the Senate declared that it would want to exclude "from the scope of bargaining matters of faculty governance including academic freedom, tenure, curriculum, and other presently internal personnel matters, such as the allocation of merit salary increase money."[23]

Finally, it remains to be noted that on May 7, 1973, the Faculty Senate authorized the University Committee to appoint a committee to revise and recodify the laws and regulations of the University. A seven-member committee completed its formidable task by January 1974, and a newly codified body of *Rules and Regulations* for the Madison campus was debated by the Senate section by section at the meetings of February 4, March 4, March 18, April 1, and April 8, 1974. Finally, approval to the new code was agreed upon at the Senate meeting of April 29, 1974. The new code built upon the foundations of the previous one, but took into account the changed situation of the Madison campus as a result of state-wide merger. Thus, unlike the previous code, the 1974 code is concerned solely with the Madison faculty. Perhaps the greatest amount of innovation in the new code related to a more precise definition of the various types of faculty appointments and faculty status.

Thus, the University of Wisconsin-Madison, a quarter-century ago, was fully committed to meaningful faculty self-determination through freely chosen faculty bodies. That tradition was, in 1974, as robust and as functional as ever in the past. As Richard Hartshorne, now emeritus professor of geography, and then an active faculty leader, said at the faculty meeting of January 7, 1952, in protesting the publication of unsigned letters by a faculty member in a Madison newspaper: "We believe that the University of Wisconsin should and does encourage that fearless discussion of university policies, in faculty meetings and between the faculty and the Board of Regents, by which alone sound educational policies may be achieved. If there has been no dramatic fight for this principle by the faculty in recent years that is not because of timidity but because there has been no need. The tradition of this faculty is strong; its administrative officers have been bred in that tradition; by and large they have demonstrated, both in word and deed, their concern to support and enhance it. Should they at any time fail to do so, this faculty does not lack those who will remind them of their obligation to maintain democratic faculty government."[24]

NOTES

1 *Revised Statutes 1849,* chap. 18, sec. 9, Act of July 26, 1848.

2 *Laws 1866,* chap. 114, sec. 11, Act of April 12, 1866.

3 *Laws 1971,* chap. 100, sec. 20 (13)(d), Act of October 11, 1971.

4 *Laws 1973,* chap. 335, sec. 36.09(4), Act of July 8, 1974.

5 In 1967 the number of petitioning faculty members was raised to ten. *Laws and Regulations,* as amended in 1967, in Faculty Document 120, chap. 21, sec. 21.02(2).

6 Committee on University Functions and Policies, *First Report* (Madison, October 1948), p. 73.

7 Committee on University Functions and Policies, *Second Report, Internal Survey* (Madison, November 1949), chap. 3, p. 18.

8 *Ibid.,* p. 13.

9 *Ibid.,* chap. 4, pp. 29-30.

10 *Ibid.,* chap. 8, pp. 11-12.

11 University Faculty Special Meeting Minutes, March 20, 1950, p. 2.

12 University Faculty Assembly Document 24, approved by the University Faculty Assembly on February 26, 1969, and by the Board of Regents on April 11, 1969, sec. 6.09.

13 See sec. 5.05, Faculty Document 1654, approved by the faculty on May 25, 1966, and by the Board of Regents on June 10, 1966.

14 *Laws 1955,* chap. 619, Act of October 15, 1955.

15 For a detailed account see J. Martin Klotsche, *The University of Wisconsin-Milwaukee: An Urban University* (Milwaukee, 1972). Dr. Klotsche was president of the Milwaukee State College, and the first provost (later called chancellor) of the merged system.

16 The process of inserting UWM faculty members into University faculty committees was a gradual one. The faculty meeting of October 1, 1956, placed three persons from UWM on the Committee on Courses; on December 3, 1956, a UWM faculty member was added to the Committee on Nominations; on January 7, 1957, a member of the UWM faculty was added to the University Committee, two were added to the Regent-Faculty Conference Committee, and one to the Knapp Bequest Committee; on February 11, 1957, two professors and the Librarian from UWM were added to the Library Committee.

17 *Laws 1955,* chap. 619, sec. 39.024(3)(h). It is gratifying to note that the tradition of faculty self-government which was so firmly rooted in Madison has flowered in Milwaukee. Thus Chancellor Klotsche writes in *The University of Wisconsin-Milwaukee,* p. 117: "University governance is now viewed as both a *means* to achieve institutional objectives and an *end* in itself to permit people in the University community to participate in the decision making process. Search and screen committees are now commonly used in the making of administrative appointments, while the University Committee serves as an important watchdog of faculty prerogatives. Program development, personnel matters involving faculty grievances and general questions of University policy are now all matters of its continuous concern, while standing committees of the faculty devote a great deal of time and effort to particular assignments."

18 Board of Regents Minutes, January 10, 1964, p. 3.

19 Sec. 36.13(5).

20 Faculty Document 142, May 7, 1973.

21 University Faculty Special Meeting Minutes, January 4, 1971, p. 4.

22 University Senate Minutes, February 5, 1973, p. 1.

23 Faculty Senate Minutes, April 2, 1973, p. 4.

24 University Faculty Minutes, January 7, 1952, p. 3.

CHAPTER 6

The University of Wisconsin System

CLARA PENNIMAN

BY the twentieth century the University of Wisconsin had become known as a great state university with a developing reputation both as a research institution and as an institution which carried that research out into the state for the general good of the state's citizens. There were a number of distinguished scholars among its faculty members who either directly or indirectly contributed to the growing reputation of the University. Many of its alumni with bachelor or graduate degrees held eminent positions in business and in the professions. Many of these remembered their university in generous gifts. Although some faculty members were largely teaching in Extension or, especially in the post-World War II years, at a center out in the state, these faculty members too, and their students, were recognized as part of the one University of Wisconsin. From 1955 onward, however, the name "University of Wisconsin" became attached to an increasing number of separate institutions: first, in 1955, to the University of Wisconsin-Milwaukee; then to separated Extension and Center Systems; then to Parkside and Green Bay; and now, since 1971, as the result of merger of the University with the state universities under Governor Patrick Lucey, to an additional nine degree-granting institutions. This short chapter will attempt to summarize the process and changes in the development of the University as one institution to a University of Wisconsin System with two

Clara Penniman, Oscar Rennebohm Professor of Public Administration, and a Political Science faculty member since 1953, was a member of the six-person University Committee from 1971-1974 and an appointed member of the Merger Implementation Study Committee, 1971-1973. As chairperson of the University Committee from 1973-1974, she headed the committee to revise the faculty rules and regulations to reflect the changes resulting from merger. She writes: "Much of this chapter, therefore, draws upon participation experience which may both help and hinder understanding and objectivity," and adds, "The limitations on space make it impossible to develop the political analysis either of the Merger Bill in its legislative progress or of the deliberations in the Merger Committee."

doctoral campuses, another eleven degree-granting universities, Extension, and the Center System. This brief history also suggests some of the implications of these changes for the original University of Wisconsin in Madison.

The Wisconsin Legislature originally established the University of Wisconsin in 1849 and the first of the state normal schools at Platteville in 1857 with a Board of Regents for each. Since 1895, however, governors and legislators have repeatedly sought means to assure coordinated planning between the University Board of Regents and the state normal school Board of Regents through a single governing board or a single budget commission or other means. A brief and ineffective coordination of the University and the state normal schools was legislated in 1915, at the urging of Governor Emanuel Phillipp, through a State Board of Education. The 1917 Legislature increased the size of the board and significantly undermined its powers. The 1923 Legislature eliminated what had become a board without a mission. New legislation that would provide effective coordination was proposed in almost every successive Legislature. With the increase in enrollments following World War II, several study groups made proposals for coordination.[1]

Back of the search by governors and Legislature for coordinating mechanisms was always the view that (1) existing higher education was too expensive for the state and would continue to get more so; (2) that coordination would reduce or eliminate overlapping and competitive programs; (3) that coordination would relieve the state's taxpayers of a too heavy burden; and that (4) neither governors nor legislators alone or together could secure coordination through their budget controls. What constitutes overlapping and competitive programs is, of course, often in the eyes of the beholder. And too much concern for "duplication" may blind many to considerations of program balance and quality minimums.

After an unsuccessful attempt in 1953 to establish a single Board of Regents and to make the other degree-granting institutions in the state branches of the University of Wisconsin granting U.W. degrees, Governor Kohler tried again in 1955. As in 1953, the state colleges generally supported the bills while the University opposed. Late in the session, the new president of the University regents, Charles D. Gelatt, talked about a compromise version with Governor Kohler. The new proposal left existing Boards of Regents intact, established a Coordinating Committee for Higher Education, merged the U.W. two-year Milwaukee Extension with the State Teachers College there, and put the new degree-granting institution under the president of the University. As a part of the compromise, other legislation placed both Stout Institute and the

Wisconsin Institute of Technology under the jurisdiction of the Board of Regents of the state colleges.

THE establishment of the University of Wisconsin-Milwaukee assured the state's largest metropolitan area of a strong university with graduate and professional schools as well as an undergraduate college. Both the University at Madison and the University at Milwaukee can take credit for much successful cooperation in the early years of the transfer.[2]

The success of UWM was not duplicated in the Coordinating Committee. Both the 1955 Coordinating Committee and its successor, the Coordinating Council, failed in planning either for the rush of students by the middle 1960s or the decline in growth rate that has typified the 1970s. The committee and the council regularly either gave both the WSU and U.W. systems essentially what they asked in budgets, new programs, and buildings or were by-passed by the administrators and boards of the two systems. In part, the failure was due to the limitations in funds and staff of the council but also due to the inability of the council to secure the political support in the Legislature that the University and the state universities did.

As the Coordinating Council was failing to coordinate, the University grew. E. B. Fred, who had become president ten years before the 1955 "coordination," was succeeded by Conrad A. Elvehjem in 1958. Four years later, with Elvehjem's sudden death, Fred H. Harrington became president of the University of Wisconsin. All three of these presidents had been distinguished faculty members at Madison, and their appointments were generally applauded by the faculty. President E. B. Fred saw enrollments at Madison fluctuate from 9,028 to 18,693 and back to 15,928. Elvehjem had growing enrollments in his few years, 16,590 in the fall of 1958 and 20,118 in the fall of 1961.

Fred Harvey Harrington presided during years of rapid and continued expansion. The moods of the nation, the University, and the president were well matched. Harrington liked to expand and build, and the increasing enrollment from 21,733 at Madison in 1962 to a total of 35,549 on the Madison campus in 1970 and another 29,708 elsewhere in what had now become a multiversity required a president willing to push for the big decisions. State, federal, and other contract research funds grew from $3.5 million in 1955 to $25.9 million in 1963 fiscal year when Harrington became president to $42.3 million in 1970 when he resigned (no overhead is included in these figures). State appropriations that were $31.179 million in Harrington's first fiscal year of 1963 were $78.437 million seven years later in 1970, his last.[3]

The growth in enrollment and finances required new administrative arrangements. The chancellor at UWM was matched with a chancellor at Madison when Robben Fleming (named president of the University of Michigan in 1967) was appointed by Harrington and the board in 1964. In 1966 a further reorganization separated the Center System and Extension from Madison and placed a chancellor at the head of each. Harrington made these changes in organization with the approval of the Board of Regents but with essentially no faculty input and little consultation with the Madison University administration. Criticism seldom followed. The expansionist mood of the president was part of the faculty and administration mood too. Large classes to teach, many opportunities to secure research grants, needed effort to recruit more and more faculty members, and soon a series of student disturbances on campus left little time for worry about what was happening at the top of Van Hise.[4] "Anyway Harrington and Clodius [the Academic Vice President] would look after Madison." Unfortunately, some of these decisions would later come back to haunt the Madison campus.[5]

Conflict developed during the later premerger years over use of funds that Madison campus administrators and faculty members felt belonged exclusively to Madison. In the expansionist climate of the late fifties and sixties, not much attention or concern was expressed at the beginning in viewing Milwaukee, the centers, or Extension as all members of the same institution with Madison and therefore permitting faculty members throughout the institution to compete for research grants and even teaching awards that presumably had been originally intended for Madison. But, of course, that "Madison" had then included the centers and Extension, plus the Milwaukee two-year Extension. By the 1969-1970 academic year, however, a number of faculty members, administrators, and the University Committee began openly to discuss and to complain about the use of "Madison's funds" elsewhere. Initial attention concentrated on the research "overhead" paid by the federal government to offset costs to the University as a result of federal research performed here; this was "earned" largely by Madison faculty members and used on occasion by the University System Central Administration in the early years of developing the Parkside and Green Bay campuses. The Medical School, in particular, complained that it was not being allotted the overhead moneys it "earned" and which were needed for clerical and other staff positions.[6] Until 1971 overhead funds were placed in a nonlapsing fund without specific designation of use. In the earlier years some approximation of the amount of overhead "earned" by the departments or schools in which the research was carried on was made available to them for staff or other outlays, which state appropriations did not always cover but that the department or school or college wanted. Gradually Central Administration assumed control of the overhead funds in large part and used the funds to provide flexibility in the total system that legislative appropriations often did not provide. Significant funds came to Madison, but the total was considerably less than the 95 percent portion that Madison was earning. By 1971 all overhead moneys were being controlled by the state Department of Administration, with the result that the earlier convenient flexibility of these funds was available neither to the departments nor to central. Presumably, each department or school received through the approved University budget sufficient funds either through state appropriations or "overhead" to meet administrative expenditures necessary as a result of contract research plus, of course, the direct research funds. Both central and the later state control reduced the previous flexibility of departmental and college budgets in Madison. Student tuition enrollment funding earned at the Madison campus, in addition to research overhead, also provided the Central Administration flexibility in developing the Parkside and Green Bay campuses and, to a lesser extent, Milwaukee. In the period of rapid growth, Madison almost necessarily absorbed initially many of the additional students on its campus either by larger classes or more teaching assistants. The growing receipts in student tuition and the lagging, but growing, matching state moneys, together with the research overhead, were available to start up or otherwise assist the newer institutions. The state then appropriated the necessary subsequent funds.

At the time of President Harrington's resignation, faculty members of the University Committee had a long discussion with him and with Vice President Clodius.[7] The president urged the University Committee to work toward a larger degree of autonomy and separateness for Madison than the pattern had been during the past fifteen years of growth and development as a multi-campus system. Apparently everyone present recognized the need for Madison to identify itself as an entity in the system and for faculty members and administrators to accept Madison as their university without routine recourse to central. It was also recognized that this would necessitate more formal drawing of lines between central and Madison administrations. A time of change in the presidency in 1970 appeared to be the ideal point for a cutting of the casual relations that were probably the inevitable outgrowth of a presidency that had evolved from being the chief administrative officer for Madison alone to the chief administrative officer for a system of institutions where all but Madison were not only physically more remote but which in many respects operated more independently of central than Madison did.

O UT of the background of enormous growth of higher education in the state, together with student disruptions on the campuses, Governor Patrick J. Lucey in his budget message of February 25, 1971 stated: "We can no longer afford to support an archaic organization of higher education which is the product of historic accident and ignores the converging social missions of the two systems that have been developing over recent decades. . . . I have eliminated from the executive budget the Coordinating Council for Higher Education and the central administrative costs of the State Universities and the University of Wisconsin." Rumors of a higher education merger proposal had floated for some time. University friends, faculty members, and administrators were too involved in immediate University concerns on the campus to have paid much attention to the candidate's speech on June 11, 1970, when he called for a single Board of Regents. Even the planted statement calling for merger by Lee Dreyfus, president of the Wisconsin State University at Stevens Point, at governor-elect Lucey's University budget hearing in December did not alert many faculty members to the possibility of the governor actually proposing, and then insisting on, merger of the two higher education systems in the state. The bombing of Sterling Hall in August 1970 as a culmination of student activism of several years, the possibility of another legislative investigation of campuses and student activism, insufficient budget funding, and the probability of having to live with a new type of coordinating council or committee loomed as larger and more immediate problems. A new University president and central administration and a new governor had to be watched but presumably in the context of issues of the last decade. Only after Governor Lucey took office in January 1971 did it seem possible that he might not be a "friend" of the University as defined by those who wished little more than that the University be funded as requested and then left alone by the governor and Legislature.[8]

Governor Lucey himself has always insisted he was and is a friend of the University at Madison. He holds his degree from here, and many of its individual faculty members and administrators have been long-time friends and acquaintances. He simply argued that the ease of higher education budget funding of the 1960s was gone and that, in view of campus activism, a slowing-down of the job market, and numerous social

issues, universities would have to justify their existence more satisfactorily
in the future. To him, Madison appeared particularly vulnerable, and
the merger controversy could be a protection. Of course, the balance of
his argument was that the Coordinating Council for Higher Education
had failed to plan and coordinate the two systems.[9] Hence, the council
had to go if higher education in the state were to be effectively planned
and organized for the future.[10]

In any event, more than six months would elapse between Governor
Lucey's higher education merger proposal in February 1971 and October
8, 1971, when he would have a bill mandating merger on his desk.
Another three years would follow that February address before July 3,
1974, when he would sign a completed, revised Chapter 36 of the
Wisconsin Statutes outlining state law governing the merged University of
Wisconsin System.[11] Faculty members, administrators, regents, and
friends of both systems as well as legislators and governor's staff people
would spend much time opposing, negotiating, compromising over those
years. As one much-involved university lawyer commented, "Merger
almost became a career for some of us."

Although a few Madison campus administrators and faculty members
supported merger from the beginning either from conviction or from
party loyalty, it is probable that in the early months of discussion many,
many more were stunned, angry, or disappointed in the governor and
anxious about the future of Madison. To many of these individuals, it
often seemed an especially unfair blow after the past five years or so of
student enrollments growing faster than the budgeted faculty positions, of
student unrest and campus turmoil, and of continuing change in campus
relations to Central Administration. Faculty and administrators who had
managed to maintain, expand, and increase the prestige of the University
throughout the sixties frequently felt that they had earned the right to be
exempt from controversy for a few years. Instead, University administrators and faculty leaders found it necessary to analyze every merger
proposal, formal or informal; to formulate Madison positions on many
issues; and to seek allies not only within the campus or within the
University of Wisconsin as it existed at the beginning of 1971 but also
among regents, legislators, and within the Wisconsin State University
institutions. Political parameters did not always allow for firm principles.
At bottom was always the question whether merger in some form would
inevitably clear the legislature. For those who thought it improbable,
including Regent Ody Fish, any negotiating weakened their opposition
efforts. For those who believed merger likely, despite their preference,
then it was wise to negotiate for the best possible terms. Neutrality or
all-out opposition to a bill that was going to pass could only produce

legislation with the worst features. During the spring and summer of 1971 political estimates were made, revised, and reversed by administrators, faculty members, and regents. There was never full agreement among any of these groups or with others interested in the welfare of the Madison campus.

For perhaps some of the same reasons, the Wisconsin Alumni Association never mounted the type of opposition campaign to merger that it had successfully done on this and other issues in the past. Of the Milwaukee and Madison newspapers, only the *Wisconsin State Journal* opposed merger. *The Capital Times, The Milwaukee Journal,* and *The Milwaukee Sentinel* all supported the governor's position. John Wyngaard, in his columns in various papers, but especially in the *Green Bay Press Gazette,* repeatedly supported merger of higher education in the state.

An alumnus and friend of the University, as well as a long-time legislative observer, late in the summer of 1971 (when merger was beginning to appear more and more inevitable) said to this author: "Where *has* the University *been?*" The trouble with the question was that there was no longer a clear identification of *who* was the University. Legally, by 1971 the University of Wisconsin was the Board of Regents and Central Administration, together with Parkside, Green Bay, Milwaukee, Extension, and the Center System, as well as Madison. Even the Wisconsin Alumni Association no longer viewed itself as representing Madison exclusively. The totally Republican Board of Regents, no doubt from reasons of party as well as conviction, eventually voted unanimously to oppose merger. This decision was not formally made until June 1971. President John C. Weaver and Vice President Donald E. Percy eventually supported merger.[12] Parkside and Green Bay administrations and faculty members saw only the disadvantage for them of being two of eleven primarily undergraduate institutions in the new system. Extension and the centers remainded divided. Although the Milwaukee chancellor in a legislative hearing neither supported nor opposed merger, his faculty took a formal position supporting the governor and merger *if* certain conditions were met. The Madison faculty essentially took the opposite tack of opposing merger *unless* certain conditions were met. Madison Chancellor Edwin Young took no public position on merger but privately worked for the best possible terms. Given such a mix of groups and decisions, it becomes fairly obvious why reservations or opposition to merger by many on the Madison campus was frequently lost downtown.

As early as April or May, the Democratic-controlled Assembly was expected to pass merger despite the reservations or even opposition of the Democratic delegation from Dane County.[13] The Republican-controlled

Senate was necessarily viewed as the real battleground. There merger never fully divided along party lines. Senator Ray Heinzen had drafted his own merger bill even before the governor's bill was public. By July, several other Republican senators were supporting merger in some form. Even Dane County Democratic senators divided on merger, with Senator Carl Thompson supporting the governor on the issue and Senator Fred Risser, Democratic minority leader of the Senate, opposing.

To help convince the Madison faculty, aides of Governor Lucey asked that the University invite the governor on two separate occasions to address the faculty. On July 8, 1971, the governor spoke to a special faculty meeting for about twenty minutes and invited questions about merger. It is doubtful that he changed many minds, but there was no question the faculty found him forceful, informed, and generally direct in response to all questions.[14] A year and a half later, December 1972, after the initial consolidation of the boards and central administrations had been achieved but when there had been questions on tenure and budget, Governor Lucey again addressed the faculty and showed the same ability to secure attention from his audience.

The role of the WSU System in all of the political negotiation requires some attention since its role, no doubt, contributed to passage of the merger bill. The WSU Board of Regents had split on the issue of merger in June with the two regents appointed by Governor Lucey plus Republican-appointed Mary Williams supporting merger and the others opposing. The Conference of Presidents of WSU institutions agreed to merger only if twenty improbable conditions were met. Faculty members were represented through their Association of Wisconsin State University Faculty (AWSUF), which in April 1971 voted to support merger. Professor Marshall Wick from Eau Claire was president and supported by his executive council proved an excellent politician. He achieved close relations with members of the governor's staff, and negotiated actively. Although he took little public role, it is clear that WSU Executive Director Eugene R. McPhee also supported merger and privately assisted.

If consolidation of the two systems was going to occur, what were the terms on which Madison could presumably live with merger? Although discussed occasionally during the winter and early spring, most of the attention of the faculty University Committee during the summer and fall months preceding passage of the bill was directed to these issues. "Unit autonomy" and "unit or institutional tenure" became two issues on which there was broad agreement.[15] Guarantees that grant funds, overhead, and bequests would remain with the campus to which initially given; identification of Madison as the land-grant institution of the state; faculty governance; institutional control of student admission standards and credit transfer standards were others on which Madison administrators and faculty members could easily agree.[16]

The merger bill (S-213 as amended and separated from the state's budget) passed the Senate on September 22, 1971, by a one-vote margin, passed the Assembly on October 5, 1971, and was signed by Governor Lucey on October 8, 1971. The law contained some of the guarantees the University had asked and provided for study of others. Both Boards of Regents held their last meetings as individual entities on the same day. Henceforth there would be a single Board of Regents and a consolidated Central Administration to govern this new University of Wisconsin System. Although a fully revised Chapter 36 had to be written and passed to establish the basic law for the system, few individuals had the temerity in the next years to suggest reestablishing the separate systems as a political possibility.

CHAPTER 100 of the Session Laws of 1971 (the merger bill) not only provided for a single Board of Regents and a consolidated Central Administration but also for a Merger Implementation Study Committee composed of three regents from each board (selected by the individual boards), the legislative cochairmen of Joint Finance and of the Senate and Assembly Education committees, one student and one faculty member from each system, and three citizen members. Governor Lucey was authorized to make these last seven appointments.[17] The governor named Regent James G. Solberg as chairman. Under the legislation President John C. Weaver was secretary of the committee. The committee named Donald E. Percy and Eugene R. McPhee as consultants. After an uncertain start, committee members at their second meeting agreed to make the writing of a revised Chapter 36 governing this new University system the major order of business. During the winter and spring of 1972, opportunity was given to citizens, faculty members, students, and administrators to provide statements concerning higher educational issues that they believed significant. Although many letters and statements poured in, only a few actually addressed themselves to matters that would be a part of the statute.

After the fourth meeting of the full committee in May, the ad hoc subcommittee chaired by Regent Frank J. Pelisek worked throughout much of the summer on a draft for the new statute.[18] Of major importance in the drafting was the March agreement reached between the University Faculty Council (representing faculty members in the former U.W.) and the Association of University Faculty (TAUWF—renamed from the Association of Wisconsin State University Faculty). Their agreements as to faculty tenure, unit autonomy, and faculty governance removed from controversy a number of what might otherwise have been difficult issues.[19] Nevertheless, there remained dozens of items for discussions and agreement within the drafting committee: definition of faculty, definition of academic staff apart from both faculty and civil service, and limited term appointments; definition of the roles of the Board of Regents, system president, chancellors, faculties in each university, and students; safeguarding special grants to an institution; and so on. In all, the ad hoc subcommittee met eight times.

The full Merger Committee reviewed the subcommittee's draft of the proposed Chapter 36 in the statutes at a series of meetings from November through January 1973. Only a few matters drew substantial committee discussion and brought additions and revisions to the subcommittee's draft.[20]

The final report of the Merger Implementation Study Committee was completed on January 31, 1973, and forwarded for legislative consideration. After review and technical amendments by the Legislative Reference Library and subsequent review by the Department of Administration, it reached the Assembly in early May. Other business appeared more pressing to the leadership, and hearings were not scheduled until June and again late in the summer. It was not reported out by the Education Committee of the Assembly until the legislative budget session in 1974. Failure of the Assembly then to give final approval to the bill before the close of the session resulted in the Senate taking it up first when the governor called the Legislature back into special session.[21] During the Senate's consideration of merger in May 1974 there was much activity by TAUWF, Central Administration, and others to achieve their particular version of merger. Several former members of the Merger Implementation Study Committee urged senators to accept the proposed statute just as recommended by the committee. TAUWF secured the introduction of a series of amendments to: (1) require Central Administration to be located off the Madison campus; (2) eliminate the language permitting layoffs of tenured faculty as a result of budget exigency; (3) change tenure from an institutional basis to a system basis; (4) require geographic representation by regent appointees of the governor; (5) require the board to consider "comparable funding for similar programs" in all institutions and "equity" in faculty salaries across the system. Professor Marshall Wick had been unsuccessful in securing (1) and (2) in the Merger Committee. The Senate approved amendments for a modified version of (2), (4), and (5) above, but the governor would later exercise his item veto on (2) and (4). The final bill passed by the Senate included these TAUWF amendments plus a number of others introduced by individual senators. The Assembly Democratic leadership and the governor generally preferred the bill without most of these amendments, but a tactical decision was made for the Assembly to pass the bill in the Senate's form and then to rely on the governor to item veto several of the more undesirable amendments.[22]

At a brief public ceremony in the Governor's Reception Room on July 3, 1974, Governor Lucey signed the new Chapter 36 of the Wisconsin Statutes which then became the governing law for the University of Wisconsin System.[23] His item vetoes had largely restored the language of the act to the bill proposed by the Merger Implementation Study Committee more than a year earlier.

THE University of Wisconsin System and its administration created by the Session Law of 1971 could not stand aside to await the final merger bill of 1974. Both the consolidated Board of Regents and the Central Administration worked from the late fall of 1971 on as if merger had been completed. By December plans were going forward for a consolidated biennial budget. The administrative decisions for regent budget review were later made by President Weaver and Vice President Percy conferring with regents on the Budget and Finance Committee but without involvement of individual campus chancellors. As a surety of the merged system, the 1973-1975 biennial budget request for the University of Wisconsin System went to the governor from central administration and the regents with no identification of appropriations sought for individual campuses. The result did not credit Madison with the large sums in federal overhead, grants, and bequests generated by the activities of this campus alone. Cluster subtotals did appear at times.[24]

Madison administrators or faculty leaders were more successful in influencing a number of early decisions other than budget matters by the Board of Regents and Central Administration.[25] Discussions at the May and June 1972 meetings of the Board of Regents (following an attorney general's opinion) assured that grants, bequests, or other contributions presumably intended for a particular institution in the system would be made available to that university only. Regents Milton E. Neshek and David Carley, among others, deserve credit for this decision. As noted earlier in this chapter, Madison administrators and faculty members had become worried about the integrity of grants and bequests to the campus and the disposition of overhead moneys earned by research carried on at

Madison. Dean Robert Bock of the Graduate School had early proposed language for the merger bill that would attempt to insure that such funds for Madison would be available only to Madison. Chapter 100 of the Session Laws mandating merger carried a provision with such intent. (The final version of Chapter 36 repeated this language.) A tentative decision of the secretary of the Board of Regents in early 1972 appeared to translate wills and bequests to the University of Wisconsin as meaning the new University of Wisconsin System. As a result of this preliminary adverse decision, Madison faculty members and others urged on regents the legitimacy of each institution retaining those special funds given it. The May-June board decision was most reassuring that merger would not spread through the system the WARF, Vilas, Knapp, and many other grants and bequests that have meant so much in Madison's continued development as a major research university in the nation.[26]

In this 125th year of the existence of the University of Wisconsin at Madison, challenges to the quality and integrity of the University abound. There have always been threats to the quality of the University. These differ somewhat today. A persistent difficulty is the growing tendency here, and in most public universities, to remove more and more decisions from the campus to a central administration and to a state fiscal agency. This frequently means, as in Wisconsin, that fiscal flexibility and some control in central is achieved only by some "management" of the nonstate tax resources (such as student tuition or fees, research "overhead", and the like) of the largest institution or institutions in the system. This lengthened hierarchy of control, reinforced by computer formula analysis of a limited number of quantitative measures, removes some of the past autonomy of the institution and may fail to recognize nonquantitative measures of quality with which campus faculty members and administrators are familiar. Innovation may suffer from an inability of administrators to assign quantitative weight to the unknown on which research universities have flourished. The Madison chancellor and the faculty will almost inevitably have different perspectives on most issues than the University president and Central Administration. In the University of Wisconsin System, these differences must be considered both normal and necessary if Madison's needs are to be met.[27] Where agreement cannot be reached within the system, the regents and ultimately the governor and Legislature will be called on for policy decisions.

Gone are the days before 1955 when the University had its president and staff in Bascom Hall with a Board of Regents concerned only with decisions for this campus. Both the boards and university presidents prior to 1955 attempted to make educational policy of value to the whole state. Whether some of their decisions were parochial in terms of the needs of higher education in the state is debatable. There is no question, the University grew and flourished. By most statistical measures, it is still flourishing.

NOTES

1 In 1945 the Joint Committee of the Wisconsin Association of Elementary School Principals, Wisconsin Association of Secondary School Principals, Wisconsin Association of School Administrators, Association of Wisconsin Teachers Colleges, and Wisconsin Association of Directors of Vocational and Adult Education urged a state board of education for all education in the state; a 1947 report, "Junior College Needs in Wisconsin," by John Guy Fowlkes and Henry Ahrnsbrak (two faculty members in the U.W. School of Education), stressed the need for coordination of education in the state; in 1948 Kenneth Little, vice president of the University, published a report, "State Institutions of Higher Learning," that discussed methods of coordinating higher education; later in 1948 a U.W. Committee on Functions and Policies chaired by Mark H. Ingraham, dean of the College of Letters and Science, criticized the existing state administration of higher education and recommended a single Board of Regents, a single major institution (Madison), together with several four-year colleges and a number of junior colleges throughout the state. The U.W. Board of Regents in 1950 pointedly ignored this part of the Ingraham Report.

   Another report in 1948, this time by the legislative Commission on Improvement of the Educational System recommended integration of the state's higher education system and the establishment of a single Board of Regents. Although Governor Oscar Rennebohm recommended a bill that incorporated this idea, opposition by the University, the teachers colleges, and the State Federation of Labor brought its defeat.

   It should be noted that although the University was often praised or blamed for the defeat of bills to coordinate the state's higher education system, the Normal School (the successively State Teachers College, State College, and in 1963, by the board's action, State University) regents often also opposed.

   A good summary of coordinating proposals is contained in a doctoral dissertation by Joseph C. Rost, "The Merger of the University of Wisconsin and the Wisconsin State University Systems: A Case Study in the Politics of Education" (Madison, 1973), pp. 133-168.

2 The Madison Department of Political Science, for example, worked hard to assist the Milwaukee Department of Political Science. For a number of years after the Milwaukee department needed any tutoring, faculty members still met for an annual dinner and social and professional conversation. Probably Madison Professor William H. Young deserves as much credit as any individual for these early efforts. Other Madison departments also ably assisted their Milwaukee counterparts. A joint University Committee and joint divisional executive committees assisted Milwaukee in establishing academic standards and strong faculty governance. As late as 1970 many Milwaukee faculty leaders gave credit to the Madison faculty members on the University Faculty Council for their

judicious handling of disciplinary cases of Milwaukee faculty members following antiwar activities on that campus in the spring of 1970.

3 Data provided by the Graduate School, Registrar's Office, and Research Administration.

4 President Harrington has moved his offices to the seventeenth floor of Van Hise when it opened in 1967. The chancellor for Madison took over the president's offices in Bascom.

5 Although Extension had been one of the special prides of Wisconsin and an integral part of the responsibilities of most departments, it is probable most faculty members were unconcerned in 1966 about its removal. By the 1970s, there was much more concern. A significant loss was developing in the previous close association of Extension faculty members and campus faculty members so that statewide application of campus research had lost some of its reality. A separate issue was the fact that when the budget for Extension was removed from the Madison chancellor's control, nothing had been done about removing from Madison responsibility the tenure commitments for the more than one hundred faculty members whose only or major appointment was in Extension. See Chapter 14 for further discussion.

6 The issue of "overhead" is a particularly complex issue. All federal research contracts were entered into between the University, the faculty member or members, and the specific federal agency, whether HEW or Defense or whatever. Most such contracts provided the required funds for the specific research and then a percentage of the grant as an additional federal allotment for "overhead." "Overhead" varied for individual universities and represented the institution's calculation of the cost of housing, utilities, and so so required for the research project. Often these costs were an estimate based on the total expenditures of the institution for such items. In early grants to Madison faculty, the costs were thus calculated on the basis of the Madison campus. Later, however, they were based on such costs for the multi-campus University. This new basis of calculation could affect Madison adversely either by understating true costs or even, perhaps, by overstating Madison's true costs and making contract with us less attractive.

7 Much of the discussion of the University Committee members with President Harrington and Vice President Clodius can be inferred from the minutes of the University Committee on May 20, 1970, that report a conversation on these subjects with Chancellor Young.

8 Few faculty members or University administrators expect state gubernatorial and legislative "friends" to be quite as generous or as uninterested in what goes on at the University as this statement suggests. This would simply be optimal behavior against which actual behavior is likely to be measured. See Leon D. Epstein, *Governing the University* (San Francisco, 1974), especially chap. 3, pp. 36-67.

9 What constitutes coordination may not easily be defined. When the merged Board of Regents and the Central Administration in 1973 (presumably under legislative mandate) attempted to limit graduate programs in many of the out-state institutions, legislators in affected districts led the protests!

10 Various estimates were also given as to potential savings from elimination of the council staff and merger of the central administrations of the U.W. and WSU. It is almost impossible to prove "savings" putatively or subsequently in such reorganizations. Would more state funds have been required and secured during the past three fiscal years without merger? This author is doubtful and believes any measure of the desirability and success of merger would have to rest on other grounds.

11 Since the revision of the Wisconsin Statutes in 1911, Chapter 36 of the statutes has contained the state law governing the University of Wisconsin, and Chapter 37 has contained state law governing the Wisconsin State University System (including its previous names). Before passage of the Merger Bill in 1974, the combined Board of Regents and the Central Administration were required to operate part of the system under Chapter 36 and the remainder under Chapter 37. These statutory chapter references became the short-

hand for the former U.W. and the former WSU parts of the new University of Wisconsin System.

12 The governor early made it clear that new U.W. President Weaver was his choice for the president of the merged system. Since Eugene R. McPhee, executive director of the Board of Regents for the Wisconsin State Universities was retiring in 1972, the expressed prefer- ence of the governor for Weaver removed arguments over who would be the president of the merged system. It tended to silence Republican critics who might otherwise have accused the governor of wishing to replace Republican Weaver with a Democratic U.W. president. It also limited Weaver's field of maneuverability. Although Donald E. Percy early supported the wisdom of merger for planning higher education in the state, there were times when he attempted to remain out of the picture.

13 Dane County Democratic representatives were not the only ones unhappy about merger. The Democratic co-chairman of the powerful legislative Joint Finance Committee, George Molinaro, objected strenuously to merger. He had worked hard a few years before to get a four-year University of Wisconsin institution at Parkside (between Racine and Kenosha and in his senate district) and was proud of his achievement. He opposed a merger of higher education that would make Parkside one of eleven four-year campuses with less probability of the distinction that might develop over the years if more tightly related to Madison.

14 In at least one case the governor not only took the question seriously at the time but later wrote the particular faculty member a more detailed statement of his views (letter to Professor Robert Kingdon, July 22, 1971).

15 The University Committee saw "unit autonomy" as embracing academic planning and curriculum; degree requirements; admission standards; faculty appointments, promo- tions, and salaries; control of financial resources earned; faculty voice in selecting major administrators; adequate unit administrative staff; no central faculty legislative body . . . (University Committee Minutes of September 13, 1971).

16 At first, the committee had supported statutory mission statements for each institution; but when WSU representatives managed a bill version that enlarged the mission of each of their institutions, it seemed preferable that no mission statements be included. Another issue that caused confusion was the initial position of the University Committee in de- manding a strong central administration. Later, as more and more support of institu- tional autonomy developed, the earlier position for a strong central administration was overlooked. Similarly, the Association of Wisconsin State University Faculty shifted back and forth on the issue of institutional and system tenure in view of changing enrollments.

17 The members of the MISC, as finally named, were Regents Fish, Renk, and Pelisek from the former U.W. board and Regents Neshek, Christenson, and Solberg from the former WSU board. As citizen members, the governor named his appointee to the WSU board, Regent Lavine; Edward E. Hales, a lawyer from Racine whom the governor would soon name to the Board of Regents; and Joe E. Nusbaum, secretary of the Department of Reve- nue and part of the governor's inner circle. For the faculty members, the governor named Marshall Wick from Eau Claire and Clara Penniman from Madison (both had been among those nominated to the governor by appropriate faculty groups). Students named were Randy Nilsestuen from River Falls and Robert Brabham of the University of Wis- consin-Milwaukee. Legislators were automatically Senator Hollander of Joint Finance, Senator Heinzen from the Senate Education Committee, Representative Molinaro of Joint Finance, and Representative Brown of the Assembly Education Committee.

18 The initial ad hoc subcommittee appointed by Chairman Solberg had consisted of Regent Pelisek, Joe E. Nusbaum, Donald E. Percy, Eugene McPhee, (both consultants), Bonnie Reese (Legislative Council), Gary Goetz (Legislative Fiscal Bureau), Mike Vaughn (LRB). It appeared to faculty members that other continuing inputs were needed. Beginning in

June, Clara Penniman and Marshall Wick, as well as other faculty members from each system, plus the student, Randy Nilsestuen, regularly attended and participated in the ad hoc committee meetings. In the fall, when the report went to the full committee, both Penniman and Wick were identified as part of the ad hoc committee. From Madison David Hanson, attorney in the chancellor's office, and Professors Ray Bowen and E. David Cronon from the University Committee attended most meetings of both the subcommittee and the Merger Implementation Study Committee. Chairman Pelisek was astonishingly successful in allowing discussion by almost anyone in the committee room without losing control of the subcommittee's direction.

19 This agreement had been reached at a private meeting between the two groups, and the resulting document had been released on March 7, 1972. In the case of faculty tenure, TAUWF essentially accepted the previous practice in the University of Wisconsin, but the University Faculty Council agreed to support TAUWF's desire to include specific provisions on tenure in the statute. In the past, Madison faculty members had had tenure under rules of the regents. The U.W. faculty members had found this eminently satisfactory, and it had the advantage of permitting minor changes without the formality of changing statute law.

20 MISC initiation and approval of a proposal to provide mandatory periodic review of each faculty member's tenure status was subsequently rescinded. Regardless of the seeming reasonableness of such proposal and even the fact that review normally occurs, faculty members saw the proposed statutory language as a threat. Several regents were particularly helpful in securing a reversal of the decision. Another issue that brought serious disagreement in the committee was the role of students. For the first time in the history of the University, students were recognized as having a formal right to be heard in some University policy making. The difficult identification of which students on each campus is likely to be a source of continuing controversy in the next few years.

21 Merger was one of several matters for which the governor called the Legislature back into special session on April 29, 1974.

22 Central Administration, campus administrators, and faculty members were more than ready to advise the governor on item vetoes, but they were not his only source of advice.

23 The governor used twenty-seven pens to sign the bill, and members of the Merger Implementation Study Committee, legislative leaders, and University administrators who were there each received one of the pens.

24 By the completion of the budget, agreement had rather generally been reached that certain decisions would be made on a cluster basis: the doctoral cluster (Madison and Milwaukee), the university cluster (other degree-granting universities in the system), and, in separate clusters, the Center System and Extension.

25 Since this is a history of the University of Wisconsin-Madison, the roles of faculties at other institutions, especially UWM, are not adequately covered. Most of the faculty successes in influencing regent policies were achieved through the support of the UFC, which continued to the summer of 1973 to represent the institutions formerly comprising the U.W. On some issues such as search and screen, proper hearings for faculty members dismissed under fiscal exigency and systemwide faculty rules for appointments, tenure, dismissal, and the like, TAUWF and UFC leaders agreed on a common position before the regents. Several individual regents were extremely helpful in these decisions apart from their actual voting role.

26 A more complex problem is insuring that appropriations are not reduced by the amount of such funds. Thus if x fund provides y dollars for research, does either the Legislature in appropriating or central in allotting reduce Madison's appropriation by y dollars? This is a complex question to answer since we don't know what would have happened without x funds; yet the answer to date seems to be that research appropriations and allotments have

not been reduced by the amount of nontax resources.

27 In many of these disputes, there is likely to be much common interest between Madison
    and UWM. During the present years when enrollments in most former state universities
    are stabilizing, if not declining drastically, and Madison's enrollment is growing slightly,
    with Milwaukee's growing faster, controversy with the Central Administration and the
    board has arisen over Madison's (and Milwaukee's) share of the state enrollment funding.
    In December 1973 the board after much debate agreed to postpone giving Madison (and
    Milwaukee) their appropriate shares under the state's enrollment formula in order to
    soften the effect of declining enrollments on four institutions. At the July 1974 board
    meeting, the majority, with dissent from Regents Dixon, McNamara, Pelisek, Renk, and
    Sandin, agreed to keep tuition at the four-year institutions down by the expedient of re-
    quiring freshmen and sophomores at Madison and Milwaukee to pay a higher portion of
    costs than the formula provided and transferring these state tax resources of approxi-
    mately $1 million to the other institutions.

CHAPTER 7

On the Importance of Students, 1949-1974

F. CHANDLER YOUNG

THE new freedoms granted to students, the demise of *in loco parentis,* and the short but important era of campus unrest—these were the most remarkable developments in student life during the past quarter-century. Students were granted greater freedoms to live and to learn than at any time in University history. Attitudes toward students changed markedly. Students had long been regarded as children in need of parental guidance. They finally became known as adults in need of enlightenment. Student complaints and protests, common throughout University history, became more pronounced and more persistent than ever before. Intense feelings of anger and frustration about war, bigotry, powerlessness, and related matters generated dramatic events on the campus and in the community of the kind that had never before occurred. My discussion of these and other matters about student life support the thesis that students have contributed significantly to the greatness of the University of Wisconsin-Madison. My discussion is based mainly on my own on-the-scene observations throughout the past twenty-five years. It is therefore quite subjective and perhaps somewhat in variance with the views of other observers and commentators.

Excluded from this discussion are a number of important topics. Athletics is one. Not only were there the Rose Bowl games and a host of stellar victories, but also some important developments such as the discontinuation of boxing, the return of hockey, the charges of exploitation by some minorities, and the effects of the women's movement. In student government there were political changes from conservative to radical to

F. Chandler Young is the associate dean for student academic affairs, College of Letters and Science, University of Wisconsin-Madison. He has been on the dean's staff of this college continuously since 1946 except for the five years (1968-1973) when he served the University as vice chancellor for student affairs. His research and publications have been about student scholastic progress patterns.

131

moderate, the rise and fall of student support, the adversary role of student leaders in times of University stress, and a shift from advocates of social change to providers of service like the Wisconsin Student Association's Store and the WSA Pharmacy, and finally the emergence of a United Council of University Student Governments as the voice of students for the whole University of Wisconsin System. In student housing there was first the enthusiastic welcome of economical dormitory living. Then came the rejection of institutional living and a migration to apartment living. Then a return to residence hall living, where greater freedoms and more options in living were permitted then ever before. There were important changes in cooperative and coeducational living. Financial aids began with a faculty committee administering a few modest loans and scholarships and grew to a large complex program involving millions of dollars of private, state, and federal funds. Concerning drugs: In the late 1940s, hardly any students had had any experience even with marijuana. By the 1970s, however, most students seemed to know a great deal about the dangers, uses, abuses, and laws about many drugs. The Wisconsin Union's very concept and operating philosophies have been used as a model by universities throughout the world. Its history this past quarter-century begins with its important role in responding to the needs of returning veterans in the late 1940s, continues through its enthusiastic support by the campus community and the building of Union South, and closes with its extreme financial difficulties in the early 1970s. Concerning student publications: The *Daily Cardinal* has long been regarded as the greatest student newspaper in the country, but there were times when some denounced it as an irresponsible political rag. The introduction and rise of the *Badger Herald*, the discontinuation of the *Badger Yearbook*, and, most recently, an effort to revive it, were other notable developments. Fraternities and sororities flourished for a long time, often providing most of the student leadership throughout the campus, and at times setting the pace for campus social life. By the late 1960s they had been rejected by students as being too conservative, too traditional, or too much a part of the establishment. Membership declined and financial difficulties intensified. By the early 1970s, however, they seemed to be making a comeback. Perhaps someday the fascinating accounts of these and other topics will be included in a comprehensive history of the University.

MY discussion begins with some constants, some characteristics of the student body which were essentially the same throughout the past quarter-century and probably before. Perhaps the most important but often ignored one is heterogeneity.

The Madison campus student body has always included a vast array of different individual human beings, each one with his or her own unique set of characteristics, each one responding in his or her own particular way to whatever was happening, and each one experiencing only a part of the totality of student life. There have always been many more differences than similarities among students. There has always been such an abundance of opportunities to learn and ways to live that no one student ever could take advantage of but a few of them. These diversities and variations in behaviors, in attitudes, and in living and learning experiences have been so extensive that they almost defy description. Nonetheless I have identified some extremes of behaviors and attitudes and left it up to the reader to imagine what may have been in between.

Some students entered the classroom with confidence in their knowledge and intellectual skills. Others entered with fears of failure. There were times when some saw Wisconsin play in the Rose Bowl while others remained in Madison to work to make ends meet. Fun lovers took part in Humorology to raise funds for charities. Others used the time to study for six-weeks' exams. Some wrote for the liberal *Daily Cardinal,* others for the conservative *Badger Herald.* Many students liked ice carnivals, beauty queens, and fraternity-sorority living. Others preferred libraries, laboratories, and apartment living. Students in the 1950s participated in rallies and marches in fun-loving celebration of Homecoming or in the spring time exuberance over "panty raids." Students in the 1960s participated in rallies and marches in serious hopes of helping solve the pressing problems of the University and society. Some students leapt to the podium to expound their views with either ego-satisfying rhetoric or genuine concern. Others cowered in the crowd. Some prayed for peace in a quiet place of worship. Others protested war by throwing rocks from a noisy crowd. There were those whose beliefs were disturbed when they acquired knowledge which was new to them. There were others who became excited when they joined in the discovery of knowledge which was new to the world. Some sought positions of leadership. Others could not be persuaded to vote. There were those who abstained from all mind-altering substances like liquor and marijuana, while some got heavily involved in their use. Many students were genuinely concerned and active regarding the urgent problems of society. Others were selfish and inactive. Sports fans eagerly awaited every football and hockey game. Other students were more interested in chess. Some played varsity football. Others threw frisbees. One student surprised me with a kiss because, she explained, I was the vice chancellor who kept the tear gas out of residence halls. Someone else firebombed my office to stop me, as a dean, from doing business as usual. In between the extremes of these and other attitudes and actions in an ever-changing campus scene was a broad spectrum of beliefs and behaviors. These many differences among students need to be recognized whenever appraising student life.

Students have always had important effects upon the quality of teaching and research. Student enrollment, of course, affects the University budget, which in turn determines the number and quality of faculty available to teach. Perhaps more important is the interaction of students with each other and with the faculty. Every professor knows the difference between a classroom full of intelligent, academically well-prepared, highly motivated students and one where students' intellectual skills, basic knowledge, and interest in learning leave much to be desired. Faculty members have maintained high academic standards and by doing so have attracted the most able and most highly motivated students while discouraging those less able and less willing to learn. This continuous interaction of serious-minded students with each other and with the faculty has maintained the quality of instruction at a very high level.

Whenever courses were poorly taught or whenever academic standards were lowered, students often responded in ways which tended to eliminate the course or upgrade its quality. In some cases, students simply did not register for a course and it was subsequently abandoned because of low enrollment. In other cases, through student evaluations of a course and its instructor, strengths and weaknesses were identified and the quality of education improved.

When one considers the internationally renowned record of the faculty in research, one must recognize that the graduate students who worked with the principal investigators were also making important contributions of their own to research. Many of these students have published the results of their own research at Wisconsin in books and scholarly journals.

Students interacted not just with faculty and each other in classrooms and laboratories. They also interacted with the important people on and off the campus who have shaped the policies and guided the course of events on the Madison campus. Even though they have not been in positions of authority like those of governors, legislators, regents, administrators, and faculty, they have nevertheless had their effects upon the decision-making processes. There are many examples which could be used to illustrate this. I have chosen one which is fairly recent (1969) and quite exciting.

Concerns for minorities, especially black persons, were at an all-time high. Everyone and every imaginable group got into the act in one way or another. The off-campus University publics, and there have always been many different ones, flooded the mails and the media with their comments. The Legislature, pressured by the public to keep the campus quiet, introduced bills and conducted investigative hearings. The regents, while criticizing administrators for being too permissive and while seeking more effective disciplinary measures, considered ways of responding to the needs of minorities. The faculty held numerous meetings, at times with emotions drowning out the more traditional intellectual approach. They talked about ways to respond to the troubled conditions. They voted on motions. They signed petitions showing their full support of the chancellor's strong position of keeping the University open. College administrators, buffeted from all sides, were holding steadfastly to the traditional course of truth and freedom. Loosely organized student groups held meetings, distributed leaflets, circulated position papers, pumped out editorials, organized picket lines, posted notices, and led protest marches. Religious groups held numerous meetings to discuss the issues and events and to relate what was happening to belief systems and to deep humanistic concerns. Radicals and militants, not always in accord, unfortunately used some violent methods. At times their rhetoric was highly sophisticated like "dare to struggle, dare to win" or "if you're not part of the solution you're part of the problem." Even the apathetic were confronted with soul-searching decisions as whether to cross a given picket line, join the line, or go away. Many National Guardsmen were also students. In more than one case a student left his position of obstructing entrance to a building to return later with bayonet to keep the entrance open. Policemen, sometimes run ragged, tried to keep some measure of control without being brutal about it. Taken all around, every person and every group had some kind of an effect upon the troubled conditions and, perhaps most important, some effect upon the final outcomes. Some outcomes were disastrous, but others were beneficial. Some people were hurt, some property destroyed, and some faith in the worth of the University diminished. On the other hand, the pace in responding to the needs of minorities was quickened, and some new policies about minorities and about student disciplinary matters were shaped, which meant, finally, a greater University.

Throughout the years, students have employed a variety of tactics in their interactions with those responsible for the governance of the University. There is an abundance of examples of what students have done in this regard, ranging from student petitions in the early 1950s to raise academic standards to their placards in the late 1960s reading "on strike, shut it down," from their polite formal dinner engagements with legislators to angry confrontations in the State Capitol, from discussions in committee meetings to violence in the street.

Student members of the Committee on Student Housing argued for and against changes in rules about when they had to be in at night and when they could visit with the opposite sex. Students and faculty on the Committee on Student Life and Interests fought for the freedom to have controversial speakers on campus. Students published their own newspapers completely free of University control. The *Daily Cardinal* and the *Badger Herald* helped shape student opinion. They helped arouse students to action and wrote sharp editorial criticisms of University policies. Both publications advocated policies of their own. The *Cardinal,* at times, used shocking vocabulary to press its views. Students spoke out at regents' meetings, at regent subcommittee meetings, and to individual regents. They attended meetings of the Legislature and appeared before important legislative committees such as the Joint Finance Committee. They met with governors and with governors' task forces. They formed bargaining units. The Teaching Assistants Association, the Memorial Union Labor Organization, and the Residence Halls Student Labor Organization were three of the most notable. These units bargained with University authorities for a greater say in their conditions of employment. Students boycotted University functions, using picket lines for persuasion and even for intimidation. Some boycotts were concerned with national issues, such as those involved with the lettuce and grape industries. Other boycotts concerned University policies, such as those pertaining to teaching assistants or to policies in residence halls. Students marched to Bascom Hall. They marched to the State Capitol. They marched in Alabama. They marched in Washington, D.C. Some resorted to violence, like rock throwing and bombing. These highly visible violent tactics, however, involved only a few persons, some of them not even students. These few people disrupted classes and faculty meetings. They obstructed entrances to buildings. These disruptions and obstructions, however, were few and short-lived. One peaceful tactic used to protest the war was that of making the mall on Bascom Hill look like a cemetery for friends killed in Vietnam by inserting a great many wooden crosses.

WHATEVER one's views of the many and varied tactics used by students over the years, students did succeed more often than not in persuading those in authority to make decisions which advanced the students' points of view and which in the long run strengthened the University.

Students contributed to the greatness of the University in the mid-1950s when important freedoms were won for student organizations. Even though the regents had made declarations pertaining to student freedoms, there were strict rules on the books prior to 1950 seemingly designed to protect student organizations not only from financial disaster and other deterrents to internal viability, but also to protect them from domination by off-campus groups.

In 1894 the regents had declared that the University "should ever encourage that continual and fearless sifting and winnowing by which alone the truth can be found."[1] It was not until 1922, however, that the regents made it clear that this policy applied not only to the classroom but also "to the use of University halls for public addresses."[2]

In 1953, when suspicions and fears of Communists were at their peak, an irate state senator publicly criticized the University, outraged because the University had permitted a Communist student organization, the Labor Youth League, to invite a Communist to speak on campus. President Fred's answer to the senator was widely hailed. He declared: "I do not believe that the people of the state would wish the University to assume the authority of censorship of ideas."[3] Public outcries and legislative threats resulting from this incident were quieted not only by President Fred's statement but also by assurances that the University would "review and examine its rules and regulations governing the registration and advising of student organizations."[4] The problem was to reinforce the regents' statements of 1894 and of 1922 about student freedoms while at the same time lessening public criticism.

An unpublished report tells the story of what happened in the four-year period, 1953-1956, regarding a review of policies about student organizations.[5] Students, faculty, administrators, regents, legislators, and citizens, acting as groups and as individuals, took a part in this important development. The final outcomes were in support of the basic belief that students and student organizations should have the same freedoms of speech and assembly which are granted all other citizens. The principle of "sifting and winnowing" was to be adhered to in extracurricular as well as curricular learning. The freedom of students to use the name and facilities of the University was assured, not just on constitutional grounds but, perhaps more important, in terms of sound educational policy and practice. Student groups were not to be discriminated against because of opinions or affiliations which citizens off the campus were legally permitted to have. The difference between University "sponsorship" and "permission" of what student organizations did or who they invited to speak was clarified. Permissions were to be freely given.

Student organizations exercised the freedoms that had been won for them. When they invited controversial speakers to campus to arouse students to a greater awareness of the important issues of the war in Vietnam, discriminations against minorities, and other matters, they used their freedoms effectively. When these organizations led students into illegal acts of obstruction, destruction, and violence, however, they abused their freedoms. Some argued that student organizations had heightened obstructive and destructive behaviors, that they had created such antagonisms toward the University that the people of the state would lose their faith in the University. Others argued that whatever the loss of faith in the University, it would be only minimal and temporary, that the University would, in the long run, become stronger than ever before. Students, many said, had played an important part in educating each other, in extricating the United States from a tragic war, and in advancing the cause of oppressed minorities.

IN addition to freedoms for student organizations, new freedoms for individual students were won, reflecting significant changes in attitudes toward students. The published rules at the beginning of this past quarter-century reflected a persistent attitude that students are so immature that they need protection from temptation and protection from new ideas which might hurt them or which might be adopted and promoted by them to the ruination of society. The 1950 rules had their roots in earlier history.

In 1925 the dean of men published a pocket-sized edition of paternal advice: "Loafing—an easily acquired pernicious habit. Profanity—a useless inane habit which stamps the habitué as of low ideals and vulgar mind. Gambling—a fascinating vice which consumes time, money, and moral tissue in quantities too large for any student to afford."[6]

The published rules in 1951 apparently were designed to prevent students from being led into these and other temptations: "All social functions, on or off campus, at which both men and women are present must be registered in advance. At all social functions which both men

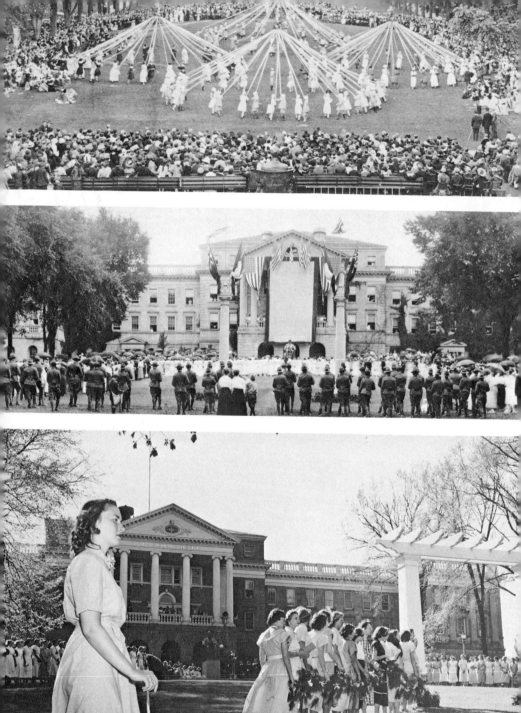

Bascom Hill has felt the change in student mood throughout Madison campus history. Around 1880 there was drill for war (see preceding pages). The maypole dance preceded World War I; the dedication of the Lincoln statue and memorial services for the war dead followed. Senior swingout for many years honored women soon to graduate; this scene around 1950. Student protestors and police charged back and forth across the Hill in the late 1960s. But by 1974 the "streaking" fad had a short Bascom Hill appearance.

Madison campus students were active in civil rights protests in the early 1960s, and began teach-ins and demonstrations to protest the Vietnam War by the middle of the decade (top). Violent protest began on campus with the Dow interview disruption in 1967 at the Commerce building (middle), and ended with the bombing of Sterling Hall and the death of a young scientist on August 24, 1970 (left).

Lower campus scenes: The Bag Rush in 1919; Homecoming bonfire in 1921; Quonsets and cars around 1949. On following page: President E. B. Fred is joined by Regents and small friends in breaking ground for the Memorial Library, which opened in 1953; students find the new Mall handy for protests, serious and in fun.

Independent student government and a free student press have been hallmarks of Wisconsin through the years. Above, President Van Hise meets with Student Senate in 1917. Middle, the Daily Cardinal staff in 1914. Bottom, the National Student Association 14th Congress in the Wisconsin Theater in 1961. Wisconsin students provided leadership in NSA throughout the 1960s.

Major student activities on the campus for many years were the Junior Prom (above), this one the 1913 edition in the Men's Gymnasium, and the Engineers Day Parade (below), this one about 1928. In more recent years, major activities were centered on issues and demonstrations, usually planned by ad hoc groups. But through it all, a wiener roast (left)—this one in connection with the 1952 Union Summer Open House—always held its attraction.

and women attend, chaperons must be present."[7] Cocktail parties were not permitted on or off campus, nor was dancing permitted in student housing on Sunday or during the week.

The University's rules about the nonacademic conduct of individual students were extremely vague until the late 1960s. The attitude of the faculty apparently had remained unchanged since the faculty's statement of more than a century ago. In 1871 the faculty stated "that a code of written laws for the government of students is not advisable—that, the least display of rules, the better. Young men should be made to understand that the faculty regard them as gentlemen who understand the general rules of propriety and are disposed to conform to them." As late as 1965, there was only a single sentence in regard to student conduct: "In addition to the civil code and specific regulations of the University, the student must adhere to a high standard of conduct."[8] This meant that the Student Conduct Committee itself had to define misconduct as each case came along.

There were, however, many specific rules about housing, especially about fraternities and sororities. The most interesting feature of these rules is that most of them pertained to women, few to men. Women were required to be in at certain early hours; men could stay out all night. Women were required to live in University-approved housing units; men could live anywhere.

Whether students paid any attention to the strict rules in effect in the early 1950s is an open question. Judging from the very few cases of record of disciplinary probation and expulsion and knowing students as I do, I doubt if the rules had much effect upon student behaviors. Students themselves, their own moral codes, and their own relationships with each other determined student conduct. The rules which were designed to prevent sexual promiscuity, for example, probably had less effect on behavior than students' own thoughts on the matter. These thoughts may have been about their own moral code or about their own appraisals of the likelihood of pregnancy or disease.

By the late 1960s, prompted by the courts, the regents had spelled out exactly what was meant by nonacademic misconduct on the part of individual students. The regents made it clear that the University could discipline students in nonacademic matters involving the damaging of University property, the endangering of the personal safety of others, the obstructing of University activities, criminal acts affecting the University, and other rule violations. Each of these nonacademic matters was defined in legal terms, complete with illustrations. For example, in the section prohibiting the obstruction of University activities is this illustration of possible obstruction: "A student would be in violation if, in attending a speech or program on campus sponsored by or with permission of the University, he engaged in shouted interruptions, whistling, derisive laughter, or other means which by itself or in conjunction with the conduct of others, prevented or seriously interfered with, a fair hearing of the speech or program."[9] In addition to specific rules, the regents adopted a complete set of disciplinary procedures and penalties designed to assure both due process and fairness in penalties.

Notwithstanding the great care in defining misconduct and establishing ways for processing alleged cases of misconduct, it was extremely difficult to identify persons who presumably violated the rules. Even if a person were caught in the act, it was difficult to obtain sufficient evidence to prove that the person was in violation of the rules. The first problem was to identify the suspect and to make sure that he or she was enrolled as a student. The second problem was to obtain sufficient evidence to make a case. For example, if one witness were to testify that a person threw a rock from a shouting crowd, the alleged rock thrower would often find several witnesses to testify that he was in fact in another part of town at the time. Some questioned the rules themselves. For example, when is derisive laughter a freedom of expression and when is it an infringement on the right of the speaker to speak freely? The difficulties of identifying suspects and of then obtaining sufficient evidence to make a case were so great that even when obstructive and destructive behaviors were many, very few students were expelled or suspended.

The legend of former Dean of Men Scott H. Goodnight waiting in a rocking chair outside an apartment to identify someone the dean of women suspected of sexual misconduct illustrates the inherent, ever present difficulties of monitoring and controlling student behavior.

By the early 1970s students were free from parental-type rules which seemingly had been derived from a perceived need to monitor and control student behaviors. The new rules recognized students as adults. These rules were designed to assure due process and fairness in penalties and to protect the University, its people, and its functions.

The important but short period of campus unrest began with the disastrous encounter of police and students over Dow Chemical employment interviews on October 18, 1967, and ended with the tragic bombing of Sterling Hall on August 24, 1970. These two nationally publicized events mark an era. There was a gradual build-up to the 1967 beginning and an abrupt ending in 1970. The origins of the build-up could probably be found in the freedom-of-speech movement at the University of California, Berkeley. Then there was the sit-in about the draft, followed by other protests on the Madison campus. The quieting effect of the loss of human life and loss of years of treasured research resulting from the bombing of Sterling Hall brought the era to an abrupt end. This event had such an impact that subsequent efforts of radical leaders to arouse the general student body failed.

The two major concerns, and there were many other important ones, which caused the unrest of this period were United States involvement in the war in South Vietnam and a new awareness of American society's unfairness to minorities. Students seemingly knew that they had neither the economic nor the political power to end the war or to advance civil rights. They did know, however, that they had the freedom and opportunity to protest and hoped to thus change the course of events.

Concerns about war were not new to this era of turmoil. On May 11, 1950, for example, eighteen students marched with banners at the annual ROTC review denouncing compulsory ROTC in particular and militarism in general. Interestingly enough, at that time the *Daily Cardinal* said that the protestors were "guilty of poor manners"[10] and should be disciplined like the discourteous students who carried banners at a football game demanding that the coach resign and the students who let animals run loose in a women's dormitory.

In October of 1967 concerns about the war in Vienam, which were "tearing this nation and its institutions, including the University, apart at the seams," reached a new high. The Dow Chemical Company had become a symbol of the establishment's support of the war in Vietnam. On Tuesday, October 17, Dow Company interviewers were picketed peacefully but on Wednesday the peaceful anti-Dow protest turned into "a bloody, glass breaking, club wielding, tear gassing battle."[11] The underlying issue was the war but other issues, most notably "police brutality," increased the intensity of emotional reactions.

Tense feelings about the war persisted. These feelings played a major part in the disturbances of the "Black Strike" of February 1969 and of the TAA strike of March-April 1970. Even though war was not the major issue during these events, angers and frustrations about the war transferred easily to other issues. War did not become the central issue again until May of 1970, when President Nixon expanded the Southeast Asian war into Cambodia and when war-protesting students were killed on the campus of Kent State University. These off-campus events intensified feelings on the Madison campus to the point where mass rallies, marches, violence and threats to shut down the University became so great that the National Guard was again called in to assist the police in restoring order.

As United States involvement in the Southeast Asian war came to an end, student concerns about war subsided. In the early 1970s, at this writing, there seemed to be a mood of apathy and uncertainty, a feeling of making the best of the present, a characteristic of young people sometimes labeled "the now generation." Students seemed to have shifted from a lashing out at all of society's problems at once to a diligent pursuit of one or another set of problems, to prepare himself or herself intellectually and professionally to take a place of authority in the professions, in business and industry, in politics, or elsewhere. Many seemed to hope that they could find a place where they could be effective in solving some, but not all, of society's problems.

Concerns about minorities were not new. One of the landmark responses to students' complaints about racial and religious bigotry had occurred in 1950. At that time, the University Committee prepared "a report on human rights for students." The committee called for "a positive, vigorous, and continuing program against prejudice, discrimination and segregation at the University and by the University."[12] Subsequently, very definite steps were taken, especially regarding the banning of discrimination in fraternities, in sororities, in dormitories, and in private housing.

On April 5, 1968, ten to fifteen thousand people took part in a rally and march to honor the memory of assassinated civil rights leader, Dr. Martin Luther King, Jr. In February 1969 a conference was held entitled "The Black Revolution: To What Ends." Exercising the freedoms granted them in the mid-1950s, students planned and organized a week-long conference of thirty-three programs to consider the future nature of the black person's participation in American life. Just what effects this conference had on the attempted "black strike" which began just before the conference ended is still an open question. On February 7, 1969, the University was presented with thirteen demands and some students began marching and chanting "on strike, shut it down." The following week obstructive and disruptive behaviors continued to increase until duty-weary police, joined by National Guardsmen, finally quelled the disturbances.

The University remained open. The demands were not met. The University did respond, however, to each demand. Full explanations were given as to what was being done and hopefully would be done to meet the needs of minorities.

The faculty quickly recognized that some students had seriously abused their freedoms. The faculty signed a petition in support of Chancellor Edwin Young and his administration in keeping the University open and in not surrendering to mob pressure. The two-paragraph petition signed in a matter of hours in February of 1969 by 1,372 faculty members, said in part: "We support the administration of the University in its refusal to surrender to mob pressures and lawless force, in its determination to continue normal educational activities, in its efforts to deal with problems, including those involving the disadvantaged members of society, through rational methods."[13]

This position, held jointly by faculty and administration, supported by law enforcement personnel when necessary, provided the strength the University needed to carry on its functions as a teaching and research institution. Somewhat similar faculty support had been given Chancellor William H. Sewell in 1967 following the Dow protest incident. The great majority of students rejected violence as a tactic even though the *Daily Cardinal* and the Wisconsin Student Association at times advocated violence and deliberately opposed the faculty and administration on many matters.

Student concerns about minorities continued into the early 1970s. One of the most interesting developments was the major shift in the emphasis of concerns from religious and racial prejudices to prejudices against women. The women's liberation movement was gaining in strength. Students were thus continuing their battles against the tendency of human beings to prejudge other persons on such irrational bases as age, race, color, creed, sex, and national origins.

THE manners, morals, and lifestyles of students have presented ever-changing variations, complexities, and puzzlements over the past quarter-century. They have had an effect upon the interactions and persuasive tactics previously discussed and were reflective of the attitudes and feelings of students. Shoulder length hair on men in the 1960s, for example, may have been a symbol of students' defiance of the status quo and an assertion of independence. Women and men began to dress in similar ways, perhaps reflecting some attitudes of the women's liberation movement. The likeness in appearance of men and women may have been an expression of the need to regard both men and women as individual human beings entitled to the same rights and privileges regardless of sex.

Length of hair, for some strange reason, has always been of special concern. In the seventeenth century the Harvard Magistrates declared that it "was contrary to the rule of God for a man to wear long hairs."[14] In the twentieth century, however, a Wisconsin professor judged hair length more wisely when he pointed out that there is no known correlation between intelligence and length of hair. Opinions about hair and other life-styles have varied considerably, depending both upon the era and the person making the appraisal.

Distinctions in dress between men and women faded. Both men and women had worn saddle shoes and knit sweaters for many years, but women had worn skirts, men had worn slacks, and women's hair had been longer than men's. Later, both men and women dressed in blue jeans, sweatshirts, and sandals and wore their hair long.

Some of the changes in social life over the past twenty-five years reflected changes in attitudes. Illegal cocktail parties were replaced with illegal pot parties. Formal dances, complete with long dresses and white ties, disappeared. Block parties and rock and roll concerts, complete with blue jeans and sweatshirts, became popular. Soft swing music of the Glenn Miller kind was replaced by loud rock music and by soul-searching folk music of the Joan Baez kind. Casual, spontaneous parties replaced the preplanned social events and formal dating. Casual attendance at student film society showings became more popular than dating for a movie on State Street. Vacation-time ski trips, once limited to Wisconsin, came to include the Rockies and the Alps.

Consistent with the student freedoms previously discussed was the growth of freedom from conformity. Put another way, it was a new emphasis on individualism. "Do your own thing" became popular. One student summed up this new freedom when he said: "Odd is normal. Normality is odd."[15]

In the 1950s there was an unwritten rule that students could not attend class in shorts. Some faculty members even excluded students who refused to comply. At the Wisconsin Union, shorts were permitted in the Rathskeller but not in the theater. Later on, some faculty members began wearing shorts to class. The various kinds of dress which later appeared in the Rathskeller shocked some people but delighted others.

An especially delicate subject, but nevertheless a popular one, is sex. Students in the early 1950s were secretive about sex; those in the 1970s were more candid in their discussions and actions, some of them openly advocating sex for recreation as well as for procreation.

It was really only during the era of campus turmoil that many students confronted faculty and administrators with rudeness, hostility, and aggressive criticism. At other times throughout the past quarter-century practically all students were friendly and courteous, showed respect for the faculty, and were appreciative of their opportunities to further their education.

A student statement about student life in the 1950s shows a greater affection for tradition and a more structured way of life than existed in the early 1970s. "The green beer on St. Pat's day mixed with the curly beards of the engineers, the lawyers throwing their canes over the goal post on Homecoming, Haresfoot, Senior Swingout, 'The oldest station in the nation,' star gazing from Observatory Hill, and dates on Picnic Point, are all part of the Wisconsin scene."[16]

Two student statements about student life capture the free-flowing, freedom-loving, person-loving outlook of students in the early 1970s. "The place is Madison — multifaceted, existing as a unique entity because for each person it is a separate way of life — academic, political, social, ecological, philosophical, and all the combinations thereof." "Madison is a mini-culture with varied social sub-groups — and sifting, moving, changing, their definition illusive, as intermixing causes prejudicial boundaries to fade and the curiosity and need of one personality for another dominates."[17]

Student affairs professionals helped to advance student freedoms, hastened the demise of *in loco parentis,* and helped keep the University open in times of campus unrest. They maximized the opportunities to learn. They minimized the deterrents to the learning process. They provided economical and educational housing. They made possible financial assistance through loans, scholarships, and employment. They enabled students to program cultural and social events in the Wisconsin Union which were both supportive of their academic work and recreational in nature. They gave disadvantaged persons opportunities for an education not otherwise possible. They helped students find jobs after graduation. They helped to personalize the University's responses to individual needs by counseling with them about their own problems or by advising them on how best to proceed in launching a program, organizing a group, or promoting change within the system. They were not monitors and controllers or parents-in-residence. They were providing information, advice, and assistance to the men and women who sought it so that they could make the very most of the educational opportunities provided them by the people of the State of Wisconsin. They began treating students as adults long before the age of majority was set at eighteen. They worked with students as adults. They worked with the faculty in obtaining student freedoms. During periods of campus unrest, they dissuaded persons from implementing plans which would likely lead to violence, comforted the hurt and frightened, and counseled those who became seriously disturbed. They participated in the disciplinary processes of suspected violators of University rules.

Student affairs personnel were, however, often misunderstood. Some people regarded them only as the monitors and controllers of student life, as those responsible for seeing to it that students studied hard, behaved properly, kept out of trouble, and did not tarnish the bright image of a great university. Others thought of them only as people to whom students could be referred to get them out of difficulty. Still others thought of them as no longer needed because students had attained adult status and did not need parents in residence. In the early 1970s it was a combination of these misunderstandings with an over-all campus budget cutback that caused a significant reduction in the numbers of these professionals and a corresponding weakening of student affairs programs. This development was inconsistent with a 1965 faculty resolution: "The University of Wisconsin should increase its efforts to improve the non-academic facilities and programs available on the Madison Campus for the physical, cultural, and social development of its students."[18]

The marvelous human beings who have come and gone over the past twenty-five years to live and to learn at the University of Wisconsin-Madison were offered a high quality education. The great majority of them obtained an excellent education which not only is serving them well but also is enabling them to serve society well. Importantly, many of them contributed significantly to the greatness of this University.

NOTES

1 Report of the Investigating Committee, in Papers of the Board of Regents, September 18, 1894.
2 Records of the Board of Regents, May 2, 1922, vol. K, pp. 180-181.
3 Statement by President E. B. Fred on January 14, 1953, in Richard Hartshorne, "Shall Student Groups Be Free to Present Guest Speakers of Their Own Choosing? A History of the Controversy at the University of Wisconsin, 1953-1956," xeroxed report dated March 20, 1957, p. 10, in University Archives.
4 President E. B. Fred's request to the Student Life and Interests Committee, in Hartshorne, "Shall Student Groups?," p. 11.
5 Hartshorne, "Shall Student Groups?"
6 S. H. Goodnight, *The Gray Book, A Booklet of Information for Freshmen* (Madison, July 1925), p. 17.
7 University of Wisconsin, *Student Handbook* (Madison, 1951), p. 65.
8 "The Report of the Non-curricular Life of Students Committee" (Frank R. Remington, Chairman), August 12, 1965; mimeographed copy in University Archives.
9 University of Wisconsin, *Rule Book* (Madison, 1972-1973), p. 34.
10 *Daily Cardinal,* May 19, 1950.
11 *Daily Cardinal,* October 19, 1967.
12 Faculty Document 933 (revised), October 2, 1950, p. 1.
13 Petitions transmitted to Chancellor Edwin Young in February 1969.
14 Harvard Laws and Liberties, March 28, 1650; as quoted in *Like It is,* vol. 2, no. 12 (March 18, 1970), p. 6 (Madison: Division of Student Affairs).
15 *Wisconsin Badger,* 1972, p. 39.
16 *Wisconsin Badger,* 1954, p. 12.
17 *Wisconsin Badger,* 1972, pp. 6, 58.
18 Faculty Document 38, December 6, 1965, p. 2.

Quality education was always Madison's aim, whether it was a history lecture by Carl Russell Fish in 1916 (top), married students studying in temporary housing at Truax Field in 1946 (middle), or an evening in the Memorial Library (right)—this one around 1963.

University athletic fortunes rose and fell throughout its history. The crew (top)— shown here in about 1900—at times won international acclaim. The football team was thrice beaten in the Rose Bowl—shown here (left) is the celebration of Wisconsin's first bid, in 1952. But—win or lose—through many years, Professor Raymond F. Dvorak was always ready to lead the singing of "Varsity" (above).

CHAPTER 8

Evolving Undergraduate and Graduate Curricula, 1949-1974

CHESTER H. RUEDISILI

TWENTY-FIVE years ago the Committee on University Functions and Policies was appointed at the request of the Board of Regents to make a self-analysis of the University of Wisconsin. The committee defined the nature and purpose of the University, investigated how well it met these standards, and suggested constructive ways to correct deficiencies. Noting that the initial purpose of the University was "to furnish liberal and professional education at the post-high school level to the youth of Wisconsin," the committee posited three basic and inter-related objects of such an education: "to train the individual to earn a living in a socially useful manner, to develop in him the highest cultural and intellectual interests, and to make him a moral, intelligent, and well-informed citizen with a deep sense of his obligation to the community."[1] Two other major purposes were stressed: productive scholarship (research) and public services closely connected with this research. All three functions worked together to form "a community of scholars made as useful as possible."

More recently, the Interdisciplinary Studies Committee on the Future of Man described the primary purpose of the University as being that of providing "an environment in which faculty and students can discover, examine critically, preserve, and transmit the knowledge, wisdom, and values that will help ensure the survival of the present and future generations with improvement in the quality of life."[2]

The two committees agreed, though separated by twenty years, that the University met its obligation for professional education very well, but

Chester H. Ruedisili is associate dean of the College of Letters and Science, and has been chairman of its Honors Program since 1963. He started in the dean's office in 1937 while still a graduate student, received the Ph.D. (psychology) in 1941, taught in the Psychology Department from 1941-1966, and, except for a one-year assignment working with Japanese universities, has been associated with the academic programs of the college and University for thirty-seven years.

the same could not be said for liberal (cultural, moral, and intellectual) education. Both reports, especially the latter, were critical of the efforts expended in this direction.

How does a university accomplish the goals and purposes it sets for itself? How are instruction, research, and public service meshed together to form a community of scholars? The mainspring in this process is the curriculum which at any particular time is the result of three interacting variables: the size and quality of the faculty, the size and needs of the student body, and the courses offered. The latter sprout and flourish in some fields, and wither in others, depending on various influences. Federal and state legislatures may provide appropriations that create specific curricula (as the science explosion did after Sputnik), or these agencies may cut funds with the opposite results. Requirements in some professional programs are established because of pressures from accrediting associations and professional societies, as in social work or medicine. Economic and political events may affect supply and demand needs in particular departments or colleges (as in Agriculture or Business). Society itself often encourages (and sometimes deprecates) the development of new fields of knowledge and thus is a factor in making the curriculum.

When the University of Wisconsin was founded in 1849, it consisted of three professors (and one tutor), fifty-six students, and fifteen subject areas. After 125 years, the Madison campus has expanded to 2,094 faculty (of professorial status), 34,365 students, and 7,669 courses listed in college and school bulletins. This spectacular growth has been especially rapid in the past twenty-five years and has resulted in a plethora of curriculum changes. This chapter, in attempting to describe the "evolving undergraduate and graduate curricula, 1949-1974" for the eleven colleges and schools in the University, can include only the highlights that are the most significant developments during the exciting twenty-five years of four presidents: E. B. Fred, Conrad A. Elvehjem, Fred H. Harrington, and John C. Weaver; of three Madison campus chancellors: Robben W. Fleming, William H. Sewell, and Edwin Young; and of four deans in the largest college on campus, the College of Letters and Science: Mark H. Ingraham, Edwin Young, Leon D. Epstein, and Stephen C. Kleene.*

*Many faculty members, including deans and departmental chairmen, provided comprehensive descriptions of their curricula. (These are available in the University Archives.) The writer is grateful for this assistance and regrets the strict editing and cutting that was necessary. What remains is his interpretation and judgment of the changes and trends that have occurred.

TABLE 8.1 shows the number and percentage of students, faculty, and courses in the colleges and schools (hereinafter "college" will include "school") that constituted the University in 1949-1950 and in 1973-1974. (All figures are for the first semester of the year designated.)

Student enrollment (excluding special students) increased from 17,639

Table 8.1. Number and Percentage of Students, Faculty, and Courses in U.W. Colleges and Schools (1949-1950 & 1973-1974*) (omitting specials and unclassified students)

| College/School | Students | | | | Faculty (prof. ranks) | | | | Courses (in bulletins) | | | |
| | 1949-1950 | | 1973-1974 | | 1949-1950 | | 1973-1974 | | 1949-1950 | | 1973-1974 | |
	No.	% of total	No.	% of total	No.	% of total	No.	% of total	No.	% of total	No.	% of total
Agriculture	1045	5.9	1475	4.3	145	20.2	264	12.6	299	10.5	672	8.8
Business	1085	6.2	962	2.8	17	2.4	60	2.9	102	3.6	262	3.4
Education	1379	7.8	2666	7.8	56	7.8	185	8.8	267	9.4	714	9.3
Engineering	2229	12.6	1874	5.5	72	10.0	173	8.3	264	9.3	677	8.8
Family Resources	601	3.4	773	2.2	25	3.5	38	1.8	65	2.3	157	2.0
Graduate School	2822	16.0	9239	26.9	–	–	–	–	(705)		(2790)	
Law	723	4.1	936	2.7	18	2.5	41	2.0	43	1.5	147	1.9
Letters & Science	6819	38.7	14202	41.3	283	39.4	865	41.3	1634	57.4	4629	60.4
Medicine	302	1.7	562	1.6	90	12.5	404	19.3	104	3.7	272	3.6
Nursing	223	1.3	1168	3.4	4	0.6	35	1.7	24	0.8	54	0.7
Pharmacy	411	2.3	508	1.5	9	1.2	29	1.4	43	1.5	85	1.1
Total	17639	100.0	34365	100.0	719	100.1	2094	100.1	2845	100.0	7669	100.0

Source: Unless otherwise noted, the data in the tables of this chapter are taken from the *Bulletins,* the records of the Graduate School, the Business Office, the Office of the Registrar, and the Chancellor's Office of the University of Wisconsin. Most of the relevant 1949 records are now in the University Archives.

*The data in all tables in this chapter are first semester figures.

to 34,365, a 95 percent increase. The largest percentage increases were Nursing (424 percent) and Graduate School (227 percent), but on a percentage basis of total enrollment, the Graduate School showed the largest jump (from 16.0 percent to 26.9 percent), with Nursing next. Business, Engineering, and Law had lower percentages in 1974, probably a reflection of the attentuated 1949 figures caused by the continuing high enrollment figures of World War II veterans. Engineering enrollment actually dropped by 16 percent and Business by 11 percent. The growth of special students was amazing—from 51 to 1,552 (2,943 percent increase).

The marked increase in the number and percentage of women students within each college is noted in Table 8.2. In 1949 they constituted 24.4 percent of the student body, but by 1973 this figure had risen to 40.4 percent (from one in four of all students to two in five). Colleges showing the greatest percentage growth were Agriculture* (from 1.5 percent to 27.6 percent), Law (2.2 percent to 20.6 percent), Business (4.1 percent to 13.2 percent), and Pharmacy (9.5 percent to 23.4 percent).

Table 8.2. Number and Percentage of U.W. Students by College and Sex
(1949-1950 and 1973-1974)

College/School	1949-1950					1973-1974				
	Men	% of college	Women	% of college	Total	Men	% of college	Women	% of college	Total
Agriculture	1029	98.5	16	1.5	1045	1068	72.4	407	27.6	1475
Business	1040	95.9	45	4.1	1085	835	86.8	127	13.2	962
Education	663	48.1	716	51.9	1379	638	23.9	2028	76.1	2666
Engineering	2224	99.8	5	0.2	2229	1832	97.8	42	2.2	1874
Family Resources	2	0.3	599	99.7	601	18	2.3	755	97.7	773
Graduate School	2348	83.2	474	16.8	2822	6292	68.1	2947	31.9	9239
Law	707	97.8	16	2.2	723	743	79.4	193	20.6	936
Letters and Science	4677	68.6	2142	31.4	6819	8152	57.4	6050	42.6	14202
Medicine	270	89.4	32	10.6	302	463	82.4	99	17.6	562
Nursing	—	0.0	223	100.0	223	47	4.0	1121	96.0	1168
Pharmacy	372	90.5	39	9.5	411	389	76.6	119	23.4	508
Total	13332	75.6	4307	24.4	17639	20477	59.6	13888	40.4	34365

Table 8.3. Undergraduate and Graduate U.W. Students by College and School
(1949-1950 and 1973-1974)

College/School	1949-1950				1973-1974			
	Under- grad. & profess.	Grad.	Total	% Univ. total	Under- grad. & profess.	Grad.	Total	% Univ. total
Agriculture	1045	552	1597	9.0	1475	992	2467	7.2
Business	1085	62	1147	6.5	962	710	1672	4.9
Education	1379	258	1637	9.2	2666	1419	4085	11.9
Engineering	2229	276	2505	14.1	1874	627	2501	7.3
Family Resources	601	27	628	3.5	773	84	857	2.5
Law	723	1	724	4.1	936	—	936	2.7
Letters and Science	6819	1639	8458	47.7	14202	5095	19297	56.1
Medicine	302	59	361	2.0	562	194	756	2.2
Nursing	223	—	223	1.3	1168	68	1236	3.6
Pharmacy	411	26	437	2.5	508	73	581	1.7
Total number	14817	2900	17717		25126	9262	34388	
Total percentage	83.6%	16.4%	100.0%	99.9%	73.1%	26.9%	100.0%	100.1%

Graduate enrollment, shown in Table 8.3 (including specials) expanded by 219 percent over the twenty-five-year period (from 2,900 students in 1949-1950 to 9,262 in 1973-1974), whereas undergrads

*For simplicity's sake, "Agriculture" designates the College of Agricultural and Life Sciences, "Family Resources" is the School of Family Resources and Consumer Sciences, and "L&S" is the College of Letters and Science.

showed only a 70 percent increase. When graduate students are classified by the college of their field of knowledge, L&S showed the greatest percentage increase of total university enrollment (from 47.7 percent to 56.1 percent); over half of all students—undergraduate and graduate—are enrolled in this college. Engineering had the sharpest drop. The colleges with the greatest percentage increases (see Table 8.4) were Business (1,045 percent) and Education (450 percent); they also showed the largest percentage increases of total graduate enrollment.

The first year for which complete undergraduate enrollment figures by majors is available was 1953-1954. That year, 42 percent of the students listed specific majors. By 1973 this figure increased to 51 percent, indicating more students were progressing into the junior and senior years of college. Majors are chosen, or changed, for many different reasons or combinations of reasons. During the past quarter of a century, some majors have mushroomed and a few have disappeared. The most marked expansion in numbers of undergraduate majors by college is found in these departments: Agriculture (Bacteriology, Biochemistry, and Horticulture); Business (Accounting and Finance Investment and Banking); Education (Art, Art Education, Elementary Education, Music Education, Occupational Therapy, and Men's Physical Education); Engineering (Civil and Electrical); and Family Resources (Dietetics, Food Science, and Related Art).

The College of Letters and Science, with 60.1 percent of all undergraduate students in the University, offers seventy-four fields of major study. A comparison of the ten largest undergraduate major departments in 1952 with those in 1973 reveals some surprising shifts of student interest. Economics, ranking first in 1952, dropped to tenth in 1973. Other downward changes were English, Sociology, and Chemistry. In 1973 Psychology had the largest number of undergraduate majors in the

Table 8.4. U.W. Graduate Enrollment by College (1949-1950 and 1973-1974)

College/School	1949-1950		1973-1974		
	No.	%total	No.	% total	% increase
Agriculture	552	19.0	992	10.7	80
Business	62	2.1	710	7.7	1,045
Education	258	8.9	1419	15.3	450
Engineering	276	9.5	627	6.8	127
Family Resources	27	0.9	84	0.9	211
Law	1	0.0	—	—	—
Letters and Science	1639	56.5	5095	55.0	211
Medicine	59	2.0	194	2.1	229
Nursing	—	—	68	0.7	—
Pharmacy	26	0.9	73	0.8	181
Total	2900	99.9	9262	100.0	219

college (490). Departments showing an upward trend were Zoology, History, Journalism, Communication Arts, and Social Work. A popular new development (since 1971) is the Individual Major, for the student who with faculty assistance designs his own tailor-made curriculum in a field not currently available (ecology, for example).

Thirty departments in the University have over one hundred graduate majors at the present time. Business ranks first (698 students) and is followed by History (496), Curriculum and Instruction (408), English (379), Social Work (319), Chemistry (264), Library Science (214), Economics (209), Mathematics (209), Communication Arts (206), and Educational Administration (203). L&S, with 55 percent of the graduate students enrolled in this college, currently has twenty departments with more than one hundred graduate students. Interesting shifts have occured in the positions of the top ten L&S departments. Chemistry, ranking first in 1949, dropped to fourth in 1973. Other downward changes are Economics, Physics, Zoology, and Geology. Departments showing a rising trend are Social Work, Communication Arts, and Sociology. Two departments not existing in 1949 now rank in the top ten: Library Science is fifth and Computer Sciences is tenth.

"A University is great because it has an outstanding faculty." This statement, universally accepted as a criterion for evaluating an institution of higher education, describes the faculty of the University of Wisconsin now and has for many years. Three members of this distinguished faculty have served as presidents of the American Association of University Professors: Mark H. Ingraham, Helen C. White, and David Fellman. Surveys going back to the 1930s consistently have ranked the University among the best in the nation.

Table 8.5. U.W. Faculty Budgeted Positions (1949-1950 and 1973-1974)

College/School	1949-1950					1973-1974				
	Prof.	Assoc. prof.	Asst. prof.	Total	% of total	Prof.	Assoc. prof.	Asst. prof.	Total	% of total
Agriculture	73	33	39	145	20.2	159	58	47	264	12.6
Business	8	3	6	17	2.4	26	19	15	60	2.9
Education	21	15	20	56	7.8	100	40	45	185	8.8
Engineering	28	22	22	72	10.0	96	44	33	173	8.3
Family Resources	7	5	13	25	3.5	16	6	16	38	1.8
Law	11	3	4	18	2.5	23	1	17	41	2.0
Letters and Science	130	72	81	283	39.4	464	186	215	865	41.3
Medicine	34	29	27	90	12.5	141	100	163	404	19.3
Nursing	—	2	2	4	0.6	2	12	21	35	1.7
Pharmacy	4	1	4	9	1.2	11	5	13	29	1.4
Total number	316	185	218	719		1038	471	585	2094	
Total percentage	43.9%	25.7%	30.3%	99.9%	100.1	49.6%	22.5%	27.9%	100.0%	100.1

Table 8.1 lists the number and percentage of faculty budgeted positions (professors, associate professors, assistant professors) by college in 1949-1950 and 1973-1974. The expansion from 719 to 2,094 amounts to a 191.2 percent increase. Faculty at the professor rank (indicated in Table 8.5) showed the greatest growth (228 percent), associate professors had a 155 percent increase, and assistant professors, 168 percent. If a comparison of the 1949 and 1973 figures by rank and by percentage of total faculty is made, professors increased while associate and assistant professors decreased. Changes that occurred within college faculties reveal shifts in both directions: Medicine jumped from 12.5 percent of the total faculty to 19.3 percent and Nursing also rose; in the other direction, Agriculture dropped from 20.2 percent to 12.6 percent as did Engineering and Family Resources by smaller degrees.

A tabulation of faculty by departments (using staff directories as the source but omitting the emeriti) for the current year reveals twenty-eight departments in the University with twenty-five or more members. Heading the list is the Department of Medicine in the Medical School with seventy-eight, followed by Mathematics (seventy-three), History (sixty-six), Sociology (sixty-three), English (sixty-two), Curriculum and Instruction (fifty-nine), Physics (fifty-three), Music (fifty-two), Economics (fifty-one), Agricultural Economics (forty-six), and Electrical Engineering (forty-four).

Table 8.6. U.W. Academic Staff by Rank and Sex (1949-1950 and 1973-1974)*

| | 1949-1950 | | | | | | 1973-1974 | | | | | |
| | Men | | Women | | Total | | Men | | Women | | Total | |
Rank	No.	% of rank	No.	% of rank	No.	% of total	No.	% of rank	No.	% of rank	No.	% of total
Administration	21	91.3	2	8.7	23	0.7	190	87.2	28	12.8	218**	3.4
Professors	359	92.5	29	7.5	388	11.0	981	95.0	52	5.0	1033	16.3
Associate prof.	209	85.3	36	14.7	245	7.0	392	87.9	54	12.1	446	7.0
Assistant prof.	316	80.4	77	19.6	393	11.2	415	82.7	87	17.3	502	7.9
Lecturers (excl. Forest Products)	35	88.6	4	11.4	39	1.1	146	63.2	85	36.8	231	3.6
Associates	37	80.4	9	19.6	46	1.3	455	82.1	99	17.9	554***	8.7
Instructors	505	69.2	225	30.8	730	20.8	32	42.1	44	57.9	76	1.2
Assistants (tchg., resch., project)	1298	78.6	353	21.4	1651	47.0	2522	76.9	758	23.1	3280	51.7
Total number	2780		735		3515	100.1	5133		1207		6340	99.8
Total percentage	79.1%		20.9%		100%	100.1%	81.0%		19.0%		100%	99.8%

*1949-1950 figures from 1950-1952 General Announcement Catalogue.
**Includes many more administrative positions than in 1949.
***Includes associates (project, research, program) scientists (senior, associate, assistant), PD fellows, and trainees.

Statistics that describe data from different time periods always are difficult to interpret. Groups that appear to be the same may be quite different because of changes in classification or definition. This should be kept in mind in considering Table 8.6, which shows academic staff by rank and sex for 1949-1950 and 1973-1974. The number of women on the academic staff increased 64.2 percent (from 735 to 1,207); men increased 84.6 percent (from 2,780 to 5,133). In 1973 women constituted 19.0 percent of the total academic staff, down from 20.9 percent in 1949. This loss is especially marked at the professorial ranks. Higher percentages for women were noted in 1973 at the administrative level, lecturers, and instructors.

When the total academic staff in 1949 and 1973 is analyzed by ranks, increases were noted for administration, professors, lecturers, associates, and assistants. Decreases were found for assistant professors and instructors. Especially to be noted is the expansion in number of professors and the very great contraction of instructors.

The appendix to the U.W. Regents' Reports for 1849 lists the following as the course of study: "English Grammar; Arithmetic; Ancient and Modern Geography; Elements of History; Algebra; Caesar's Commentaries; Aeneid of Virgil (six books); Sallust; Select Orations of Cicero; Greek Lessons; Anabasis of Xenophon; Antiquities of Greece and Rome; Exercises in Penmanship, Reading, Composition and Declamation. Instruction . . . to all who desire it, in Bookkeeping; Elements of Geometry and Surveying."[3] After one hundred years, the original fifteen courses of study had increased to 2,845 and now, twenty-five years later, the total has exploded to 7,669 courses.

Curricula and courses offered in the University are in a constant state of flux, and they must be to meet the changing problems of society and the needs of students. Individual faculty members at the University of Wisconsin always have been free—and encouraged—to initiate curriculum changes. The 1949 report of the University Functions and Policies Committee, criticizing the overspecialization of curricula in some of the professional fields, stressed the importance of insuring a continuous and concerned review of departmental and college curricula. Its recommendations urged the faculty to develop a better balance of broad general education and of specialized education, because this combination is essential to produce well-rounded, moral, and responsible citizens in a democracy—a worthy goal to be sought in this age of Watergate. The explosive expansion of new information in the past twenty-five years requires extensive and constant broadening of the curriculum to keep pace with this proliferation of knowledge.

Table 8.1 lists the number and percentage of courses for 1949 and

Table 8.7. Undergraduate and Graduate Courses Listed in U.W. College and
School Catalogues (1948-1950 and 1974-1976)

	1948-1950						1974-1976					
	Undergrad.		Grad.		Total		Undergrad.		Grad.		Total	
College/School	No.	% of coll.	No.	% of coll.	No.	% of total	No.	% of coll.	No.	% of coll.	No.	% of total
Agriculture	245	81.9	54	18.1	299	10.5	495	73.7	177	26.3	672	8.8
Business	87	85.3	15	14.7	102	3.6	115	43.9	147	56.1	262	3.4
Education	211	79.0	56	21.0	267	9.4	456	63.9	258	36.1	714	9.3
Engineering	220	83.3	44	16.7	264	9.3	479	80.8	198	29.2	677	8.8
Family Resources	52	80.0	13	20.0	65	2.3	120	76.4	37	23.6	157	2.0
Law	—	0.0	43	100.0	43	1.5	—	0.0	147	100.0	147	1.9
Letters & Science	1220	74.7	414	25.3	1634	57.4	3012	65.1	1617	34.9	4629	60.4
Medicine	45	43.3	59	56.7	104	3.7	108	39.7	164	60.3	272	3.6
Nursing	24	100.0	—	0.0	24	0.8	31	57.4	23	42.6	54	0.7
Pharmacy	36	83.7	7	16.3	43	1.5	63	74.1	22	25.9	85	1.1
Total number	2140		705		2845		4879		2790		7669	
Total percentage	75.2%		24.8%			100.0%	63.6%		36.4%			100.0%

1973. It should be noted that these are not all offered every semester or even every year. The tremendous growth from 2,845 courses to 7,669 (170 percent) is staggering. Undergraduate courses listed in Table 8.7 jumped from 2,140 in the 1948-1950 catalogue to 4,879 in the 1974-1976 bulletins (a 128 percent increase). Graduate level courses showed an even sharper growth, from 705 to 2,790 (296 percent increase), constituting 36.4 percent of all courses offered in 1974, whereas in 1949 they comprised 24.8 percent of the listings. This emphasis at the graduate level is true for all colleges, but is most evident in Business, Education, Engineering, and Pharmacy.

IN the past twenty-five years, the University faculty has found little need to tamper with the undergraduate degree requirements that apply to all students. A strong and solid foundation had been laid by earlier faculties, but some changes have occurred during these years.

The physical education requirement for both freshman and sophomore men and women was four semester courses (two hours per week) for many years, but this has been reduced now to a noncredit one-semester requirement (with opportunity for exemption).

All freshman and sophomore men in 1949 were required to enroll in the elementary course of military science unless exempted, a requirement of the World War II years replacing an earlier voluntary program. In the early 1960s the faculty and regents again placed military training on a voluntary basis, although a short orientation course was still required of male freshmen. Late in the 1960s this latter requirement also was eliminated.

A year of freshman English was required by all colleges of first-year students in 1949 unless they earned exemption on the basis of placement tests or by receiving an A in the first semester course. By 1971 the requirement had been eliminated except for those few students (7 percent in 1973) showing deficiencies in English skills on placement tests. These students now must complete one semester of composition or public speaking.

Early in the 1950s the University faculty established a U.S. History and Institutions requirement for all undergraduate degrees. This requirement continued for a decade but was eliminated by all colleges between 1962-1965.

If University undergraduate degree requirements did not change materially during these years, the same cannot be said for curriculum and degree changes within the colleges. Undergraduate degree programs have remained remarkably stable in number since 1949, when forty-three were offered. Now there are forty-five, but in the interim eight were dropped (three in L&S: Nursing and Pharmacy, which became separate entities, and Naval Science; Biochemical Engineering; and four combined programs with Education), while eleven new B.S. degrees were added: five in Agriculture (Agricultural Engineering, Landscape Architecture, Natural Resources, Natural Science, Agricultural Business Management); and six in Engineering (Civil and City Planning, Civil and Construction Administration, Engineering Mechanics, Nuclear Engineering, Industrial Engineering, and Agricultural Engineering).

Programs for departmental majors in the undergraduate colleges have expanded from 120 in 1949 to 159 currently (33 percent increase). Most of this growth is found in Agriculture, Family Resources, and L&S. Because of majors that were dropped or had their titles revised, there now are sixty-four majors that did not exist twenty-five years ago. In L&S, thirty (41 percent) of the seventy-four current majors have evolved since 1949.

Departments of instruction increased from 93 to 146 (57 percent increase). The greatest growth took place in Engineering (including new fields like Bioengineering, Plasmas, Space Engineering and Sciences), Education (examples are Curriculum and Instruction, Educational Policy Studies, Educational Psychology), and L&S (African Languages and Literature, Afro-American Studies, Cartography, Linguistics, Literature in Translation, Statistics, Urban and Regional Planning, for example).

To describe all of the curriculum changes within the colleges during these twenty-five years would require a complete book by itself. Only some of the most significant trends can be mentioned.

In 1961 the College of Agriculture, recognizing a needed shift in purpose from on-farm activities to the business industry that services farm activities, adopted a curricular option system that permits multiple approaches to the study of many of its majors. A greater emphasis on the science facet of agriculture rather than the production facet is reflected in a change of departmental names: Dairy and Food Industries to Food Science, Animal Husbandry to Meat and Animal Science, and Soils to Soil Science. The college itself changed its title in 1968 to Agricultural and Life Sciences to depict its revised program and concern. With increasing interest in the environmental sciences, a School of Natural Resources was approved within the college in 1967. Now 60 percent of the student body come from urban areas where previously a majority had been farm-reared, and almost 30 percent of the college's students are women.

With the advent of the computer and quantitative techniques for solving problems in both the private and public sectors of business, the School of Business (changed from Commerce in 1966) added new majors and attracted a burgeoning number of graduate students. New graduate programs in arts administration, health services administration, and public management reflect the recent emphasis on the not-for-profit segment of society. A revised undergraduate degree curriculum in 1973 changed the distribution of credits in business and economics courses. Students complete their first two years in L&S and then transfer to Business.

In the School of Education, students preparing to teach at the secondary level before 1957 were required to complete eighteen credits of professional courses. This sequence was revised with the advent of the block teaching and internship programs. Two new programs had been approved a little earlier, the Business Teacher Education Program in 1950 (with a B.B.A. degree in Commerce) and the Elementary Teacher Education sequence in 1952. Students carry their beginning liberal arts work while registered in L&S (one year for the elementary program and two years for the secondary), and must include thirty-six credits of liberal studies in their programs. Wisconsin High School had served as the educational laboratory school for fifty years, but closed its doors in 1964. About the same time (1962), the Educational Psychology Department was formed (separating from the Department of Education) and soon thereafter a further subdivision produced the departments of Educational Administration, Educational Policy Studies, Counseling and Guidance,

Special Education (now named Behavioral Disabilities), and Curriculum and Instruction.

Technological advancements in many areas, developing and changing needs of modern society, and the additional emphasis given to the consideration of social values in engineering work account for the curriculum changes in the College of Engineering. New undergraduate degrees in Engineering Mechanics, Industrial Engineering, and Nuclear Engineering were formulated; usually these programs followed those begun earlier at the graduate level (an interesting time lag). Like Agriculture and Education, several departments revised their titles: Civil Engineering adding Environmental to its name, Electrical Engineering including Computer in its title, and Engineering Graphics changing to General Engineering. Emphasis on interdisciplinary programs (Engineering and Medicine, for example) is evidenced by the increasing number of joint faculty appointments that cross traditional departmental boundaries.

Starting as a department in L&S in 1908, the School of Family Resources and Consumer Sciences has seen three changes in title and status during the last twenty-five years. In 1951 the Department of Home Economics in the College of Agriculture became a school; in 1968, the School of Home Economics was renamed Family Resources and Consumer Sciences; and in 1973 the School of Family Resources and Consumer Sciences became an autonomous unit apart from the College of Agricultural and Life Sciences. (A school, too, can have an "identity crisis"!) Majors in the school must include two integrated courses that cover environmental resources, and the humanistic factors affecting professional, personal, and family life.

In 1949 three curricula in nursing were offered: in the School of Nursing and in L&S with a Bachelor of Science (Hygiene); in a combined program with Home Economics; and a Certificate of Graduate Nurse program (which was discontinued in 1960). A five-year B.S. (Nursing) degree was approved in 1951 and was revised to a four-year program in 1956. Registered nurses who were graduates of hospital diploma programs followed a specially designed baccalaureate curriculum until 1967, when the two options were merged. The most drastic curriculum change came in 1971 after several years of planning. The redesigned program conforms to the long-held belief of the faculty that a strong liberal arts component is essential, and general education courses constitute over half of the required credits. A common core program is followed throughout the four years, but students during the last two select an area of concentration that prepares them for different and expanding roles in either of two specialized fields of practice: primary health care or secondary health care; that is, nursing practice outside the hospital in the first instance, or in the care of the acutely ill in the latter.

Established by the Wisconsin Legislature in 1883, the School of Pharmacy was the first in the country to develop a four-year curriculum leading to a degree. This was phased into a five-year program in 1964 when two years of prepharmacy studies in L&S were introduced as the prerequisite to three years of professional study in Pharmacy. The focus of the curriculum has shifted from emphasis on "product preparation and orientation" to "patient orientation." Primary concern now is not on the technical aspects of drug manufacture but on how the drug affects the patient and the best therapeutic regimen for various disease states. Because 70 percent of the drugs handled by the pharmacist today did not exist in 1960, the preparation of the pharmacy student includes courses in chemistry, pathology, physiology, bacteriology, and pharmacology; in addition the student observes various therapeutic treatments of patients in U.W. Hospitals and attends lectures and discussions with practicing physicians and pharmacists.

The largest liberal arts college in the state, the College of Letters and Science, at the present time includes over 14,000 students, approximately 900 faculty at the professorial level, more than 4,600 courses, and sixty-eight departments of instruction. The diversity of its course offerings and its curriculum structure is overwhelming (and often confusing!). Most students in the college earn general Bachelor of Arts or Bachelor of Science degrees, but some more specialized degrees are conferred as well, such as B.A. (Journalism), B.S. (Chemistry), B.S. (Medical Technology), and Bachelor of Music. The curriculum of the B.A. General Course in 1949 required English language and literature, foreign language, and one of three options: the humanities, the social studies, or the natural sciences. For the B.S. General Course, the requirements included English language, literature, composition, and one of two options in social studies or natural sciences.

Since then, two college committees have studied the curriculum and recommended changes. The Curriculum Committee of 1962, chaired by Professor James S. Watrous, recommended proposals that hopefully would provide an opportunity for students in the college to obtain a more liberal education, while at the same time the degree would be strengthened through a more rigorous academic program.[4] The requirements included the following: a basic knowledge of the tools of communication (English language, mathematics, and foreign languages) needed to understand the major areas of knowledge (previously students were allowed to omit both foreign language and mathematics); a proficiency in either foreign languages or mathematics; and a strengthening and broader experience in the three areas of the humanities, social studies, and natural sciences. Course distributions for both the B.A. and B.S. were identical, but the B.S. degree required sixty credits or more in mathematics and natural science.

Almost a decade later, the faculty again recognized the need to bring more flexibility into the curriculum while still retaining the college's traditional high academic standards. The Curriculum Review Committee (Professor E. David Cronon, chairman — now dean of the college) in 1971 described the elements of a liberal education in these terms: "the ability to think critically and communicate one's ideas effectively, some awareness of the vast extent and variety of man's accumulated experience and knowledge, and the mastery of at least one subject sufficiently well to appreciate its sublety and complexity."[5] The curriculum proposed by the committee was designed to attain these goals. Distribution requirements for the B.A. and B.S. degrees no longer are similar except in English, where there is little change from that previously in effect. The B.A. requires four or five high school units (or the college equivalent) of foreign language, and three high school units (or the college equivalent) of mathematics. For the B.S., only three units of foreign language are required, but five units of mathematics (including generally two college semesters of calculus, computer sciences, or statistics) must be completed. The breadth requirement for both degrees now includes forty credits spread almost evenly among humanities, social studies, and natural sciences. Other recommendations of the committee that were approved include an extension of the maximum study load in a semester to twenty credits, and a stipulation that at least 60 of the 120 credits required for a degree be earned in intermediate or advanced level courses.

One other college committee reviewed the academic programs during this period. At the request of Chancellor Robben Fleming, the Internal Study Committee was formed in response to the prevailing discontent with undergraduate education.[6] The report of the committee (chaired by Dean Leon D. Epstein) included forty-two recommendations designed to make improvements in undergraduate teaching. Among the areas covered were professorial participation in undergraduate teaching; communicating with undergraduate majors; special, Honors, and experimental classes; structural innovations; student program planning; evaluation of teaching; and grading.

Wıтн knowledge accumulating at a mind-boggling rate, departments are constantly reevaluating their objectives and priorities: eliminating the outmoded aspects, introducing novel approaches, and striving to strengthen and invigorate their programs. To attempt to describe the significant developments in some forty-five L&S fields is impossible. Determining what to mention when so many new and exciting programs have been introduced is a difficult assignment. Only a few highlights can be given as examples.

In the humanities, Art History, with a greatly enriched course offering (particularly introductory), has enrolled an expanding number of students (more than 2,200 in 1973-1974). The opening of the Elvehjem Art Center (1970) created an outstanding teaching resource, and the Kohler Art Library in the center is the largest in a Midwest public college or university. The degree programs in English are pyramidal in conception, starting with a broad chronological range of English and American literature at the undergraduate level and advancing to specialization in a major period of literary history at the Ph.D. level; this specialist approach is emphasized to a greater extent at U.W. than at most universities. The central dominating focus of teaching literature in this department is interpreting literature in its historical context. The new area of concentration in English linguistics is one of the most comprehensive and extensive in the country. The School of Music, a department in L&S, has excellent teaching facilities in the new Humanities Building (practice rooms, listening laboratories, auditoriums, and classrooms equipped with the latest electronic devices for recording and reproduction), and its courses attract many nonmajors. A change in the philosophy and purpose of this department has taken place, from emphasis on history, theory, and music education to performance by solo, ensemble, and organizations, with the main thrust in the applied performance area. A primary focal point of the Spanish and Portuguese Department is the growth of monographic courses for undergraduates. These are devoted to a narrow topic (author, genre, or a movement) and provide a taste of specialization and the opportunity to work closely with a professor in a research situation. Foreign language instruction has changed radically in the past twenty-five years, shifting from the traditional grammar-reading program to the audio-lingual technique, and the use of the language laboratory has given new life and meaning to the acquisition of language skills. The newest department in L&S, Theatre and Drama (separated from Communication Arts in 1973), made an auspicious start with its move into Vilas Hall. Because of the outstanding accommodations, its production program became a working laboratory tied into the regular classroom teaching. Other curriculum ramifications of importance are those in scene, costume, lighting design, and technical theater (one of the country's best), and the unique interdisciplinary program in Asian Theatre.

Of the departments classified as social studies, Economics (once the largest department in the college in terms of majors) has contracted somewhat both in faculty and in students. Its subject matter has changed, too, from an institutional approach and emphasis on labor economics in 1949, first to such areas as international trade and economic development, and currently to fields like public finance and the economics of health, education, and poverty. Increasingly, the approach to economic problems has involved mathematical and econometric methods. Among the top three largest graduate programs in the country, History ranks first in this regard in L&S. New areas have evolved in African, Latin American, South Asian, Far Eastern, and Middle Eastern history. Quantification is playing an increasingly important role in this field. The School of Journalism and Mass Communications has grown especially in nonskills conceptual courses like communication and public opinion, international communication, literary aspects of journalism, and communication in developing nations. New sequences in advertising, public relations, broadcast news, and mass media and minorities have been established, as well as a summer internship course. Curriculum changes in Political Science reflect an increased emphasis on quantitative measurements of political reality concurrently with decreased interest in formalistic or legalistic theories of political activity. A corresponding shift from an institutional, descriptive approach to government toward a more dynamic process orientation also has occurred. Efforts have been expanded in comparative politics and regional studies. The current trend is to make political science a policy science that emphasizes policy outcomes, their impact, their process of creation, and occasionally their worth. The Psychology Department has experienced the greatest burgeoning of students (majors and nonmajors) in the college and ranks first in number of undergraduate majors. This explosion of students necessitated a shift from the small-class format to larger classes for most courses. Only in the advanced undergraduate courses (largely for majors) can classes of twenty-five be maintained. Student interest in the social and clinical aspects of psychology has multiplied. The instructional orientation of the department is to teach psychology as a science rather than applied psychology. Emphasis in teaching at the graduate level shifted in the 1960s from a general basic training in all fields to specialization in one area and a minor in another. The School of Social Work (an L&S department) resisted the national trend in social work education during the 1950s that emphasized psychiatric theory and practice, and completion of a two-year Master in Social Work degree. The pendulum finally swung in the 1960s and 1970s toward the Wisconsin point of view that the social world of the client deserved major consideration. This directed attention on matters like poverty, housing, minority group problems, and public welfare policy. The field returned to the social sciences, where the emphasis had been in the 1920s. The University's school has played a national leadership role in designing a five-year professional training program — four years of undergraduate work and a one-year master's degree.

As one of the physical science departments, Chemistry, with its move into new and expanded facilities in 1963 and 1967, was able to meet the challenges of mushrooming enrollments and scientific developments created by the "Sputnik era." An increased emphasis on instrumentation was made possible: in general chemistry, precise analyses rather than qualitative measurements; in organic, nuclear magnetic resonance; in physical, electron spin resonance; and so on. Enrollment expansion was particularly a problem in the elementary courses and required the utilization of audio-visual instruction to maximize routine information transmitted to students, thus allowing more time to deal with individual learning difficulties. Another department that was initiated during this twenty-five-year period is Computer Sciences. Starting as Numerical Analysis in 1961, it now has a faculty of thirty members, 187 undergraduate majors, and 163 graduate students — a phenomenal growth since its birth. The computers in the University are not operated by this department (which has its own Computer Systems Laboratory), but by the Madison Academic Computing Center. Geology and Geophysics (the latter term added in 1969) moved to its new home in Weeks Hall in 1974; it has added courses in such subdisciplines as x-ray crystallography, palynology, geochemistry, oceanography, and carbonate petrology. Most of the undergraduate work in Mathematics once was taught as "how" courses (referred to as "cookbook" math), but with the emphasis on science after Sputnik a shift was made (especially at the calculus level and above) to "why," stressing the mathematical theory essential for graduate study. Greatly increased enrollments in the 1960s required a shift from small sections of twenty-five students taught by professors to sections of 100-150, with discussion groups handled by teaching assistants. A more recent trend, with the decreased emphasis on science in the nation and the government, appears to be a shift of enrollment from calculus-level courses to precalculus courses. Organized in 1948, Meteorology has probably offered over the past six or seven years the nation's most comprehensive academic program in the atmospheric sciences. Concerned with the welfare of man through the study of his environment, the department has played prime roles in the Space Science and Engineering Center, Marine Studies Center, Oceanography and Limnology Program, and the Institute for Environmental Studies. Recent developments in the Physics Department include special courses for nonmajors (Ideas of Modern Physics, Physics in the Arts, Physics in the Contemporary World), and curricula in new areas (medical, plasma, high energy, solid state, biophysics, modern "atomic" physics). As in Chemistry, the program for majors has a stronger emphasis on modern experimental work, particularly involving realistic experience with a variety of sophisticated up-to-date equipment.

Botany, one of the few biological science departments in the college, in the past five years has recognized the need for a broader undergraduate mission than preparation for graduate school. Focusing on making students more aware of their natural surroundings, three programs for majors were designed: the biotechnician option, the field sciences, and the molecular, biochemical, and physiological major. The recent interest in environmental and population problems has led to an amalgamation of Botany and Zoology, such that ecological offerings consider both plants and animals (as well as microorganisms) as integral and interdependent components of the ecosystem. Other new approaches include courses for nonscience majors (Chemistry, Physics, and Zoology have developed similar courses) and junior-senior tutorials for majors. The second largest L&S department in terms of undergraduate majors, preparing many students for Medical School, Zoology strengthened its instructional program with its move to the new Noland Zoology Building (1972). New courses, especially in ecology, have been initiated (ecology of fishes, human population ecology, acquatic populations) and several old courses have changed their names (cellular biology instead of cytology, and developmental biology for embryology). A popular introductory course, "Biological Principles and Their Impact on Society," employs the latest techniques and hardware in audio-tutorial methods.

Twenty-five years ago the University Functions and Policies Committee encouraged the development of interdisciplinary programs, pointing out that it is rare (though desirable) to have Liberal Arts, Medicine, Agriculture, and Engineering all on the same campus, as at Wisconsin. Of the various efforts to build relationships among the disciplines, several should be mentioned.

Starting from a base of strong language departments and related disciplines and assisted by grants from the Ford Foundation and the National Defense Education Act, area study programs mushroomed during this period, although the beginnings of the Ibero-American curriculum date back to the 1930s. Current programs associated with our International Studies and Programs Office are listed (with starting dates):

Scandinavian (1949), Asian (early 1950s), Russian (1958), South Asian (in 1958 was Indian Studies), African (1961), Ibero-American (1962), East Asian (1963), Southeast Asian (1966), Western European (1967), and Middle Eastern (1972, but in committee stage only at present time). Degrees are offered at both the undergraduate and graduate levels, with work being carried in Agriculture, Business, Education, Engineering, Law, and L&S.

Searching for answers to the growing environmental problems, the University established the Institute for Environmental Studies in 1970. Involving over fifty faculty members in its instructional programs for both undergraduate and graduate students (drawn from departments like Agricultural Economics, Anthropology, Bacteriology, Botany, Civil Engineering, Economics, Geography, Geology, History, Meterology, Nuclear Engineering, Political Science, Urban and Regional Planning, Zoology) and approximately four hundred faculty and students in research, the institute attempts "to bridge the expanding concepts of ecology with the pressing problems of population growth, pollution, resource consumption, and the efficiency with which we use resources."

A more limited interdisciplinary program that applies only to undergraduate work is the Biology Core Curriculum organized in 1966. Designed for students interested in science, but undecided between biological and physical, this integrated program is a joint venture of Letters and Science, Agriculture, and Medicine. It has proved particularly popular with students heading toward Medical School. Elective elementary courses are available in the freshman year, with a four-semester sequence starting in the sophomore year. Biology courses, divided into lectures and laboratories, include cellular, developmental, organismal, and population. During the past year, approximately 1,100 students were attracted to this program.

The Integrated Liberal Studies (ILS) program, established in 1948, provides small groups of students in L&S an alternate way to satisfy the "breadth" requirement. Initiated as a four-semester content-oriented program primarily concerned with the history and development of Western Civilization, it has evolved into a program more concerned with processes and issues, and with ways of seeing and understanding the problems of contemporary America as viewed from an interdisciplinary perspective.

According to Merle Curti and Vernon Carstensen, the Regents' Biennial Report for 1915-1916 recommended that in order to improve undergraduate instruction "special attention be given to the needs and the development of students of exceptional talent."[7] The Functions and Policies Committee likewise urged colleges and departments to provide gifted students with academic work commensurate with their abilities. Currently, four colleges are attempting to do this with Honors Programs: Agriculture, Business, Family Resources, and L&S. The first program in L&S (1960) established courses of significantly improved depth and challenge and recognized the need for increasing individual freedom and responsibility of students, especially in their last two years.[8] Honors work now includes specially designed Honors courses either "enriched" (of greater depth, scope, and originality) or "accelerated," separate Honors sections of existing courses, special Honors lab and discussion sections attached to regular courses, and independent work (such as individual reading, term papers, Senior Honors Thesis, etc.). Approximately 9-10 percent of all L&S students are enrolled in the Honors Program in any year.

Interest in study abroad programs is evidenced by their growth on the campus since they were initiated in 1961 in India and at Monterrey, Mexico (for Engineering students). Since then, others have been established in France, Germany, England, Mexico, Italy, and Spain. In any year, approximately 90-110 U.W. students participate in these programs, along with students from other institutions. After supplementing their basic language preparation with an intensive language and orientation session of several weeks in the country itself, students enroll in the regular university courses taught in the native tongue.

A series of undergraduate seminars particularly for freshmen was conceived in the spring of 1969 as a unique and valuable educational experience in a large university. Designed to give students the opportunity to meet weekly with a distinguished faculty member in a small-group give-and-take atmosphere, their number jumped from seven sections originally to a total of thirty during 1973-1974. All professors volunteer their time, and the subject matter covers a wide spectrum: Behaviorism and B. F. Skinner; Plagues, Politics, and Population; The Science of Creative Intelligence; Discovering Beauty with a Camera (taught by President John C. Weaver). Other courses previously closed to freshmen were made available to them during this twenty-five-year period (in Anthropology, Art History, Comparative Literature, Economics, History, Linguistics, Philosophy, Political Science, Psychology, and Sociology).

For many years, most departments offered independent study courses to qualified juniors and seniors, but this approach was not particularly popular with students. In the last five to ten years this attitude has changed materially, and now in a typical semester 500-600 L&S students register for such work. Even freshmen and sophomores are eligible to elect these courses, now named Directed Study.

Since 1961, when Professor Michael B. Petrovich first used an automated system of audio-visual equipment for his Russian history course, the Multimedia Instructional Laboratory (within the School of Education) has been helping to improve the quality of large-group instruction on the campus. Now located in the new Educational Sciences Building, its wide array of modern facilities provides professional assistance to any faculty member regarding instructional design, production, programming, and presentation (including the use of graphics, photographics, audio-recording, and television). Specially designed lecture rooms are available and all types of projection equipment are involved. Another division, the Media Distribution Center, includes a videotape library of over two hundred programs and a system for viewing. Its micro-teaching program makes possible the videotaping of student teachers in a simulated class situation to critique student performance — a highly effective learning experience.

Other service departments have evolved to assist students and faculty with increasingly sophisticated equipment, such as dial-access program libraries, color video-cassette players and monitors, and synchronized tape-slide programs. Examples of this type of technology for instructional improvement include the Laboratories for Recorded Instruction (extensive facilities particularly for the foreign languages, but available to other departments), the Tape Center in the College Library, listening laboratories in Music, and the audio-visual equipment in Vilas Communications Hall. The Economics Department uses videotapes of teaching assistants and faculty members in the classroom, allowing them to review their classroom performance and to improve their skills.

Another innovative teaching approach is the development of "modules" in designing courses. These are "mini" courses usually five weeks long (one-third of a semester) and count for one credit. Such courses are available in General Engineering, Educational Policy Studies, and Educational Psychology.

Students now may earn degree credit in L&S (and a few of the other colleges) by special examinations for some elementary and intermediate level courses. The foreign language departments permit such credit for previous language work completed in high school (or elsewhere) and determine "credit by examination," using performance in a foreign language course completed on the Madison campus as the criterion. Credit in calculus and in general chemistry also can be achieved on the basis of special departmental examinations. Nationally devised tests likewise can be used by students to demonstrate their achievement and to receive degree credit. This is possible with the Advanced Placement Program and with the College Level Examination Program (both sponsored by the College Entrance Examination Board).

Starting with the 1972-1973 year, a revised academic calendar has been in effect on the campus. Following suggestions of students and faculty, the school year now begins in late August, and the first semester ends prior to Christmas, thus eliminating the former brief "lame-duck" session after the holidays. The second semester is able to start early in January and is completed by the middle of May.

Before leaving this section that deals with undergraduate curriculum changes, the grading system should be mentioned since this issue has been of concern both to students and faculty. The present pass-fail plan began in 1962 as a senior elective privilege in L&S—with grades of S (satisfactory) and U (unsatisfactory). By January 1969 this privilege was available to all students with a 2.5 cumulative grade-point average; a maximum of ten courses (elective only) may be carried. Both student and faculty interest in this option seems to be declining.

After several years of study in the early 1970s by faculty committees and the Faculty Senate, the grading system was amended as follows: to permit the repeating of courses that had been failed (retaining the "F" on the record, but not counting it in the grade-point average); to allow certain courses to be graded with "CR" for credit and "N" for no credit; to institute new grades of "AB" and "BC"; and to require at least a "C" for credit under the pass-fail option.[9] A charting of the undergraduate grade-point average during the twenty-five years shows minimal changes from 1949 to 1965. Beginning in 1966 the curve rises precipitously until 1970, when it started to level off. In 1949 the first semester average was 2.62 and for the second semester it was 2.69; corresponding figures for the 1973-1974 year were 2.88 and 2.95 (the highest ever attained). The reasons for this can lead to interesting conjectures!

THE past quarter-century has seen a spectacular growth in graduate education nationally, with Ph.D. output expanding at a compound rate of about 12 percent annually. Normally, about 60 percent of these scholars have been absorbed in the academic marketplace and two-thirds of the remainder in research and development funded by the government. This picture now is changing because of curtailed budgets and cutbacks in governmental support; as a result, growth at the graduate level has been slowed.

On the Madison campus, Graduate School enrollment since 1949 has increased 227 percent, Law School by 30 percent, and Medical School by 90 percent, and these three schools together now constitute almost a third of all students. It should be noted, also, that the number of women in these post-bachelor areas has expanded greatly, showing an increase from 522 to 3,239 (520 percent), whereas men increased from 3,325 to 7,498 (126 percent). In 1949 women constituted 14 percent of the total enrollment in these schools, but by 1973 the figure had doubled to 30 percent.

The growth in enrollment in the Graduate School has been accompanied by a concomitant development in the curriculum. In 1949 the Graduate School conferred five degrees: Ph.D., M.A., M.S., M.B.A. (Business Administration), and M.M. (Music). Now, eleven are granted, with the addition of M.S. (Arts), M.S. (Nursing), M.F.A. (Fine Arts), M.L. (Laws), M.A.S. (Actuarial Science), and Second Degrees in Engineering. Fields of study (major and minor) in Social Sciences and Humanities have grown from thirty-four in 1949 to fifty-eight (71 percent increase), while in Natural Science and Engineering the increase from fifty-five to sixty-seven shows a 22 percent expansion. Social Sciences and Humanities constituted about 38 percent of the total graduate programs in 1949 and have increased somewhat (to 46 percent at the present time). A breakdown of graduate major programs by college shows the following with some majors listed in several colleges: twenty-nine in Agriculture, twenty in Business, thirty-five in Education, sixteen in Engineering, six in Family Resources, two in Law, eighty-three in L&S, one in Medicine, one in Nursing, and eight in Pharmacy (a total of 201). Of these, almost ninety have evolved since 1949.

A national trend in graduate education is a growing pressure for broader training, with much less emphasis on the narrow specialities within disciplines. This breakdown of boundaries between departments, colleges, and fields of knowledge is revealed in the multiplication of interdisciplinary courses in recent years. Area studies programs on our campus draw on a wide variety of University resources, especially in the humanities and the social studies. Additional programs designed to bring skills of more than one discipline into focus on a problem are Biomedical Engineering, Molecular Biology, Neurosciences, Oceanography and Limnology, and Plant Breeding and Plant Genetics. Some curricula born during this era grew rapidly and vigorously and now are well recognized and established (for example, Behavioral Disabilities, Meteorology, Nuclear Engineering, Nutritional Sciences, and Statistics).

A recent emphasis in graduate programs has been a sharp turn toward professionalized training at the master's level. This has been noted in fields like Landscape Architecture, Ocean Engineering, and Water Resources Management. An analogous trend toward professionalization in method is found in the social sciences. In the biological sciences there is increasing concern with the acquisition by students of core understanding at the system, organism, cell, organelle, and molecular level; students may specialize at one or two levels, but must have a solid foundation in all of them. In the physical sciences a blurring of traditional divisional lines in graduate research has occurred, with increasing overlapping of fields of interest encompassed by chemists, biochemists, physicists, and applied mathematicians. This has involved an expansion of sophisticated instrumentation dealing with such diverse areas as mass spectroscopy, photo-electron spectroscopy, nuclear magnetic resonance, and nuclear activation analysis. Humanities research was stimulated in 1959 with the establishment of the Institute for Research in the Humanities that includes history (art, music, and science), philosophy, languages, and literature. Examples of other research institutes and centers that have been initiated are the Industrial Relations Research Center, Land Tenure Center, Mathematics Research Center, Seminary for Medieval Spanish Studies, Institute for Research on Poverty, Primate Research Center, Wisconsin Research and Development Center for Cognitive Learning, and the Wisconsin Survey Research Laboratory.

For many years the foreign language requirement for the Ph.D. — reading proficiency in two foreign languages of which one had to be French or German — proved to be a difficult hurdle for many students. But since 1969 each department or unit administering a doctoral program has been responsible for setting its own language requirement and some have modified the old provisions.

At the beginning of this era, a student received a Bachelor of Laws degree if he had three years of residence in law schools (the last year at Wisconsin), completed eighty credits with a weighted average of seventy-seven, and satisfied a six months' apprenticeship in a law office (with certain exceptions). Now, a student must earn ninety credits in law schools, the apprenticeship has been discontinued, and the degree of Doctor of Law (J.D.) is conferred. Students with exceptional academic records in L&S, Engineering, and Business may be admitted to Law School after earning at least ninety credits and may count the law work toward their undergraduate degrees. Graduate law degrees — Master of Laws (LL.M.) or Doctor of Juridical Science (S.J.D.) — may be earned by advanced students with LL.B. or J.D. degrees, and are research degrees. The Graduate School, in addition, accepts a minor in law toward the Ph.D. degree in a related field, and also offers a Master of Arts or of Science in Legal Institutions to qualified foreign law graduates interested in a program that relates the processes of law to social and economic factors.

The current curriculum reflects a broadening and deepening of trends that already were in motion twenty-five years ago, evidence that this Law

School was a pioneer in its approach at the time. The basic courses remain; their goal is to present law in relation to the social functions it is supposed to serve. Some course titles have been changed, as was noted earlier in other fields. The most obvious change from the earlier curriculum, caused by the flux in public policy, is the substantial enlargement of seminar offerings in such areas as civil liberties, psychiatry and the law, corporate reorganization, water resources management, and consumer credit. New courses evolved as a result of law's relationship to broader areas of public regulation and concern, such as criminal and juvenile justice administration, environmental litigation, and welfare law and administration. As the curriculum expands, the faculty continues to relate its law teaching to knowledge gained in the social studies quite apart from the law. Courses like the sociology of law and foreign legal systems enlist the efforts of faculty colleagues in other departments, and indicate the desire to keep the curriculum in significant contact with the frontiers of public policy. An area of recent change and continuing growth is the teaching of practice skills: a general practice course; advanced legal writing taught by practitioners; trial and appellate advocacy; and clinical internships with district attorneys, judges, state government agencies, and with lawyers providing legal services to the poor or to inmates of penal or mental institutions.

The Medical School, now a part of the University Center for Health Sciences (which includes Pharmacy, Nursing, University Health Service, University Hospitals, State Laboratory of Hygiene, and the Wisconsin Psychiatric Institute), has made changes and additions to the basic science, clinical science, housestaff, and continuing education phases of its curriculum during this twenty-five-year period. No change has occurred in the degrees conferred. Student enrollment has greatly expanded from the 84 students in the 1949 freshman class (and a total enrollment in all four years of 302) to 159 freshmen in 1973 (and 550 totally). When the new Center for Health Services, now under construction on the west side of the campus, is completed in 1977, two hundred incoming students will be admitted.

A thoroughly revised M.D. program was instituted in 1967. Previously, the basic science phase involved two years of instruction in anatomy, physiology, physiological chemistry, pharmacology, medical microbiology, pathology, preventive medicine, and genetics. The new program reduced the discipline-oriented approach to the first year by developing core curricula involving basic concepts and special experimental techniques. In the second year the primary thrust is on the basic science principles that underlie clinical care. A year course in patho-physiology of disease is organized in blocks of time by organ systems (such as cardiovascular, skeletomuscular, respiratory, gastrointestinal) and by systemic disease areas (for example, infectious disease and neoplastic disease). Another group of courses provides basic clinical skills and techniques in physical diagnosis, psychiatry, and autopsy pathology. The third year remains essentially unchanged, consisting of forty-eight weeks of basic clinical clerkships. The final year has been reconstructed into time blocks of eight weeks each to provide the greatest possible flexibility in selecting elective courses, except that one block is a mandatory preceptorship served with a practicing physician in Wisconsin.

An alternate to the regular curriculum for the first two years of Medical School was initiated in 1973 with the development of the Independent Study Program. This innovative program provides statements of learning objectives for each course in the regular curriculum, and students proceed to achieve them with their own patterns of sequencing and self-pacing. Study materials of various types are available, and faculty members function as resource persons to facilitate learning rather than to direct it. Lectures and formalized class experiences have been eliminated and students are expected to assume a high degree of responsibility for monitoring their progress.

Substantial changes in the departmental structure of the school have evolved in the last twenty-five years. Among those created or attaining independent status are Clinical Oncology, Family Medicine, Medical Genetics, Medical Sciences, Neurology, Neurophysiology, Psychiatry, and Rehabilitation Medicine. Of particular current interest is Family Medicine, established to counteract the fragmentation of health care brought about by specialization. Intended to provide individuals for doctor-shortage areas, it attempts to utilize the total health system to meet the health needs of the patient (including appropriate referrals to other specialists) rather than have the doctor practice in isolation.

THIS chronicle of the evolving undergraduate and graduate curricula in the eleven colleges and schools on the Madison campus for the past twenty-five years reveals the amazing changes that have occurred in students, faculty, courses, departments, programs, and requirements. Each change was made at the time "to move further toward excellence."

Throughout this era the University of Wisconsin has been in the front rank of American universities. But how is excellence in this particular endeavor measured? Typical yardsticks or gauges are subsequent accomplishments of students, professional success of alumni, and recognition of faculty usually by peer ratings. The most recent study by the American

Council on Education, based on a national survey of leading scholars, rates graduate departments on the basis of "quality of faculty" or "effectiveness of doctoral program" and shows that Wisconsin is at least "adequate" or "acceptable" in all thirty-six fields; in thirty-one of the thirty-six, the University's departments are above this qualifying level.[10] If U.W. departments ranking in the top ten on either rating (faculty or program) are tabulated, the results are remarkable: in Humanities they qualify in five of the ten fields; in Social Sciences, six of the seven; in Biological Sciences, eight of ten; in Physical Sciences, four of five; and in Engineering, one in four. Rankings in the top three nationally were earned by Chemical Engineering, Spanish, Geography, Botany, and Entomology. Other studies during this era ranked the School of Education fourth nationally; the School of Business was in the top five; the School of Pharmacy stood fourth; and the School of Journalism and Mass Communications was rated first in research productivity and fifth overall.

These citations, and the previous review of evolving curricula, highlight the variety of programs initiated and strengthened during the past twenty-five years. The progress, growth, and success of these curricula growing out of concerned faculty and student interaction in eleven different colleges and schools located on the same campus can be summarized in one phrase that exemplifies the University of Wisconsin: "the excellence of its diversity."

NOTES

1 Committee on University Functions and Policies, *Second Report, Internal Survey* (Madison, November 1949), chap. 1, p. 1.

2 The Interdisciplinary Studies Committee on the Future of Man, "The Purpose and Function of the University," in Faculty Document 279, May 20, 1969, p. 2.

3 Regents' *Annual Report* (Madison, 1849), appendix, p. 797.

4 The Report of the Letters and Science Curriculum Committee, in Letters and Science Faculty Document 119, November 19, 1962.

5 The Report of the Curriculum Review Committee, in Letters and Science Faculty Document 156, April 19, 1971, p. 3.

6 The Report of the Internal Study Committee of the College of Letters and Science, in Letters and Science Faculty Document 134, May 15, 1967.

7 Merle Curti and Vernon Carstensen, *The University of Wisconsin* (Madison, 1949), vol. 2, p. 313.

8 Committee to Study the Development of a General Honors Program, "Recommendations for the Establishment of an Honors Program in the College of Letters and Science," in Letters and Science Document 111, February 23, 1959.

9 Resolution on the Grading System (in Relation to Faculty Document 121), Faculty Senate Minutes Addendum, January 15, 1973.

10 Kenneth D. Roose and Charles J. Andersen, *A Rating of Graduate Programs* (Washington, D.C.: American Council on Education, 1970).

CHAPTER 9

Development of Research in the Physical Sciences, 1949-1974

JAMES A. LARSEN

FOR perspective let us look briefly at the history of the earth and of mankind, and of that particular human endeavor known as the pursuit of scientific knowledge. The age of the earth has been estimated roughly at some five billion years. Life apparently has been present since Precambrian time — some fossils are at least three billion years old. On this geological time scale, man is a newcomer to the scene. And science, as a conscious application of thought and effort to the study of nature, is at the most three or four centuries old.

Science has changed much of the world rapidly during the past two or three decades, not only in the way the peoples of at least the advanced nations spend their lives but in views of the world and the universe. Science is not only a force in what are termed practical affairs, it is a cultural force, one capable of rapidly changing both ways of living and philosophical attitudes and beliefs. Universities have traditionally carried out most of the basic research conducted in the United States. Industrial research efforts have been directed largely toward utilization of new basic knowledge for improvement of old products and creation of new ones. The federal government has consistently been third in the amount of basic research conducted and second in applied and developmental work although it financed much of the research by both universities and industry. During recent decades the University of Wisconsin has ranked among the nation's leaders in size of its research program and significance of the discoveries that have resulted. Described in the following pages are a few

James A. Larsen is science editor of the University-Industry Research Program at the University of Wisconsin-Madison and has both observed and described in publications the development and progress of research programs at Wisconsin during recent decades. Obtaining all three degrees at Wisconsin, the first in economics and both master's and doctorate in ecology, he has conducted research on the plant life and environment of the Arctic and Subarctic in programs sponsored by federal agencies.

examples of the contributions to knowledge of the physical sciences and engineering made by Wisconsin scientists during this period.

WHILE the gross structure of atoms and the reactions between atoms have now largely been described with mathematical precision, physicists in recent decades have been confronted with a vast and inelegant profusion of new information concerning a large number of extremely small particles which appear to be constituents of the protons and neutrons forming the nuclei of the atoms. Some of these particles, such as the rho particle discovered at Wisconsin in 1961 are in the range of 10^{-14} centimeters in diameter and exist for less than 10^{-20} seconds. Essentially, nuclear physicists today are attempting to determine the forces at work between nuclear particles. Prior to 1930 most nuclear research was carried on principally in England, Germany, and France. During the 1930s refugees from Europe gave great impetus to American research but most important were the machines developed by three Americans to accelerate protons to speeds necessary for penetration of atomic nuclei. One type of machine, the electrostatic generator, was invented by Van de Graaff at Princeton. Another, the cyclotron, was developed by E. O. Lawrence at Berkeley. Shortly after Van de Graaff's initial work, R. G. Herb at Wisconsin made innovations in design which rendered Van de Graaff's electrostatic generator a practical device for studying atomic nuclei. Enclosed and insulated by high pressure gases, the Herb generator was more compact than the original, and after 1935 most electrostatic generators followed the pattern of the Wisconsin development. The development by Herb's group of a practical source of hydrogen negative ions (1956) made possible a new type of accelerator, the so-called "tandem" generator. The Atomic Energy Commission located the first of these tandem accelerators in the United States at Wisconsin in 1958 and today this type of accelerator dominates the field. A 1969 spot-check of papers given at the American Physical Society meetings revealed that 83 percent of the new results came from electrostatic accelerators and these were chiefly of the tandem design.

Another important contribution to nuclear physics was the development in 1964 by Willy Haeberli of the first source of polarized negative ions. Polarized ions have spin axes aligned and are invaluable for probing the spin dependence of nuclear forces. One of the truly fundamental advances in modern nuclear physics was Henry H. Barschall's systematic study of neutron scattering cross sections. Results by 1952 showed regularities which led physicists to the now very successful optical model of the nucleus. The electrostatic accelerators developed at Wisconsin give a fine degree of control over the velocities of the incident particles and precise measurements were possible of the energy, lifetime, and angular momentum of the various states of the atomic nuclei.[1]

Research with the extremely high energy machines such as the cyclotron at Berkeley and the cosmotron at the Brookhaven National Accelerator Laboratory in New York had made it apparent by the 1950s that a whole new range of nuclear phenomena could be observed by achievement of even higher energies, but it was also apparent that the cost of accelerators would make it necessary for universities to collaborate in the development of large machines available to physicists from many schools.

The Midwestern Universities Research Association (MURA) was an association of fifteen midwestern universities organized in 1954 to provide facilities for research and instruction in the field of high energy nuclear physics. Funds for research came from the National Science Foundation and from the Office of Naval Research in the early days, with the Atomic Energy Commission becoming the principal source of support as of February 1956. During the summer of 1956 interested scientists formulated plans for the design and construction of a new high energy particle accelerator. The machine was to be a proton accelerator with a beam intensity one hundred times greater than anything previously built in the high energy range. To achieve the focusing required in such a system, a fixed field alternating gradient (FFAG) system was used and a 50 MeV electron model of the accelerator was proposed for construction. Tihiro Ohkawa while at the University of Tokyo and Keith Symon at the University of Wisconsin had independently invented FFAG focusing in 1954.

In 1963 the MURA group submitted its final proposal to the AEC, with assurance that it would be funded. This did not occur and MURA was dissolved and the facilities, staff, and land became part of the Madison campus of the University of Wisconsin on July 1, 1967. The MURA director, Frederick E. Mills, undertook the problem of interfacing the laboratory with the University under the name of University of Wisconsin Physical Sciences Laboratory.[2] The giant accelerator, however, was ultimately constructed and is now in operation at the National Accelerator Laboratory at Batavia, Illinois.

By 1967 plasma physics research at Wisconsin had increased to the extent that it became desirable to build a larger version of a small early model of a reactor design known as the Wisconsin toroidal octupole. This closed plasma containment device was the first United States experiment to give quiet plasmas useful for experiments. It was proposed by D. W. Kerst and Tihiro Ohkawa while they, with H. K. Forsen, were conducting research at General Atomic in San Diego. Kerst, who had been technical director of MURA, had worked with Ohkawa and Symon at MURA during the period September 1956 to August 1957. The Wisconsin octupole was fabricated at Wisconsin's Physical Sciences Laboratory with funds from the Atomic Energy Commission. A host of experiments on plasma creation, plasma heating, and plasma analysis have been possible with the octupole. By 1974 a score of Wisconsin scientists and engineers had completed the initial design for a fusion generating plant with basic structures of stainless steel, lithium as a heat transport medium, a thermal power output of 5000 MW, and an electrical output of 1500 MW. The UWMAK-1 fusion reactor, as it is known, was designed on the basis of present-day technological capabilities and in sufficient detail to uncover potential problems as the goal of fusion power comes closer.

Along more conventional lines, construction of a nuclear fission reactor for experimental work in the College of Engineering at Madison was completed in the late 1950s and the reactor has been instrumental in a wide variety of studies. The reactor was licensed for steady-state operation and a hot cell facility adjacent to the reactor laboratory provided capability for handling highly activated materials. Associated equipment included neutron and gamma sources, detectors, counters, pulse-height analyzers, and other instrumentation.

It was thus apparent by the mid-1970s that physicists at Wisconsin had contributed in a major way to the advance of experimental and theoretical knowledge of the atom. Wisconsin was among the leaders in development of practical applications and educational programs in the field of nuclear physics. Wisconsin physicists also conducted a wide range of studies significant to astronomy, particularly in the development of highly sensitive instruments for studying faint emissions of both light and x-rays from distant galaxies and this work is described briefly in the section of this chapter on astronomical research. There were very significant programs on particle physics, solid state physics, low-temperature physics, and laser studies. The physics research at Wisconsin was at the forefront in a wide variety of fields.

THE role of chemistry has been a major one in the development of modern science and technology. One major explanation for the amazing growth of knowledge is to be found in the new experimental instruments that have made modern studies of natural phenomena possible. In chemistry these include instruments for mass and photoelectron spectroscopy, electron spin and nuclear magnetic resonance studies, x-ray crystallography, and measurement of thermoluminescence and fluorescence. Over the years, federal and Wisconsin Alumni Research Foundation grants have included funds for instrumentation and, as a consequence, equipment acquired or developed and built (under supervision of Paul Bender, director of the Chemistry Department's instrument service) has given Wisconsin an array of instrumentation surpassed by no other university in the world. These research tools have been a major factor in making it possible for Wisconsin chemists to advance knowledge at the forefront of the science.

The various specialized fields of chemistry are too numerous to include in this survey and only a few are mentioned here. These, it is hoped, will convey with some degree of accuracy the range of chemical studies at Wisconsin during recent decades.

John E. Willard has directed Wisconsin's program in radiation chemistry since it was begun in the late 1940s and has been responsible for maintaining Wisconsin as a leader in this field. The studies of the chemical effects of nuclear transformations were carried out with the aid of the nuclear reactors at the Argonne National Laboratory and the University of Wisconsin-Madison.

Research in organic chemistry at Wisconsin has a long and distinguished history and cannot be treated here in detail; mention must be made, however, of two individuals who were key figures in the field during the decades 1920-1960, Homer Adkins and Samuel M. McElvain. The former came to Wisconsin in 1919 and was joined in the organic chemistry division by McElvain in 1923. The research in the division expanded through the years as organic chemistry acquired an increasingly important role and by 1970 had come to occupy the efforts of a dozen senior researchers. Today research in the division encompasses a wide range of studies covering most if not all of the frontiers of this branch of chemistry.

In the early 1950s important studies were under way on colloids and substances of biological significance. Pioneer research into the chemistry of the colloids had been initiated by John W. Williams more than a decade previously and research on such substances as the steroid hormones was begun subsequently under the direction of W. S. Johnson and A. L. Wilds. The first (and only) Svedberg oil turbine ultracentrifuge in an American university was installed in Williams's laboratory in 1937. He and his associates applied it to diverse studies of protein digestion, antigen-antibody combination, and stability of blood plasma substitutes.

By 1950 the chemical kinetics of the nitrogen oxides had been under investigation at Wisconsin for nearly half a century. The development of what is known as the Wisconsin process for nitrogen fixation by Farrington Daniels was initially a contribution to fundamental knowledge, but the research soon had practical applications not only in technology involving nitrogen compounds but also in atomic energy, jet propulsion, and smog control. Research on low-temperature decomposition of nitric oxide led to applications in the development of catalysts to decompose nitric oxides produced in automobile engines.

Prior to 1960 relatively little information on chemical and physical properties of material at temperatures above 500° C was available. At Wisconsin, furnaces were constructed for experimentation over the range of 500-15000°K. Extensive tables of thermodynamic data were assembled and especially significant were the data for gaseous atoms and ions useful for plasma calculations up to 50,000°K.

High polymeric substances consist of chainlike or threadlike macromolecules in which thousands of atoms in linear sequence form a flexible backbone. Thermal motions in macromolecules are responsible for unusual physical phenomena, such as rubber-like elasticity. Since the late 1940s, research on the viscoelastic properties of polymers in the laboratories of John D. Ferry and associates has established Wisconsin's leadership in advancing basic understanding of the relationship of molecular structure of polymers to their physical properties.

Wisconsin became one of the first universities to promote theoretical chemistry when Farrington Daniels formed a small research group in 1934. After World War II the navy built the University of Wisconsin Naval Research Laboratory and sponsored this research under the direction of Joseph O. Hirschfelder. In 1958 the name of the group was changed to the Theoretical Chemistry Laboratory, and in 1972 the National Aeronautics and Space Administration awarded the University of Wisconsin an initial grant of $700,000 to form the present Theoretical Chemistry Institute. The work of the institute has resulted in techniques to solve equations in the fields of quantum and statistical mechanics, intermolecular forces, properties of gases and liquids, chemical kinetics, and the chemical effects of nuclear radiation.

Only the briefest mention can be made of many fields of specialized chemical research that have emerged within the past decade. Perhaps most remote from immediate practical application were Larry A. Haskin's analyses of moon rocks collected by the Apollo astronauts (see the geology section). Other work of great significance included Michael J. Berry's studies of reaction dynamics and chemical lasers, Lawrence F. Dahl's studies of bonding and organosilicon compounds and anionic reactions, John P. Walters' research on analytic techniques using the spark of electrical discharges, Howard E. Timmerman's studies of organic photochemistry, and Richard B. Bernstein's work on molecular beams. There was a great deal of research under way in such other new branches of chemistry as energy partitioning into reaction products, systems for chemical analysis separations, quantum chemistry, optical pumping, stereo-chemistry and the nature of bonding, redox behavior, free radicals, enzyme action, nucleic acids, macromolecular conformation, electroanalytic chemistry, stabilities and lifetimes of ionic states, dielectrics, solid state structure, liquid structure, and photochemistry. The branch of science known as chemistry had expanded to a degree that would have astonished even the most farsighted chemist of the early part of the century; the expansion had been a direct consequence of the burgeoning importance of chemical knowledge to nations with advancing technology.

SCIENTISTS have established the age of the earth at four and one-half to five billion years. Hints as to the nature of early life are found in fossils — and credit for discovery of some of the oldest known fossils belongs to a Wisconsin geologist, Stanley A. Tyler. Exposed along the western shore of Lake Superior is a series of Precambrian sedimentary rocks about fifty feet thick. In the middle of the sedimentary sequence is a ten-foot layer, the Gunflint Chert, the unique significance of which was not recognized until 1954, when Tyler and E. S. Barghoorn, a paleobotanist at Harvard, dissolved some of the chert and discovered a residue of filaments and spheres that were obviously fragments of primitive plants, precisely the kinds of organisms one would expect to find early in the history of plant life. Rocks of the Gunflint Chert are, according to radioactive age determinations, about two billion years old. Less abundant fragments were more recently discovered in other Precambrian formations elsewhere, some of which are as old as three billion years.

Photographs of x-ray patterns created by minerals are as characteristic as fingerprints. X-ray techniques can be used to identify minerals that are otherwise indistinguishable by sight or by methods other than laborious chemical analysis. An x-ray laboratory set up in the Wisconsin geology department in 1951 under the direction of S. W. Bailey provides x-ray analyses to scientists conducting research in geology, chemistry, physics, soils, mining and metallurgical engineering, chemical engineering, and other fields. Representative research projects carried on during the early years included studies of the crystal structure of microcline, the origin of granite, and characteristics of the opaque minerals which are important constituents of many types of ore. This latter study was carried on by Eugene N. Cameron as part of an ambitious program for microscopic identification of ore minerals. Cameron developed apparatus and techniques for quantitative measurement of anisotropism exhibited by the various minerals to provide standard data for mineral identification. Reference data were obtained for many mineral types, all of which were first identified by x-ray and chemical analytical methods.

The University of Wisconsin has been described as the gravitational center of the world, not because it lies at the true center of gravity but because here have been conducted the most extensive investigations of the subject to be carried on anywhere in the world. During the International Geophysical Year, for example, Wisconsin geophysicists, directed by George P. Woollard, conducted a major portion of the year's world-wide gravity research program. These studies revealed much exact information on the shape and structure of the earth. The scientists measured the intensity of gravity in Antarctica, observed the thickness of the earth's crust in many areas of the world and the depth of the polar ice caps, and made accurate measurements of earth tides induced by the pull of sun and moon.

Interbedded lava flows and detrital sediments are evidently to be found at depths of 20,000 feet in northern Wisconsin, and here, in connection with these very old rocks, are found extensive iron and copper deposits. Association of mineral deposits with ancient volcanic flows and sediments is of worldwide extent but, strangely, there has been no similarly extensive deposits of iron formed at any time since. By the early 1950s Woollard had begun a program to learn what geophysical methods could be applied to studies of the mineral deposits likely to occur in northern Wisconsin and Minnesota and to establish a regional network of geophysical measurements to reveal something of the kinds of rocks lying beneath the surface. Through gravity and magnetic work, the source of the ancient lavas was located. It is a major fissure, filled with dense, magnetic rock, several miles in width and extending from Superior, Wisconsin, to near Clay Center, Kansas. This implies the existence of iron deposits in the basement rocks in a belt extending 1000 miles south of the present out-crops in Minnesota and northern Wisconsin.

Not even a small fraction of Wisconsin's 56,154 square miles has been examined in detail and will not be until the state's general geological structure is known. Carl Dutton, regional geologist, United States Geological Survey, compiled an extremely useful geologic map of Wisconsin in the late 1960s on the basis of work done to that time. The office of state geologist conducted an initial series of aerial gravimetric surveys (as have some private mining companies) as a start toward systematic geological and geophysical mapping of the state. Rough estimates of possible deposits large enough to be worth mining show that a copper ore deposit of ten million tons, in an area of four hundred acres, might have a total value of $250 million.

The mission of Apollo 11 in July 1969 brought back twenty-two kilograms of samples of lunar surface material for direct scientific investigation, the first extraterrestrial objects other than meteorites ever to be available for analysis and scrutiny. Wisconsin geologist Cameron and Wisconsin chemist Larry A. Haskin, an authority on analysis for rare earth elements, were selected to be among those who would study the lunar materials. Cameron was expert in analysis of opaque minerals by means of the electron microprobe; a $100,000 instrument had been installed on the Wisconsin campus two years previously with funds from the Wisconsin Alumni Research Foundation and the National Science Foundation. Haskin had helped develop analytic methods for rare earth analyses using neutron activation techniques. The analyses contributed by the Wisconsin scientists are of great significance in the understanding of lunar origins.

THE atmospheric circulation over continents and across seas is powered by the great quantities of energy received from the sun. Ultimate understanding of weather and climate depends upon knowledge of the fate of this energy as it drives the restless winds. The most recent of the tools available for this study are the satellites which, in effect, serve as global data-gathering stations relaying information to scientists on earth.

The instruments for the first — and many subsequent — satellite stations were devised at the University of Wisconsin by meteorologist Verner Suomi and engineer Robert J. Parent. The first instruments measured the intensity of the radiation received by various regions of the earth, the amount reflected back to space, and the amount absorbed by earth surface and atmosphere. Research satellites were developed by 1966 which provided rapid sequence photographs of global cloud patterns and further amplified the power of meteorologists to probe the behavior of the atmosphere.

The successful Explorer VII experiment in 1959 revealed the enormous potential of satellite instrumentation for climatic research and it was followed in rapid succession by two other satellites, Tiros III, launched in July 1961, and Tiros IV, launched in February 1962. Other Tiros experiments followed. Then, in December 1966 a camera 22,300 miles above the Pacific Ocean began taking spectacular weather pictures of the cloud-shrouded earth. Relayed to ground stations, the photographs gave scientists a detailed picture of cloud patterns over nearly half the earth's surface.

Instrumentation for the meteorological satellites was steadily improved and gave scientists surprisingly detailed information on the atmosphere including data on temperatures, cloud heights, and other physical parameters. They were further improved to even transmit color photographs.[3] But not all information of value to the science of meteorology came from the earth. The Mariner 10 spacecraft, passing within 4,000 miles of Venus in February 1974, gave scientists their first close look at the atmosphere of that planet. Suomi and Robert Krauss were members of the team analyzing the atmospheric information from Mariner 10. Enormous jet streams, a major Mariner 10 discovery, flow in great spirals around Venus, giving meteorologists a better basic understanding of the mechanisms driving the earth's atmosphere, particularly in the tropics.

In 1972 the United States had also launched the first Earth Resources Technology Satellite, ERTS-1. This satellite began producing the first space pictures of the earth's surface taken specifically for world-wide resource management. No one was sure how many useful applications the satellite data would have, but initial efforts — from reporting forest fires in California to planning cities in New England — suggested that the potential was great.

ENGINEERING applies knowledge of the natural sciences to the needs of society. The University of Wisconsin College of Engineering has traditionally centralized research activities in the Engineering Experiment Station and during one year in the late 1960s, for example, 235 separate research projects were in progress at the station, representing chemical, civil, electrical, nuclear, and mechanical engineering, and mining and metallurgy. New directions and the interdisciplinary nature of engineering research were apparent in all engineering fields by the 1960s, and here we can describe but a few examples.

The Biomedical Engineering Center coordinated research under way in seven engineering departments and two laboratories, work carried on by many medical scientists and members of the colleges of Letters and Science and Agricultural and Life Sciences. Biomedical studies were conducted on a wide range of medical problems. The Instrumentation Systems Center, established in 1966, was another engineering program that expanded rapidly. Its major role was in support of other research programs by providing development and maintenance service of research instruments. During 1968 a Rheology Research Center was established to study the flow and deformation of polymers. The rheology program developed apparatus to measure stress functions, viscosity and rigidity, elastic recoil, and other rheological phenomena, work with many industrial applications.

In the early development of the field of chemical engineering, the work of Olaf A. Hougen and Kenneth M. Watson is of particular significance. Their research to elucidate the basic principles underlying chemical reactor design was of value to all industries engaged in process development and chemical manufacture. From these principles the most favorable conditions of operation could be predicted with respect to flow rates, temperature, pressure, composition, and catalyst selection.

It is apparent that research in engineering has in recent decades been at once broad and intensive, contributing in major ways to world industrial and technological development. The complete list of Wisconsin's contributions cannot be incorporated in a summary such as this, but a few of the fields in which accomplishments were especially worthy of note should be mentioned: engineering mechanics, metallurgical and mineral engineering, process metallurgy, powder metallurgy, new materials, industrial engineering, strategy of design, job analysis, internal combustion engine design, fluid dynamics, computer simulation, solid waste disposal and recycling, welding technology, water chemistry, and spray drying.

As an example of engineering research which possesses ever-increasing potential for immense practical benefit we could do no better than describe research at Wisconsin into new energy sources and new methods for storing and transmitting energy. A wide range of projects in electrical energy generation, storage, and transmission were under way during the 1950s and 1960s, expanding markedly by the 1970s. Research programs with potentials for immense practical importance included work on development of fusion generating plants, on utilization of solar energy, and on energy storage. A score of Wisconsin scientists and engineers centered in the Nuclear Engineering Department had by 1973 completed the initial design for a fusion generating plant. The reactor design represented an extension of existing technology with requirements that appeared attainable with reasonable developmental work. The energy of fusion is also the origin of the oldest source of energy known to man— sunlight. In the years 1950-1960 the Wisconsin solar energy research program was a cooperative effort between Farrington Daniels, Verner E. Suomi, and other Wisconsin faculty members. The program was carried on at the Solar Energy Laboratory under the direction of John A. Duffie, with several departments of the College of Engineering and departments in other colleges of the University participating. With the original four-year grant from the Rockefeller Foundation, studies of methods of utilization of solar energy and of measuring and recording radiation were carried on, with additional attention given to the development of solar operated devices for use in nonindustrialized areas. By the 1970s, electrical transmission technology was undergoing rapid changes, but even greater demands were anticipated as a result of the growing needs for increased size and efficiency in power systems. One important factor in planning for the future was superconductivity, evidently destined to be an important factor in electrical power systems by at least the end of the century. Engineers Roger Boom and Harold Peterson studied the feasibility of storing electrical energy in large superconducting magnets.

It is apparent that during the decades covered in this brief description of research in engineering at the University of Wisconsin, there was a growing trend toward multidisciplinary research—combining, for example, the efforts of engineers and medical scientists, or of engineers and physicists. There was also a growing trend for engineers to give thought and effort toward solution of economic, social, and environmental problems. As W. Robert Marshall, dean of the College of Engineering, wrote in 1971: "It is entirely possible that history could record that the last three decades of the 20th century were the golden decades for technology and its contributions in assisting to solve the problems of society which now so sorely worry mankind."[4]

T HERE are few if any branches of modern science that do not depend heavily upon mathematics and electronic computers. Much research in mathematics or computing defies easy description, but a few of the projects under way during recent history will demonstrate the variety of fields in which work at Wisconsin has been of great significance.

By the 1950s, computer development was a rapidly expanding field. At Wisconsin, exemplifying interest in the field, several corporate members of the Wisconsin Utilities Association presented a $240,000 Westinghouse alternating current network calculator to the College of Engineering. The calculator was used primarily to aid in planning power systems; a small-scale system analog, or model system could be set up, reproducing the electrical characteristics of the system generators, transformers, transmission lines and loads, existing and proposed. Development of a hybrid computer combining the capabilities of analog and digital systems was undertaken in the College of Engineering in the late 1950s and subsequent expansion of computer research and service has been extensive, giving Wisconsin a full range of computing capability from the most modern analog and digital machines to a combination of both.

In the facility known as the Academic Computing Center, Wisconsin was able to develop some of the finest numerical and statistical programs in the world and by the 1970s all campuses of the University of Wisconsin system were able to take advantage of computing power several-hundred-fold greater than existed in 1960. The availability of WARF funds for research utilizing computers was especially important. During 1960, one could identify 191 users who had benefited by direct support from WARF. By 1970, users numbered in the thousands.

Research work in the Department of Mathematics itself covered dozens of areas and impinged upon a variety of other sciences. R. H. Bing and his colleagues in topology made important advances in understanding the geometric nature of three- and four-dimensional surfaces. L. C. Young developed radically new approaches to the calculus of variations and its applications in control theory. S. C. Kleene and his colleagues made fundamental discoveries dealing with the ultimate limitations of human reasoning and the ability of a computer to simulate human behavior. Other research included that of Mary Ellen Rudin in the field of topology, for which she was granted a prize offered by a Dutch mathematical journal. Paul Erdos, virtually a legend in his own time, was Brittingham Professor and continued his work which by 1974 had resulted in the publication of more than 600 mathematical papers. Many discoveries in meteorology and oceanography were made by R. E. Meyer and M. C. Shen and their students. Joshua Chover's work included prediction of future values for quantities subject to chance disturbances, behavior of reserves of quantities subject to chance supply and demand, and the chance spread of contagion. The phenomenon of adiabatic invariance, with ramifications in quantum mechanics and plasma theory, has intrigued physicists since the day of Einstein and Lorenz. The first satisfactory mathematical treatment was obtained by J. E. Littlewood during one of his visits to Wisconsin and was developed further by Wolfgang Wasow and R. E. Meyer.

D. L. Russell studied control theory applications, and C. C. Conley carried on studies of an equation with applications in research on propagation of signals in nerves. By the 1970s a young and active group of mathematicians at Wisconsin was tackling problems of computer storage, the theory of crystals, and a variety of other subjects.

A significant development at Wisconsin in the field of mathematics was, in a sense, a collective effort since it ultimately was destined to involve many hundreds of mathematicians. The development was the Mathematics Research Center established on the Madison campus in 1956. The previous year the army had solicited numerous universities to set up a contract for such a center and the proposal submitted by Wisconsin was accepted over the others. The work of the center was described as devoted to maintaining the nation's position in science and technology among the countries of the world. Established as part of an academic community because its role was essentially academic in nature, its purpose was to give leading world mathematicians an opportunity to spend a period of time—usually nine months or a year—in study and research on mathematical topics of their own choice. The advantage, as foreseen by the army in its support of the center, was the general advancement of mathematical knowledge that would result and the availability of mathematical talent for consultation when the need arose. The work of the mathematicians at the center was of an unclassified nature, with results published in reports or journals available to anyone with an interest in the subject. A large percentage of the world's leading mathematicians, including several from Iron Curtain countries, spent a period of time at the center or participated in conferences and symposia sponsored by the center. The center, however, became the target of political attack during the years of the unpopular Vietnam War. It was bombed in 1968, the consequence, according to Director J. Barkley Rosser, of the misconceptions harbored by individuals who, lacking acquaintance with the applications of mathematics, could not believe that fundamental research in mathematics could be of general value. The were few clear conclusions to be drawn from the ultimately tragic controversy; perhaps it could only be said that even scientists whose interests were purely intellectual would no longer be spared direct involvement in political life.

WE began this discussion of recent developments in the physical sciences at Wisconsin with the story of research in nuclear physics and the smallest of particles of which modern science is aware. It is fitting that we close with the solar system, the stars, the galaxies.

Wisconsin astronomy, under the successive leaderships of Joel Stebbins, A. E. Whitford, and A. D. Code, specialized in using photoelectric methods to make accurate quantitative measurements of the radiation emitted by various astronomical sources, chiefly stars, and in interpreting these measurements in an attempt to understand the physical processes going on in the stars. Donald E. Osterbrook applied the same methods to interstellar space. Physicists, too, were carrying on research of significance in astronomy. During the 1950s physicist Julian E. Mack made important studies of nuclear properties through observations of the minute effect of nuclei on the light emitted by atoms. Mack, together with Fred Roesler, then a graduate student, developed a series of increasingly powerful Fabry-Perot interference spectrometers. In 1962 they developed the PEPSIOS all-interference spectrometer employing three Fabry-Perot interferometers. Because of its precision and sensitivity, this instrument opened up new possibilities for high-resolution spectroscopic studies of astronomical sources. Roesler pursued the application of PEPSIOS to astrophysical problems, including measurement of the deuterium to hydrogen ratio on Jupiter, and together with Frank Scherb, made a study of light emitted from the darkest regions of the sky. Other physicists, William L. Kraushaar and colleagues, made studies of the soft diffuse x-rays emanating from space.

A logical extension of the studies by Wisconsin astronomers of the distribution and intensity of starlight became practical with the development of space vehicles. The University of Wisconsin's Space Astronomy Laboratory (SAL) first used a wide variety of rocket propulsion devices to study the ultraviolet (UV) radiation from blue-white stars above the earth's atmosphere. Then, to provide a more permanent station for UV measurements, SAL began participating in NASA's Orbiting Astronomical Observatory program. The first shot of the OAO series was one of the greatest disappointments in the American space program. OAO-1 was placed in the desired circular orbit in April 1966, but before any major experiments could be activated, the satellite's power supply failed. The OAO-2 satellite was more successful—in fact, one of the most successful of any of the satellites. The largest and most complex unmanned satellite ever sent into space, it was the first true space observatory. It remained in operation for much longer than anticipated and gave astronomers a wealth of new data on the universe, including their first comprehensive view of the universe in the ultraviolet.[5] Probably the most fundamental contribution that OAO-2 made to astronomy was empirical determination of the effective temperatures and luminosities of stars. The Orbiting Astronomical Observatory carried out accurate continuous measurements of stellar radiation for fifty months unhindered by obscuration effects from the terrestrial atmosphere. The angular diameters of stars were measured by an ingenious instrument called the stellar interferometer developed by astronomers at the University of Sydney. The last step, the absolute energy calibration of stars, was made possible by the use of the synchrotron storage ring, the unique facility developed at the University of Wisconsin's Physical Sciences Laboratory (see the physics section). The synchrotron storage ring was developed to probe the smallest constituents of matter but proved to be an effective tool for exploration of the large-scale structure of the universe.

That this machine — designed to probe the secrets of the fundamental particles — should help unravel the mysteries of the stars and the evolving universe emphasizes the unity of physical science. Every investigation is a link in man's effort to understand the nature of the universe and the ultimate meaning of it all in terms of man's inhabitation of the small spaceship called earth.[6]

NOTE ON SOURCES

This is a greatly condensed version of a manuscript on the history of physical sciences at the University of Wisconsin to be published in its entirety elsewhere. Material for this chapter has been obtained from a variety of sources. Chief among them are descriptive accounts of research prepared by the author during the course of work as science editor at the University of Wisconsin (*Fifty Years of Graduate Education at Wisconsin* [Madison, 1954], *Exploring the Unknown* [Madison, 1958], *New Frontiers of Science* [Madison, 1964]); material from an article entitled "The Human Condition," which appeared in *College and University Journal,* vol. 12 (March, 1973), pp. 17-21; and articles appearing in the *UIR/Research Newsletter* (University-Industry Research Program, University of Wisconsin-Madison, vols. 1-9, 1965-1974), prepared by the author and many of the graduate students participating in the UIR science writing program. Additional information and advice on matters of emphasis were obtained in interviews with certain key individuals in the Wisconsin research program, a number of whom have also read the manuscript and offered suggestions for revisions.

This chapter is surely not intended as a definitive history but rather as a brief and far from all-inclusive account of Wisconsin research during the past two decades or so. Grateful acknowledgment is hereby given to all of those graduate students whose articles were adapted to the purpose here without special individual attribution and to those scientists who gave freely of their experience and expertise during preparation of the manuscript.

NOTES

1 See individual articles by R. G. Herb, H. T. Richards, and Willy Haeberli in *International Symposium on Nuclear Structure* (Sao Paulo, Brazil: Revista Brasilerica de Fisicas, 1972), pp. 17-35, 213-253, 187-211. The symposium was held to observe installation of a Herb generator at the University of Sao Paulo, Brazil.

2 An historical account of the development of the Wisconsin Physical Sciences Laboratory and reports by the scientists involved appears in the *UIR/Research Newsletter,* vol. 7, no. 1.

3 V. E. Suomi and T. H. Vonder Haar, *Geosynchronous Meterological Satellite,* AIAA Paper no. 68-1094 (New York: American Institute of Aeronautics and Astronautics,

1968); T. H. Vonder Haar and V. E. Suomi, "Satellite observations of the earth's radiation budget," *Science,* vol. 163 (1969), pp. 667-69.

4 W. Robert Marshall, "Foreword," *Engineering Experiment Station Annual Report 1970-71* (Madison: University of Wisconsin College of Engineering, 1971).

5 National Aeronautics and Space Administration, *The Scientific Results from the Orbiting Astronomical Observatory (OAO-2),* a collection of papers presented at a symposium held at Amherst, Mass., August 23-24, 1971, NASA SP-310 (Washington, D.C.: 1972), 590 pp.

6 In writing this summary of physical research at the University of Wisconsin between 1950-1974, I have struggled against the insuperable limitation of space and the desire to include everything of significance. Since the ultimate in condensation—an annotated bibliography of research papers produced at Wisconsin in those years—would easily fill an entire volume, it is obvious that I have made a selection of topics to cover in some greater detail. The reduction is mine, and whether these are the research fields that ultimately will prove to be the most significant neither I nor anyone else can say. I only hope that those whose work is not mentioned will realize the limitations on such an effort as this one. The real history of science at Wisconsin, not to say in the United States and the world, will await the lifetime efforts of many hundreds of future scholars.

Physical scientists at Wisconsin joined early in the now-pressing search for new, clean energy sources. Above, a solar energy panel; below, a view into the Wisconsin atomic pile, before it was sealed — perhaps forever.

Wisconsin's lake research dates from Edward A. Birge (above) and has been carried on by generations of scientists including (left) John Neese and Arthur Hasler, and (below) Reid Bryson, James Verber, and Verner Suomi. Others, not shown, number in the hundreds, from Chancey Juday to Robert Ragotzkie.

CHAPTER 10

Examples of Progress in the Biological Sciences, 1949-1974

WILLIAM B. SARLES

In the University of Wisconsin-Madison there are at present at least forty-two departments and forty-one institutes or special group-interest laboratories in which biological scientists are leaders in research projects or programs. Research in the biological sciences has become increasingly interdisciplinary in organization and practice. Intellects and skills of individuals trained in physics and biophysics, mathematics and statistics, chemistry and biochemistry, geology and soils, hydrology, meteorology and space sciences, or in one of the many branches of engineering, agricultural, or medical sciences may be needed if the research is to reach desired goals. Opportunities remain for the individual, aided by a few students or assistants, to make significant contributions, and it continues to be true that each project needs at least one leader. Emphasis in this account will be centered on accomplishments by some of the recent leaders and their colleagues at Madison.

During the past twenty-five years the contributions of faculty and students to knowledge in the biological sciences have been great in quantity, and, in many instances, truly outstanding in quality. It is impossible to describe in the space available all of the accomplishments; only a few examples can be considered. That which follows represents the author's attempt to select and to present in brief, narrative form some of the major achievements. In doing so it must be realized that, with few exceptions, one cannot give credit to all who were involved in the research and graduate instruction that was performed to discover facts and to develop

William Bowen Sarles is emeritus professor of bacteriology. He received his Ph.D. from Wisconsin in 1931, majoring in bacteriology and minoring in biochemistry. He taught bacteriology at Kansas State, Hawaii, Iowa State, and the University of Wisconsin-Madison for a total of forty-four years. He was chairman of the Department of Bacteriology at the University 1954-1968. He was editor of the *Journal of Bacteriology,* 1961-1965, and president of the American Society for Microbiology in 1967.

concepts or theories. Furthermore, it is clear that many will not agree with the author in the choices he has made, but he is faced with an embarrassment of riches and has had to make selections that others might not approve.

WHEN E. A. Birge came to Madison in 1876 as a twenty-four-year-old instructor in natural history he brought with him an unquenchable curiosity about living things in lakes and streams. He started Wisconsin's work in limnology and continued it nearly to the time of his death, at age ninety-eight, on June 9, 1950. His early studies concentrated on Lake Mendota, but he soon became interested in Trout Lake and other lakes that are nearby in northern Wisconsin. He developed the concept of a lake as a unit of environment for life within its waters. This meant that he had to study effects on aquatic organisms of temperature, wind, circulation and stratification of water, penetration of light into the water, presence and distribution of dissolved gases and of nutrients, and the reaction (hydrogen ion concentration) of the water. Thus, he was one of the earliest to introduce and to develop the interdisciplinary group method of research in the biological sciences.

Birge received expert help in his limnological work from his chief assistant, Chancey Juday, from 1900 until Juday's death in 1944. There were many students who worked with Birge, Juday, and their faculty colleagues, but it was Arthur D. Hasler (Ph.D., 1937) in whom the fire of Birge's curiosity became most firmly implanted.

Hasler, now professor of zoology and director of the Laboratory of Limnology, has worked vigorously and successfully during and since his graduate student days on the lives and environments of fishes. His research has involved especially the causes for productivity of fish of certain bodies of water and the lack of productivity of others. More recently he has been concerned primarily with the migration and homing abilities of salmon, but has also studied movements of nonsalmonid fishes, such as white bass, in Lake Mendota.

The principal question to be answered is: How do salmon remember their birthplace in a small stream or river, located usually far upstream from the ocean or lake to which they migrate, so they can return to their place of birth to spawn? The problem is complicated further by the mixture, during their open sea or lake life, with different kinds of salmon and other fishes which obey the command to return to breeding grounds often thousands of miles and even continents apart. How do they sort themselves out, and then head for their stream of origin?

Results of well-designed, fully instrumented laboratory studies, and of investigations of fish in open waters and streams, support strongly the hypothesis that the salmon identifies the stream of its birth by the characteristic odors of its water. The stream's odors were "imprinted" in the salmon as a fry or fingerling during its early life, and the fish actually smells its way home once it gets far enough upstream from the sea or from the large lake to detect the home water's scent.

Progress was made also in attempts to determine how sexually mature salmon in the open ocean or large lake sort themselves out from others of different stream origins and start to migrate back to their natal stream to spawn. Hasler and his co-workers theorized that the sun is one of the celestial bodies from which the salmon might take bearings to start and to continue their journey back home. Studies in the laboratory and in the field have demonstrated that both the azimuth and the altitude of the sun are of significance to the salmon and can be used for direction finding. There must be, as Hasler emphasizes in his monograph on the homing of salmon,[1] additional means by which these fish obtain information on direction at night or on cloudy days. These further "underwater guideposts" are the subject of continuing research.

To return to Birge. How he would have been thrilled by recent observariations on eutrophication of lakes made by use of the first Earth Resources Technology Satellite, ERTS-1, from an orbit 500 miles above the earth! Photographs taken by cameras in this satellite of images of lakes caused by reflection of near infrared and of red light differentiate clearly the eutrophic lakes: those containing heavy growths of algae and of rooted aquatic plants (so-called weeds), reflect more red light than the relatively clear, less eutrophic or oligotrophic lakes. William Kuhlow and Alden McClellan of the University's Space Science and Engineering Center report that the Man-computer Interactive Data System (McIDAS) can be used to enhance imagery obtained by ERTS-1 cameras to enable mapping of lakes and streams and to differentiate between cloudiness of water caused by sediments and that caused by aquatic plants or algae.[2] The ERTS-1 was developed from the basic research and technology of Verner Suomi, Meterology and Space Science, and Robert J. Parent, Electrical Engineering and Instrumentation Systems Center, Engineering Research.

WHEN he joined the University of Wisconsin-Madison faculty in 1913 as a bacteriologist, E. B. Fred started studies on nitrogen fixation by symbiotic action involving root-nodule bacteria and leguminous plants.

He also investigated nitrogen fixation accomplished by independent non-symbiotic nitrogen-fixing bacteria: species of the genera *Azotobacter* and *Clostridium*. With his colleagues in bacteriology, botany, agronomy, soils, and biochemistry, he established an internationally recognized center for research on fixation of nitrogen. With the aid of many graduate students, but especially I. L. Baldwin, Elizabeth McCoy, and Perry Wilson, all of whom became his colleagues in the faculty, E. B. Fred (now emeritus professor of bacteriology and emeritus president of the University) guided the interdisciplinary program with great success until he became president of the University in 1945. It was Perry W. Wilson, one of E. B. Fred's most brilliant and successful graduate students, and, in turn Robert H. Burris, one of Wilson's best students, who carried on to discover some of the biochemical secrets of the nitrogen-fixation process. This is work of fundamental importance because it helps to understand how cells of independent microorganisms and of microorganisms symbiotic with leguminous plants accomplish this unique process. Biological nitrogen fixation is one of the keys to world supplies of proteins. Its importance, great now, may well become even greater.

Their work resulted in preparation from nitrogen-fixing bacteria of cell-free, purified enzyme extracts that they separated into an iron-molybdenum-protein fraction and an iron-protein fraction. Neither fraction alone can catalyze fixation of nitrogen, but when combined under suitable conditions they yield an active, catalytic nitrogen-fixing complex known as nitrogenase. Nitrogen fixation by the nitrogenase complex requires that six electrons must be transferred to reduce N_2 to $2NH_3$. This requires an abundance of ATP and an electron donor of low oxidation-reduction potential: ferredoxin. Nitrogenase also reduces acetylene to ethylene; use of this reaction enables detection of nitrogenase activity in microorganisms or in extracts from nitrogen-fixing cells. It thus becomes possible to test nitrogen-fixing ability of many kinds of microorganisms from varied sources in nature, and has resulted in discovery of numerous species of bacteria and of blue-green algae heretofore not known to fix nitrogen.

Interest in biological nitrogen fixation is increasing at present because the Haber process to fix nitrogen chemically requires expenditure of large amounts of energy. Furthermore, biological nitrogen fixation is of great interest to limnologists investigating productivity of waters of lakes and oceans, and of over-productivity—excessive eutrophication—of such bodies of water.[3]

It has been rewarding to E. B. Fred, age eighty-eight on March 22, 1975, and to his many colleagues and students at Wisconsin, to have some of the secrets of biological nitrogen fixation revealed during their lifetimes. Once again, the "one thing leads to another" syndrome and the need for interdisciplinary group efforts have been eloquently illustrated.

THE Department of Genetics, known from the time of its founding in 1910 until 1918 as the Department of Experimental Breeding, was the first such department in the United States. It was established in the University's College of Agriculture to encourage science that, by research and teaching, could improve agriculture. Its faculty was chosen to develop basic general genetics as a distinct biological science. Members of the new department were also called upon to help specialists in animal and plant production or protection to apply pertinent findings of research in genetics and thus to serve the interests of agriculture. These objectives were achieved with distinction not only in research but also in the training of graduate students.

Genetics has become the nucleus of research in the biological sciences at the University of Wisconsin-Madison and throughout the world. Of the twenty-five professors and associate professors now in the department, nineteen hold joint appointments in other biological science departments or institutes. Modern work in genetics also involves many faculty members and advanced students who are specialists in biological sciences that are the primary responsibility of thirty-five of the forty-two departments and twenty-nine of the forty-one institutes, group interest laboratories, special programs, or centers for research to which reference was made earlier in this chapter. Thus, genetics is the nucleus of research in the biological sciences, and it has ties to practically all aspects of biology.

It is possible to describe briefly only a few examples of the genetics research of the past twenty-five years. This is unfortunate because one could devote not only a chapter but an entire book to the accomplishments and significance of genetics and genetic science at Wisconsin. There is no biological science that substantiates more effectively Louis Pasteur's 1863 statement that: "There are no applied sciences . . . there are only the applications of science, and this is a very different matter. . . the study of the applications of science is easy to anyone who is master of the theory of it. . . ."[4]

The compromise, necessitated by lack of space, is to present brief descriptions of two major contributions by Wisconsin faculty members, each of whom was awarded the Nobel Prize—in collaboration with others — for his work. These narratives will be followed by even more brief listing of additional achievements believed to be of special significance to genetics and to biological sciences.

Late in 1947 Joshua Lederberg joined the faculty of the Department of Genetics when he was twenty-two years of age and had just completed his Ph.D. work at Yale University under direction of Edward L. Tatum. It is significant that Tatum was a Wisconsin alumnus, B.A., 1931, Ph.D., 1934; his Ph.D. work was directed by the late W. H. Peterson and by E. B. Fred. Lederberg was awarded the Nobel Prize in 1958 in Medicine and Physiology with E. L. Tatum and G. W. Beadle. Lederberg left to join the faculty of the Stanford University Department of Genetics in 1959.

That which follows is taken from a summary prepared by Lederberg in 1958 for an unpublished "History of the Department of Genetics" kindly supplied by W. H. Stone. These extracts from Lederberg's summary indicate some of his principal interests and accomplishments in research on genetics of bacteria during the 1947-1958 period.

1. Discovery and proof of sexual reproduction in the bacterium, *Escherichia coli.*

2. Invention of the replica plating technique to ascertain results of cross-breeding between cells of different strains of *E. coli* and to detect mutant strains.

3. Finding that small fragments of hereditary material of a cell of one strain of a bacterium can be transmitted to a cell of a closely related strain by a bacterial virus (bacteriophage) capable of invasion of both kinds of bacteria and of being replicated within the invaded cells. This provided the first explanation of the phenomenon of transduction, one of the principal means by which hybridization of some kinds of bacteria can occur. It was fundamental to study and understanding of the immuno-genetics of bacteria of the genus *Salmonella*. This pioneering work of Lederberg has led to world-wide studies by thousands of microbiologists and geneticists. Results of such research are of great practical significance in detection of disease-producing salmonellae and in development of means to immunize persons or animals against such pathogens.

4. Discovery of spontaneous mutation among cells of large populations of bacteria to produce mutants resistant to antimicrobial agents such as antibiotics. Such drug-resistant mutant cells have a great advantage be-cause they can multiply to produce enormous numbers of cells that cannot be inhibited or killed by the drug. The practical significance of this finding to treatment of infectious diseases of man and of animals is readily apparent. Lederberg pointed out that additional means for ac-

quisition and transfer of drug resistance in bacteria would be discovered, and this has proven to be a true prediction.

While he was a member of the Genetics faculty at Wisconsin, Lederberg developed and taught a course in microbial genetics, started studies in medical genetics, gave numerous seminars and public lectures, and participated actively as a consultant to faculty members and postdoctoral research workers. He was an innovator, an instigator, and a stimulator of great ability.

In 1960, when he was thirty-eight years of age, Har Gobind Khorana joined the University of Wisconsin-Madison faculty as professor of biochemistry and a co-director of the Institute for Enzyme Research.[5] He considered himself to be a biochemist specialist in synthesis of proteins. What he accomplished, however, was first to join, by enzymatic action, chemically synthesized segments corresponding to the gene (DNA) for alanine-transfer-RNA. This gene specifies the composition of the tRNA molecule for the amino acid alanine in synthesis of proteins in yeast cells. It was for this work and achievements that led to it, that Khorana was awarded in 1968 the Nobel Prize in Medicine and Physiology. He shared the award with M. W. Nirenberg and R. W. Holley.

His second main accomplishment, reported in 1970 before he left Wisconsin to join the faculty of the Massachusetts Institute of Technology, was to complete the synthesis of the entire gene. At that time, he had started synthesis of another gene, called tyrosine-suppressor transfer-RNA, found in nature in *Escherichia coli.*

He was the master biochemist who gathered a large international group of postdoctoral fellows to work with him in the Institute for Enzyme Research. He did not claim to be a geneticist, but he most certainly worked on the very foundation of molecular genetics: the nature and structure of the gene, and finally, the complete synthesis of a gene. To do this, he had to determine the structure and the chemical composition of the gene that he was to synthesize. Next, he had to "read" its genetic code so that he could put together in correct sequence the nucleotides needed to produce molecules of transfer-RNA which in turn direct RNA in a cell's ribosomes to synthesize proteins.

ROBERT M. Bock, professor of biochemistry and molecular biology, and dean of the Graduate School, has led groups of graduate students and postdoctoral fellows to win the race to produce the first crystals of transfer-RNA.[6] This was accomplished in 1968 only a few days before a similar event was achieved by a group working at the Massachusetts Institute of Technology. The Wisconsin research involved biochemists, biophysicists, and specialists in enzyme research. It was interdisciplinary, but, essentially, the work was directed toward molecular genetics.

As described briefly in narration of Khorana's work in the preceding section of the chapter, it is the function of a tRNA molecule to transfer genetic information from DNA to ribosomes, which in turn synthesize proteins essential to life of a cell. There is one kind of tRNA specific for just one kind of amino acid that it can retrieve, that is, pick up and transport to the ribosome. As Bock explains, the tRNA molecule can translate one word of the "language" of heredity (nucleic acid code words) to a word of instruction for a life process (amino acid words of protein structure).

Crystallization of the tRNA molecules is the first step in a program to ascertain how tRNA molecules are constructed, and how they read, and finally translate and transfer genetic information. This is biochemistry, biophysics, and molecular genetics work of importance to understanding genetics and the very basis of life of a cell.

Masayasu Nomura and Peter Traub, both geneticists working in the Wisconsin Institute for Enzyme Research, with the help of Helga Bechmann and several co-workers, were the first to achieve reconstruction from their component parts of active ribosomes.[7] They separated ribosomes, which are intracellular particles that consist of RNA and several kinds of protein, and which are centers in cells for synthesis of proteins, from cells of the bacterium *Escherichia coli,* and from other kinds of bacteria representing different genera and species. The next step, also achieved by use of the ultracentrifuge, was to separate the RNA components from ribosomal proteins. They then concentrated their efforts on the 30S particle obtained by ultracentrifugation because it alone is able to recognize and respond to the "message" delivered by a tRNA molecule. They degraded a 30S particle into a mixture of component macromolecules. This mixture was further separated into three fractions which they induced to reassemble into structures that showed all of the physical and biological properties of active 30S particles from ribosomes.

The final step, in which Bechmann played a leading role, was to use protein and RNA fractions from ribosomes of different species of bacteria and to combine them to make "hybrid" active ribosomes. It was found that some kinds of "hybrid" ribosomes were fully active, but others showed lowered activity. Another finding was that RNA from yeast or from rat liver ribosomes could not replace RNA from *E. coli* ribosomes in reconstitution of *E. coli* ribosomes or the ribosomes of other kinds of bacteria.

Traub and Bechmann have left the University, but Nomura remains as the leader of Section 5 of the Institute for Enzyme Research and as professor of genetics and biochemistry. The work described is of tremendous importance to an understanding of ribosomal structure and function. It may also lead to exploration of properties and activities of "hybrid" strains of bacteria and of hybridized cells of other kinds.

Howard M. Temin became a member of the faculty of the Department of Oncology and of the McArdle Laboratory for Cancer Research in 1960, at age twenty-six. He is concerned primarily with production of tumors by viruses. His research on the Rous sarcoma virus—an RNA virus that can cause tumor formation in chickens—led him to a remarkable genetic discovery, the transfer of genetic information from RNA to DNA.[8]

In living cells, transfer of genetic information is from DNA to DNA, DNA to RNA, and finally RNA to protein. DNA-containing viruses use the same modes of information transfer. RNA-containing viruses replicate by information transfer from RNA to RNA. Some RNA-containing viruses, including all those that cause cancer, replicate by information transfer from RNA to DNA. This was the remarkable genetic discovery; the next step was to find an explanation for it. In 1970 Temin and Satoshi Mitzutani at the University's McArdle Laboratory and David Baltimore at the Massachusetts Institute of Technology simultaneously and independently discovered an enzyme in the virus particles of RNA-containing tumor-producing viruses that catalyzed the RNA to DNA transfer of information. This mode of information transfer explained how RNA-containing tumor-producing viruses can persist in cells that they invade and how they can be latent in such cells. It also may provide a mechanism for embryonic differentiation and lead to new approaches to study of cancer.

Temin is an oncologist, a virologist, a cell physiologist, and a molecular biologist, but, like Khorana, the discovery that he made has profound importance to genetics at the molecular level of action. His work again illustrates the role of genetics as the nucleus of biological sciences.

CORN is Wisconsin's major grain crop and source of ensilage used for feed.[9] During the past twenty-five years, research in genetics by R. A. Brink, O. E. Nelson, and N. P. Neal and in agronomy by N. P. Neal and A. M. Strommen resulted in development of many inbred lines of corn that could then be used for production of hybrid varieties developed especially for Wisconsin agriculture. These hybrid varieties have special properties such as rapid growth to enable corn to be grown farther north and thus widen the cornbelt in the state and hence increase total corn production; higher and more uniform yields; higher protein and lysine content of the grain; and resistance to frequently encountered causal agents of diseases. It has been estimated that the added value attributable to Wisconsin hybrids amounts to over $20,000,000 per year.

Research in genetics by R. A. Brink, in agronomy by Dale Smith, and in plant pathology by the late F. R. Jones, resulted in the development of the Vernal variety of alfalfa. This variety is relatively tolerant to winter weather, resistant to the bacterial wilt disease, and since 1954 has been grown successfully on approximately 3,000,000 acres of Wisconsin land each year for production of high-quality alfalfa forage. It is estimated that the added value to farmers attributable to production of Vernal alfalfa is over $50,000,000 per year.

Research in genetics led by the late G. H. Rieman and D. C. Cooper, and by R. W. Hougas and S. J. Peloquin, resulted in development of the potato variety known as Superior. It has proved to be "superior" because of its tolerance to the potato scab disease and because of its high quality for use in making potato chips. These workers were also responsible, with help from others, in development of the Russet Sebago, the Russet Burbank, the Antigo, and the Red Beauty varieties for table use. Cooperation between genetics, plant pathology, and horticulture also developed a Wisconsin Certified Potato Seed Industry that has been highly successful as a source of seed free from causative agents of disease, and as a center for producing and testing inbred lines and hybrid varieties. Cooperation provided by agricultural engineers to develop irrigation of Wisconsin's central sands area for production of potatoes and other crops such as snapbeans and cucumbers, has been necessary and of great value. As Dean Glenn S. Pound of the College of Agricultural and Life Sciences says, the central sands region, once considered to be of limited value for agriculture, has now become one of the most productive agricultural areas in the United States; it is now called "The Golden Sands" area.

M. R. Irwin, and more recently W. H. Stone, have demonstrated many antigenic characters in cattle and chickens, and their placement in genetic systems. Such information is of practical importance in blood-typing of cattle to prove parentage. Blood-typing of all bulls used in artificial insemination practice is now required by dairy cattle associations.

It was E. E. Heizer of Dairy Science who developed the large-scale program of artifical insemination of dairy cattle in Wisconsin. Cooperation was provided by Paul Phillips, and by Henry Lardy of Biochemistry and now a co-director of the Enzyme Institute, who solved many of the problems of extending and preserving the semen of bulls. Dairy herd improvement associations participated actively. At present there are approximately 1,500,000 dairy cows in Wisconsin that are bred annually by artificial insemination. During the past twenty-five years the yield of milk per cow has been increased by 30 to 40 percent because of artificial insemination with semen from proven bulls.

A. B. Chapman, L. E. Casida, R. H. Grummer, and A. L. Pope have been leaders in the selection, inbreeding, line crossing, and topcrossing to improve dairy cattle, swine, and sheep. These highly practical and productive efforts to apply knowledge and principles to improvement of livestock involves improvement of yields and qualities not only of milk but of meat, hides, and wool. They have also investigated reproductive efficiency, effects of hormones, and regulation of the estrous cycle of farm animals in attempts to develop better controls that can be used by breeders of livestock.

FOLKE K. Skoog, now C. Leonard Huskins Professor of Botany, came to Madison in 1947.[10] He was, and is, interested in plant physiology, particularly in nutrition of plants, and in hormones that affect growth and tissue differentiation in plants. With the collaboration of G. C. Gerloff, he contributed significantly to knowledge of the nutrition of blue-green algae, but while doing so his studies on plant hormones increased until they consumed most of his time and effort.

It was in 1956 that Skoog, Carlos Miller, F. M. Strong, and additional co-workers reported the isolation, identification, composition, and synthesis of kinetin: 6-(furfuryl-amino)-purine. This substance was found to promote cell division and growth, to enhance initiation of flowering, and to help preserve flowers, fruits, and vegetables. Experimenting with cultures of tissues of several kinds of plants but mostly with tobacco, they found that kinetin also stimulates synthesis of DNA, RNA, and proteins; induces development of organs, and of root and stem branching; activates germination of seeds; and affects movements of solutes in plants. It was shown, furthermore, that the kinetin can act when present in minute amounts—in the parts per billion range—and that its actions depend upon interactions with definite amounts of auxin (IAA) and adenine.

Since the original work of Skoog and his colleagues, co-workers, and students, more than 200 synthetic analogues of kinetin have been produced and tested for activity. This has been a program involving international research activity. So many different compounds have been identified and synthesized that the inclusive term, cytokinins, has been adopted for all substances that have effects on plants similar to those produced by what was believed to be a unique compound, kinetin. In fact, some of the newly discovered cytokinins, such as 6-dimethylallyl-aminopurine (6-DMAAP), exhibit activity ten times greater than that of kinetin.

More recently, collaboration between Skoog's and R. M. Bock's groups has revealed that the transfer-RNA isolated from bacteria, yeast, and liver cells exhibits cytokinin activity. It is apparent that cytokinins are active in gene-controlled protein biosynthesis. The extent of such activity, and the explanations for it, are subjects of continuing intensive study.

THE University of Wisconsin-Madison today is an internationally recognized center for research on cancer. There are so many research programs that have been developed during the past twenty-five years that it is impossible even to provide an inclusive listing of titles and of faculty members involved. All that can be done here is to choose and to describe briefly only three representative, productive efforts. One of these, Howard M. Temin's work on transfer by a virus of genetic information from RNA to DNA, has been reported in the genetics section of this chapter. His principal objective is to study the role of viruses as causative agents of cancer, but the remarkable discovery he made has so much significance to molecular genetics it was decided to narrate it as genetics research. The two additional programs to be described are on (1) cause of cancer by chemical carcinogens; and (2) chemotherapy of cancer.

James A. Miller and Elizabeth C. Miller, professors of oncology, and their associates, have worked to determine how chemical carcinogens act to cause cancer.[11] In 1947 they made the primary discovery that a product of metabolism in tissues of a chemical carcinogen can bind to tissue proteins. They found later that the chemical carcinogens also bind to RNA and DNA of tissues in which the cancer is caused. In 1960 the Millers found that the metabolite—the product of tissue metabolism of a carcinogen—was more carcinogenic than the original compound. They decided that the ultimate carcinogenic derivatives of most, if not all, chemical carcinogens are electrophilic reactants. Thus, the chemical structures of carcinogens may be widely different, but the ultimate metabolic products formed in affected tissues are remarkably similar in their electrophilic properties. These studies have provided facts on which to base a rationale for prediction of carcinogenic action of chemical carcinogens.

Results of studies by the Millers and their group are made available to others in cancer research concerned with (1) biochemistry of cancer cells as compared to normal cells; (2) control of cell growth and differentiation; (3) characteristics of the nucleus and cell membranes of cancer cells and what causes the cells to metastasize or spread from one part of the body to another; and (4) research on chemotherapy of cancer. These groups, as well as those engaged in clinical or surgical oncology, in turn feed back their findings to those concerned with carcinogenesis.

The program of research leading to chemotherapy of cancer by use of 5-fluorouracil (5-FU) was designed and carried to completion by Charles Heidelberger, professor of oncology, McArdle Laboratory for Cancer Research.[12] The work was based on a specific biochemical rationale.

Before cells can divide successfully, their DNA must be replicated exactly, both with respect to quantity and the genetic information contained. One of the major characteristics of cancer cells is their rapid rate of cell division. Thus, if it were possible by chemical means to block DNA synthesis, the division of cancer cells, and hence the growth of tumors, would be blocked.

There are, however, rapidly dividing normal cells in the body which are essential for maintenance of health. These are found primarily in bone marrow and in the lining of the gastrointestinal tract. Orotic acid is the principal pyrimidine used for synthesis of RNA and DNA in such normal cells. Retman and co-workers in Philadelphia had shown in 1954 that another pyrimidine, uracil, was used for synthesis of RNA and DNA in rat liver tumor tissue cells. In all kinds of tumor tissue cells studied by Heidelberger's group at Wisconsin, greater incorporation of uracil than of orotic acid was found to occur.

Thymine is an essential component of DNA, but is not found in RNA. Uracil is found in RNA, but not in DNA. All of the thymine required by cells for synthesis of DNA is made enzymatically by the attachment of a 1-carbon unit (a methyl group in this instance) to the carbon in the 5-position of uracil. Thus, the object is to prevent biosynthesis of DNA by preventing synthesis from uracil of one of its building blocks, thymine. Blockage was achieved by substitution of an atom of fluorine for the hydrogen atom normally attached to the carbon in the 5-position of uracil. 5-Fluorouracil was first synthesized by Heidelberger, and then, in large quantities by Hoffmann-La Roche, Inc.; it thus became available in quantities sufficient for research and clinical purposes. It was shown to inhibit growth of tumors by inhibiting DNA synthesis in tumor cells.

Preclinical and clinical pharmacological studies demonstrated that 5-FU is a highly toxic compound. It must be injected with great care in exact dosages suited to each use so as to minimize its toxicity to normal tissues. Some types of tumors are more susceptible to 5-FU chemotherapy than others. 5-FU is not a "magic bullet" that is specific only for cancer cells.

Chemotherapy with 5-FU alone, or combined with radiotherapy or with other drugs, is seldom curative. In spite of its toxicity, objective improvement has been consistently obtained by its use in about 25 percent of patients who have recurrent, far-advanced cancer.

Work by Heidelberger is continuing to discover new compounds related to 5-FU, such as 5-FUDR. There is also continuing clinical study on concomitant use of other drugs, radiotherapy, and possible use of heat to enhance chemotherapeutic action.

IT was in 1926 that the Wisconsin Alumni Research Foundation was established to administer the Steenbock patent based on his 1924 discovery of the use of ultraviolet light to increase vitamin D content of foods. Hector F. DeLuca, now Steenbock Research Professor of Biochemistry, and chairman of the Department of Biochemistry, has recently discovered what might be called super-vitamin D.[13] This is not one compound, but two, one from vitamin D-2, the other from vitamin D-3.

DeLuca and his colleagues have developed the biochemical techniques needed to deduce the metabolism and actions of vitamin D. The active agents existed in such microscopic amounts that they defied chemical analysis until very recently, when modern mass spectroscopy reached the capability of determining the structure of complex compounds available only in millionths of a gram.

The knowledge of these structures permitted large scale synthesis and suddenly opened the route to great advances in understanding of metabolism crucial to diseases of bone, teeth, and kidney.

This anniversary year finds University scientists enthusiastically applying the new knowledge to diseases of man and animals and exploring the avenues for basic understanding which have been opened by this research.

As pointed out in the introductory paragraphs, it has been possible to report only a few of the many significant contributions to biological science. Apologies are due to the many who have contributed so much to unreported achievements. The author has chosen to emphasize significant findings in limnology, nitrogen fixation, genetics and its applications, cytokinins, and the causes and chemotherapy of cancer. These are specialities that have yielded discoveries which have received international recognition and have brought renown to the University. They serve to illustrate the great advances that have been made and to provide evidence for that which the University can accomplish in the years to come.

NOTES

1 Arthur D. Hasler, *Underwater Guideposts: Homing of Salmon* (Madison, 1966).

2 R. Ebisch, "Earth Resources Satellite: ERTS-1," *UIR/Research Newsletter* (University-Industry Research Program, University of Wisconsin), vol. 8, no. 2 (1974), pp. 3-6; and "McIDAS: Man-Machine Computer," *ibid,* p. 7.

3 Anonymous, "Nitrogen: Key to World Protein Supplies," and "The Chemistry of Biological Nitrogen Fixation," *UIR/Research Newsletter,* vol. 8, no. 1 (1973), pp. 24-26.

4 R. J. Dubos, *Louis Pasteur: Free Lance of Science* (Boston, 1950), pp. 67-68.

5 Anonymous, "Synthesizing a Gene" (report on award of Nobel Prize to Drs. Khorana, Nirenberg, and Holley), *UIR/Research Newsletter,* vol. 3, no. 4 (1968), pp. 2, 16; N. Thorn, "The Test-Tube Synthesis of a Gene," *UIR/Research Newsletter,* vol. 5, no. 3 (1970), pp. 3-4.

6 P. Wathen, "Wisconsin Researchers Produce First Crystals of Transfer-RNA," *UIR/Research Newsletter,* vol. 4, no. 2 (1969), pp. 2-4; N. Thorn, "Deciphering a Molecular Rosetta Stone," *UIR/Research Newsletter,* vol. 6, no. 1 (1971), pp. 21-22.

7 J. Wolf, "Wisconsin Geneticists Create Artificial, Active Ribosomes," *UIR/Research Newsletter,* vol. 3, no. 4 (1968), pp. 9-11.

8 From personal communication of Howard M. Temin, McArdle Laboratory for Cancer Research, U.W.-Madison, to William B. Sarles, August 18, 1974.

9 This section is based on excerpts from an address given by Dean Glenn S. Pound, entitled "Payoffs from Agricultural Research in Wisconsin," and given in November 1971 before the Wisconsin Agri-Business Council; also some information from personal communication from W. H. Stone, Department of Genetics.

10 P. E. Miller, "Hormones Control Plant Growth," *UIR/Research Newsletter,* vol. 2, no. 2, (1967), p. 12.

11 This and the following paragraph is based on Elizabeth C. Miller to William B. Sarles, August 20, 1974.

12 Abstracted from C. Heidelberger, "A Rational Approach to Chemotherapy," *The Cancer Bulletin,* vol. 29 (1967), pp. 96-98.

13 P. E. Miller, "Biochemists Discover Super-Vitamin D," *UIR/Research Newsletter,* vol. 3, no. 4 (1968), pp. 3-5; D. Meredith, "'Super' Vitamin D Testing Leads to Remarkable Discovery," *UIR/Research Newsletter,* vol. 4, no. 3 (1969), pp. 16, 22-23.

CHAPTER 11

Development of Research in the Social Sciences, 1949-1974

WILLIAM H. SEWELL

WISCONSIN had been an acknowledged leader in American social science throughout the first half of the twentieth century. The influence of figures like Richard T. Ely, Frederick Jackson Turner, John R. Commons, Edward A. Ross, Henry C. Taylor, Clark L. Hull, John L. Gillin, John M. Gaus, Frederick A. Ogg, and Ralph Linton had been felt throughout the scholarly world, and in 1949 their shadows and their traditions still dominated social science at this University. But the world was changing, and Wisconsin's historic eminence may in fact have delayed the process of responding to new social science techniques and approaches. By 1949 Economics, Sociology, and Political Science had all lost ground in national competition. History and Geography had maintained their earlier distinction, and Psychology was moving up rapidly. By 1958 the other social sciences had begun to regain their prewar distinction, and the next fifteen years were a time of great growth and development for almost every area of social science research at Wisconsin. Departments trebled or quadrupled in size, and research programs increased manyfold.

The reasons for this have been both local and national in origins. Perhaps the three most important local factors were: First, burgeoning enrollment in the University, but particularly in the social sciences, enabled the departments to add many energetic younger scholars to their faculties. Second, the administration of the University was particularly friendly to the development of the social sciences throughout this period.[1] Third, be-

William H. Sewell was born November 27, 1909, and came to the University of Wisconsin as professor of rural sociology and sociology in 1946. He is the Vilas Research Professor of Sociology and has served as chancellor of the Madison campus 1967-1968, and chairman of the Department of Rural Sociology, 1952-1955, the Department of Sociology, 1957-1962, the Division of Social Sciences, 1950-1953, the Social Science Research Committee, 1952-1955, and the University Committee, 1967. He is a past president of the Rural Sociological Society, the Sociological Research Association, and the American Sociological Association. He is a fellow of the American Academy of Arts and Sciences and author of more than 150 books, monographs, articles, and reviews.

ginning in 1959, all funds for research coming to the Research Committee of the Graduate School were merged, thus ending the segregation of WARF funds for the support of the biological and physical sciences. Meanwhile, the outside funds available for these more traditional research fields relieved the pressure on WARF and other local sources for natural science research support. This made possible a significant increase in funds available for the social sciences. The important outside factors were: First, the rise in emphasis on scientific methodology in the social sciences—an emphasis that was especially compatible with the Wisconsin tradition. Second, the willingness of major national funding agencies to support research in the social and behavioral sciences—particularly the National Science Foundation, the National Institutes of Health, and the Ford Foundation. Third, the new interest of the federal government and the major foundations in area research and training programs. Obviously, the effects of these conditions were felt by all social science fields at Wisconsin, but their influence was greater on Economics and Sociology than on other disciplines. This was in part due to the particular situations of Economics and Sociology at Wisconsin—both had further to go and both had traditions and personnel who were particularly compatible with the trends. Psychology and Geography also benefited greatly by these new factors, but both already had impressive research staffs and programs by the beginning of the period. Political Science and History benefited somewhat less because their behavioral science component was smaller, and Anthropology, although it made great strides, had a very small base to begin with.

WISCONSIN has long been known especially for the institutional economics of John R. Commons and his students, whose ideas and research interests completely dominated Wisconsin economics for most of the first half of this century. Most notable among these men were Selig Perlman, the brilliant labor historian; Harold M. Groves, the distinguished tax economist; Edwin E. Witte, who was the main designer of the social security system; Martin G. Glaeser, who played a leading role in the planning of the Tennessee Valley Authority; and Walter A. Morton, who was prominent in money and banking. The emphasis at Wisconsin was on applied economics—particularly on the development of laws and administrative agencies to promote and regulate for the public welfare. This emphasis has continued to the present, but with new developments in recent years that have moved Wisconsin more into the mainstream of economic research.

Perhaps the most important event in the period occurred when the distinguished econometrician, Guy H. Orcutt, came to Wisconsin from Harvard. Orcutt had as his goal a total social science effort to develop a microanalytic model of the United States economy. With a large grant from the Ford Foundation for this purpose, he established the Social Systems Research Institute as an interdisciplinary unit composed of economists, sociologists, political scientists, and others interested in the quantitative study of social and economic behavior. Although the original aim of the institute was never to be realized, and although it never became a unifying force for social science research on the campus, it has had a notable impact on Wisconsin economics. Particularly, it brought to Wisconsin such distinguished econometricians as Arthur S. Goldberger and Arnold Zellner, who rapidly gave Wisconsin leadership in quantitative research in economics. Although Orcutt and Zellner have departed, they have been replaced by outstanding younger men, including Dennis Aigner, Richard H. Day, and Donald D. Hester, and Wisconsin has continued to be a leading center for econometric research.

A more recent development, which was made possible by Wisconsin's traditional interest in applied economics and its strength in econometrics, was the establishment of the Institute for Research on Poverty. This multidisciplinary center, funded by the federal government, has brought many younger economists and sociologists to Wisconsin. Its emphasis on field-based experimental studies of negative income tax programs has attracted international attention.

It would be difficult to overstate the importance of these two institutes to the recent development of economics research at Wisconsin. Literally hundreds of books, research reports, and articles have been produced by their staffs. The work of Goldberger in econometrics has attracted worldwide attention. Robert J. Lampman is noted for his many contributions to welfare economics. The work of Harold W. Watts on the negative income tax experiments and Robert H. Haveman's writings on economic policy have received national attention. Burton A. Weisbrod and W. Lee Hansen have done important research on the economics of education. Also outstanding has been the work of Robert E. Baldwin and Theodore Morgan on international economics, Gerald G. Somers on manpower economics, Jack Barbash on labor history, Jeffrey G. Williamson on economic development, David Granick on Soviet economics, Martin H. David on income and welfare, and Glen G. Cain on labor markets.

Agricultural Economics, a separate department in the College of Agriculture, attained worldwide recognition for its research, especially for its applied research in the areas of land and resource economics, marketing, and economic development. It has been closely allied with the Department of Economics and has had much the same emphasis. Among its best known research scholars are Kenneth H. Parsons for his work on institutional economics and agricultural development, Peter P. Dorner for his research on land reform and economic development, Willard F. Mueller for his studies on organization and competitive behavior of the food industries, Peter G. Helmberger for his research on industrial organization and agricultural policy, and D. Lee Bawden for his experimental work on the effects of a negative income tax on rural people. Agricultural economists, especially Raymond J. Penn, who was its first director, also were instrumental in developing and administering the Land Tenure Center, which has been a major interdisciplinary research agency on campus. Its research and training programs are internationally known and have been funded mainly by U.S. AID.

By the beginning of the period under review, Sociology at Wisconsin had declined markedly from its lofty position in the twenties and thirties as a center for sociological scholarship and training. During the earlier period Edward A. Ross, John L. Gillin, and Kimball Young had been among the nation's most important contributors to the field. By 1949 they had been replaced by Howard P. Becker, who was a prominent social theorist; Thomas C. McCormick, who was a well-known social statistician; and by two young men, Hans H. Gerth, a sociologist of knowledge, and Marshall B. Clinard, a criminologist, both of whom were to become well-known for their scholarship. However, Wisconsin had not kept pace with developments elsewhere. Things changed little until the late fifties when — in response to increased enrollments, increased opportunities for research funds, and strong leadership — a number of young, vigorous, and research-oriented sociologists were brought to Wisconsin. With encouragement from the chairman, they began to seek funds from NIMH and NSF for their research projects. By 1962, when Sociology was settled in the new Social Science building, where for the first time it had adequate research facilities, its professorial faculty had grown to twenty-two persons (the comparable numbers were six in 1949 and ten in 1958), most of whom were involved in research projects. When, in 1964 the American Council on Education made its ratings of the quality of graduate departments, Wisconsin again had become one of the most prestigious centers of sociology in the nation.[2] Wisconsin's sociology program since then has always ranked among the several most distinguished in the United States, whether in terms of the quality and size of its faculty (currently fifty in the professorial ranks in Letters and Science alone), the number of books and articles published, the number and quality of its graduate students, the amount of outside funds for research (currently thirty projects, with an annual budget of more than 1.5 million dollars), or the adequacy of its facilities.

The major developments in Wisconsin Sociology during the period have been the rapid growth of its research and training program in demography and human ecology, under the leadership of Halliman H. Winsborough; the research and training program in medical sociology, under the direction of David Mechanic; the program in social organization, which has centered around Robert R. Alford, Maurice Zeitlin, and Michael T. Aiken; the research and training program on the sociology of economic change in which Joseph T. Elder has played a leading role; the training program in quantitative methodology, which has involved especially Edgar F. Borgatta, Robert M. Hauser, and Gerald Marwell; and the establishment of a strong research program on social stratification, which has centered around William H. Sewell, Robert M. Hauser, Archibald O. Haller, and David A. Featherman. But perhaps the most striking single development has been the extent to which Wisconsin has become recognized throughout the world as the leading center for quantitative sociological research and training.

While it would be impossible to list all of the recent sociological research contributions for which Wisconsin is known, several may be mentioned that have been particularly important. These include William H. Sewell's studies of childhood socialization and of achievement in American society; Marshall B. Clinard's work in urban slums throughout the world; David Mechanic's studies in medical sociology; Leo F. Schnore's research on urban social structure; Norman B. Ryder's research on mathematical demography; Robert R. Alford's comparative studies of political behavior; Karl E. Taeuber's research on the urban Negro; Warren O. Hagstrom's studies in the sociology of science, and Elaine C. Walster's experimental studies in social psychology. In addition, the department has several brilliant younger scholars who are doing path-breaking work on the application of multivariate statistics to social behavior. These include Robert M. Hauser, Seymour Spilerman, and Aage B. Sørensen.

It should be noted that throughout the period Wisconsin has been preeminent in Rural Sociology (a separate but closely affiliated department in the College of Agriculture). The most important research in this field has been done by the late John H. Kolb on rural communities; Eugene A. Wilkening on the diffusion of innovations in rural society; Archibald O. Haller on the aspirations and achievements of rural youth; and Glenn V. Fuguitt on studies in the growth and decline of villages.

THROUGHOUT the quarter of a century under consideration, Psychology at Wisconsin has been characterized by a strong experimental emphasis best exemplified by the research of four distinguished psychologists who were associated with the department for the whole period: Harry F. Harlow, whose contributions to animal learning brought international attention and large-scale funding to Wisconsin's Psychology Department, especially for the support of the Primate Center and the Primate Laboratory, both of which he established; Wilfred J. Brogden, who did distinguished research on learning; Karl U. Smith, who has pioneered in behavioral cybernetics; and David A. Grant, who made many contributions to quantitative methodology and to research on conditioning. The research program in clinical psychology has received a strong emphasis throughout this period and is characterized, also by an experimental and quantitive approach. This is best exemplified in the research of Peter J. Lang on behavior modification and bio-feedback and Loren J. Chapman on schizophrenia. The work of John Theios on mathematical models of information processing has been outstanding. Leonard Berkowitz's research on aggression and violence has attracted international attention. Other noteworthy research on social behavior would include Sheldon M. Ebenholtz's work on verbal learning, Vernon L. Allen's work on conformity, and Howard Leventhal's studies of emotions. Although much of the research in the primate facilities is more biological than social, attention should be called to the work of Robert W. Gay on the influence of hormones on behavior.

The Psychology faculty has excellent facilities for research in its recently constructed building and the especially designed primate laboratories. Its research is well supported by federal agencies, especially NIMH and NSF, as well as by campus sources. Like other social sciences at Wisconsin, the emphasis in Psychology is on careful and systematic research on a number of central psychological problems rather than on the development of large-scale theoretical systems.

THE research program in Political Science at Wisconsin is distinguished and eclectic in style. At the beginning of the period, the focus was largely on such traditional areas as the constitution of the United States; federal, state, and municipal government; and, regional problems and regional planning. Throughout the period, David Fellman's research on constitutional law—particularly civil liberties and defendant's rights—has been widely acclaimed, as has the work of Clara Penniman and William H.

Young on public policy and administration. Also, James L. McCamy did important studies on the administration of federal government agencies. In addition to these fields, there is now a strong emphasis on area studies, with outstanding research being done by M. Crawford Young on the Belgian Congo, John A. Armstrong on Russian bureaucracy, Charles W. Anderson on Latin American politics, and Henry C. Hart on India. Wisconsin Political Science has also been greatly affected by the "behavioral revolution," with emphasis on systemization and the use of field studies and quantification. Of particular note are the studies of Bernard C. Cohen on American foreign policy, J. Austin Ranney on American parties, Leon D. Epstein on comparative western politics, Ralph K. Huitt on congressional behavior, Jack Dennis on political socialization, Murray J. Edelman on the importance of symbols in political communication, and Matthew Holden, Jr., on urban politics. Political Science is well housed in recently remodeled North Hall and has received generous support from the University, the foundations, and federal sources. The department's faculty is now one of the very best in the nation.

WISCONSIN has long been recognized for its distinguished History faculty. Its program in American history was internationally recognized by the early part of the century, especially for the work of Frederick Jackson Turner, whose frontier interpretation dominated historical thought in America from the turn of the century through the 1930s. For the period under consideration, the History faculty has been rated among the five most prestigious in the country. Its most important single figure throughout the period was Merle Curti, whose contributions to American intellectual history and to historical methodology placed him at the forefront of American history. Distinguished contributions were also made by William B. Hesseltine and Howard K. Beale on the Civil War and Reconstruction period, by Merrill M. Jensen on the colonial period, by Vernon Carstensen on the history of American agriculture, by Fred H. Harrington on American diplomatic history, and by E. David Cronon on recent American history. European history and economic history have remained strong throughout the period. Particularly distinguished contributions have been made by George L. Mosse on European intellectual history, Harvey Goldberg on French cultural history, Theodore S. Hamerow on German diplomatic history, and Domenico Sella and Rondo E. Cameron on European economic history. Wisconsin also had great strength in medieval history, with Gaines Post, Robert L. Reynolds, and Marshall Clagget having international reputations. Paul Knaplund was a distinguished

British Empire historian. William L. Sachse in British history and Charles F. Edson in classical history were major contributors to their fields throughout the period. New areas of emphasis at Wisconsin that deserve particular mention are comparative history and cliometrics. The work of Philip D. Curtin and Jan M. Vansina on Africa, John R. W. Smail on Indonesia, and John L. Phelan on Latin America has attracted great attention. Allan G. Bogue has played the leading role in cliometrics, the use of quantification in historical studies. The distinction of Wisconsin's History Department is reflected, not only in the consistently high ranking accorded its faculty, but also in the numerous Guggenheim and other prestigious fellowships and awards that have come to its members.

IN 1949 Anthropology still was combined with Sociology and had only two persons in the professorial ranks. One of these was William W. Howells, an outstanding physical anthropologist, who, along with his predecessor, Ralph Linton, established a tradition of anthropological scholarship at Wisconsin. After Anthropology separated from Sociology in 1958, its staff expanded rapidly. Its research program soon covered most areas of anthropology, particularly after the move to the new Social Science building, where, for the first time, there were adequate laboratory facilities for anthropological research. Currently, there are strong research programs in physical anthropology, archeology, and cultural anthropology. The work in cultural anthropology is often in collaboration with area programs, especially those dealing with Asia, Africa, and Latin America. Among the best known are the studies of African social structure by Aidan W. Southall and the work of Robert Miller in South Asia. In archeology, the work of Chester S. Chard on Russia and David A. Baerreis and Catherine McClellan on North American cultural history is widely recognized. The research in physical anthropology stresses genetic factors, and its major contributors have been William S. Laughlin, Richard H. Osborne, and John T. Robinson. The graduate research training programs in Anthropology at Wisconsin are well respected and by 1964, the time of the first ACE report, the quality of Wisconsin's anthropology faculty and the effectiveness of its graduate training both ranked tenth in the country — a notable achievement for a young department.

THE Wisconsin Geography program has been one of the top three in the United States throughout the last quarter-century. Geography is both a physical science and a social science, and Wisconsin has been a leader in research in both areas. Only the social science aspects will be mentioned in this brief review. The research program in historical geography, under the distinguished leadership of Andrew H. Clark, is particularly well known. Urban geography also is strong, with the research of David Ward receiving widespread attention. Wisconsin's program in cartography and quantitative methods, in which Arthur H. Robinson has been a national leader, is outstanding. Another area of great strength is cultural geography, which focuses on the influence of institutions and social systems on the land and the management of resources. All of these areas represent new thrusts during the more recent past and are at their height at the present time. Throughout much of the period under study, Richard Hartshorne made distinguished contributions in scientific methodology and in political geography as did Glenn T. Trewartha in population geography. The research program of the department has benefited from generous support from the Research Committee of the Graduate School, the NSF, Guggenheim fellowships, and NDEA fellowships.

BEFORE ending this brief discussion of research in the social sciences at Wisconsin during the past twenty-five years, two other matters must be commented on briefly. First, social science research has gone on in other than the traditional social science departments. The distinguished work of Willard Hurst on legal history, Jacob H. Beuscher on land law, and Frank J. Remington on criminal justice has made Wisconsin's Law School a leader in the law and society movement. The work of Ralph O. Nafziger, Harold Nelson, Percy H. Tannenbaum, Steven H. Chaffee, Jack M. McLeod, and Bryant E. Kearl in Journalism and Mass Communications is widely recognized. Chester W. Harris, Virgil E. Herrick, John H. Rothney, Edward A. Krug, and Herbert J. Klausmeier have made valuable social science contributions through their studies in the School of Education.

Second, the role of centers and institutes for social science research has been very important. In all, there are twenty-five such centers currently in existence on the Madison campus. Several are interdisciplinary, for example, the Social Systems Research Institute, the Institute for Research on Poverty, and the Land Tenure Center. Others tend to center around single faculties, such as the Mass Communications Research Center in the School of Journalism and the Center for Demography and Ecology in the Sociology Department. All of these have grown up to satisfy needs of the social science faculty for organized research facilities and have greatly aided research and training on campus. The two most universally used by social scientists are the Computer Center and the Wisconsin Survey Research Laboratory. These agencies have done more to facilitate individual and group research in the social sciences than any others on campus. The Survey Research Laboratory, in particular, emerged from cooperation among a wide range of social science disciplines and also reflects the contributions and dedication of persons like Burton R. Fisher (Sociology), who promoted its creation, and Harry Sharp (Sociology), who has guided it through important stages of development.

NOTES

1 The historian Fred Harvey Harrington was vice president or president throughout most of this period; Robert L. Clodius, agricultural economist, was provost, and later vice president; Robben W. Fleming, a lawyer, William H. Sewell, a sociologist, and H. Edwin Young, an economist, were chancellors of the Madison campus. Earlier, Young had been dean of the College of Letters and Science and was succeeded as dean by Leon Epstein, a political scientist. Bryant E. Kearl, agricultural journalism, also was influential as associate dean of the Graduate School, vice chancellor, and acting chancellor.

2 Allan M. Carter, *An Assessment of Quality in Graduate Education* (Washington, D.C.: American Council on Education, 1966). For later ratings see Kenneth D. Roose and Charles J. Andersen, *A Rating of Graduate Programs* (Washington, D.C.: American Council on Education, 1970).

CHAPTER 12

Research in the Humanities since 1949

MARK ECCLES

The best thing that ever happened to encourage humane studies at the University of Wisconsin was the establishment in 1959 of the Institute for Research in the Humanities. The founder and first director, the historian of science Marshall Clagett, gained support from the University and the Johnson Foundation of Racine to begin a center for humanities in Washburn Observatory, a watchtower of learning on Observatory Hill high above Lake Mendota. The institute brought to study and teach at the University such fine scholars as E. L. Bennett and Friedrich Solmsen in Greek language and literature, Diego Catalán in medieval Spanish literature, and Germaine Brée in twentieth-century French literature. Other outstanding members have been chosen from the Wisconsin faculty: Julius Weinberg in medieval philosophy, Madeleine Doran in Shakespeare and Elizabethan literature, Max Baeumer in German, Birute Ciplijauskaite in Spanish, and Robert Kingdon in the history of the Reformation. This community of scholar-teachers is joined each year by a distinguished visiting professor and by older and younger scholars from Wisconsin or other universities here and abroad. Clagett moved on to the Institute for Advanced Studies at Princeton, as did his successor, the historian Kenneth Setton. The director from 1969 to 1974 was E. David Cronon, whose field is United States history in the twentieth century. Even though research support for the humanities is only a drop in the bucket compared to support for the sciences, at least the bucket is there to catch what it can and make use of it.

Mark Eccles, R. E. Neil Dodge Professor of English, has taught at Wisconsin since 1934. A graduate of Oberlin and Ph.D. from Harvard, he has been a Research Fellow at the Huntington Library, a Guggenheim Fellow, and Fulbright Lecturer at the Shakespeare Institute in Stratford-upon-Avon. Elected to the Humanities Divisional Committee in 1962 and again in 1969, he served as chairman from 1969 to 1972.

THE Department of English, the largest among the humanities with sixty professors, has a strong tradition of excellence in Renaissance and American literature. Merritt Hughes, an internationally known authority on Spenser and Milton, edited Milton's poetry and prose and a Variorum edition of criticism on *Paradise Lost*. He became a leader in the International Association of University Professors of English and president of the Milton Society and the Modern Humanities Research Association. Helen White published important scholarly books on Tudor and Stuart religious literature, on the metaphysical poets, and on Blake. A Renaissance woman in more than one sense, she served as a delegate to UNESCO and as president of the American Association of University Professors and the American Association of University Women. Ruth Wallerstein, a brilliant scholar and critic, won the first Christian Gauss Award of Phi Beta Kappa for her *Studies in Seventeenth-Century Poetic*. Among the best-known Shakespeare scholars in the country are Madeleine Doran, author of *Endeavors of Art*, and Mark Eccles, author of *Shakespeare in Warwickshire*, while Robert Presson and Robert Kimbrough have both written books on Shakespeare's *Troilus and Cressida*.

Harry Hayden Clark explored ideas in American authors with such energy that he guided more than a hundred doctoral students in writing dissertations. Henry Pochmann published *German Culture in America* and was general editor of the works of Washington Irving. Merton Sealts is a leading authority on Emerson and Melville, William M. Gibson on Mark Twain and Howells, and G. T. Tanselle on bibliographical problems in American literature. Frederick Hoffman published *The Twenties* and other books while he was at Wisconsin. L. S. Dembo, editor of the journal *Contemporary Literature,* is an outstanding scholar on modern American poetry and criticism, as is Walter Rideout on the modern American novel.

In other fields of English, Ricardo Quintana was especially distinguished for his books *The Mind and Art of Jonathan Swift* and *Oliver Goldsmith*. Phillip Harth has published notable books on Dryden and Swift, Eric Rothstein on Restoration tragedy, Howard Weinbrot on eighteenth-century poetry, and Richard Schwartz on Samuel Johnson. James Nelson is an authority on nineteenth-century British literature, Todd Bender on Hopkins, Paul Wiley on Conrad, and Phillip Herring on Joyce. Jerome Taylor is an active scholar in medieval literature as is Charles Scott in English linguistics. The founder and editor of the *Dictionary of American Regional English,* Frederic Cassidy, is bringing to completion one of the most valuable projects in the humanities ever undertaken at Wisconsin.

The Speech Department became in 1971 the Department of Communication Arts, and a new Department of Theatre and Drama, discussed in

Chapter 13, branched off in 1973. Frederick Haberman, chairman of Speech from 1954 to 1970, was a leader in securing the building of Vilas Communication Hall, which in 1972 provided theaters for student use and studios for work in radio, television, and film. In the same year Haberman published his edition of *The Nobel Peace Prize Lectures.* Edwin Black, now chairman, is author of *Rhetorical Criticism: A Study in Method* and editor of the *Quarterly Journal of Speech.* Lloyd Bitzer, an authority on the history of rhetoric, is president-elect in 1974 of the Speech Communication Association. Research on speech communication is being actively pursued by Thomas Scheidel, editor of *Speech Monographs,* Ronald Allen, C. David Mortensen, and Gordon Whiting. L. W. Lichty is a leading scholar on the development of radio and television in the United States, Charles E. Sherman on international broadcasting, and Don LeDuc on cable television and the Federal Communications Commission. Tino Balio and Russell Merritt are experts on the history of film in America.

VAN Hise Hall, which soars to heaven like the Tower of Babel, houses under one roof Linguistics, Comparative Literature, and ten departments that teach different languages and literatures but live peaceably together. In Classics W. R. Agard, who came from Amherst with Meiklejohn in 1927 and retired in 1964, published *What Democracy Meant to the Greeks, Classical Myths in Sculpture,* and *The Greek Mind.* Paul MacKendrick specialized in Roman archeology, where he combined expert knowledge of field work with searching scholarly judgment in *The Mute Stones Speak* and a series of books which evaluate the results of archeological research in Italy, Greece, Spain and Portugal, France, and other countries. E. L. Bennett, of the Institute for Research in the Humanities, edited *The Pylos Tablets* and continued his important investigations into the mystery of Linear B, the earliest known form of writing in the Greek language. Friedrich Solmsen, also of the institute, edited the poetry of Hesiod and was an internationally known authority on Plato and Aristotle.

The most distinguished scholar in Comparative Literature was Gian Napoleone Orsini from the University of Florence, who became chairman in 1949 and retired in 1973. He published a number of books in Italian and two major works in English, *Benedetto Croce, Philosopher of Art and Literary Critic,* and *Coleridge and German Idealism, A Study in the History of Philosophy.* Vernon Hall is the author of two scholarly works, *Renaissance Literary Criticism* and *A Short History of Literary Criticism.* David Hayman, the chairman in 1974, has published *Joyce et Mallarmé* and

In its history, the College of Letters and Science had but four deans to 1965, all shown above. In the photo-within-the-photo, Edward A. Birge, 1891-1918; left to right, George Clarke Sellery, 1919-1942; Mark H. Ingraham, 1942-1961; H. Edwin Young, 1961-1965. At left, the Sifting and Winnowing plaque, bolted to the entrance of Bascom Hall, proclaiming Wisconsin's academic freedom, is a phrase from the regent statement of 1894 exonerating one of Wisconsin's pioneering social scientists, Richard T. Ely, from charges of fomenting strikes, practicing boycotts, and teaching pernicious socialist and anarchist doctrines. John R. Commons, Fredrick Jackson Turner, Ely, and a long line of scholars have given Wisconsin international leadership in the social sciences.

The Center for Research in the Humanities, set up in the former Washburn Observatory in 1959, brought top scholars to study here and enabled Wisconsin faculty to expand research.

edited a first-draft version of *Finnegans Wake*. The department grew from two professors in 1949 to eleven in 1974.

Murray Fowler, a scholar trained at Harvard, became chairman of Comparative Philology in 1946 and of Linguistics in 1954. He was master of a wide range of Indo-European languages from Sanskrit, Greek, and Latin to Old English, Old Irish, and Welsh. His publications included an analysis of the distribution of sounds in Siamese and *Materials for the Study of the Etruscan Language*. Valdis Zeps is an authority on Baltic languages, John Street on Mongolian, and Andrew Sihler on Hittite.

FRENCH, German, Norwegian, and other languages have been widely spoken in Wisconsin, and the University has long emphasized the study of modern languages. The Department of French and Italian flourished under the leadership of Julian Harris and William T. Bandy. It was especially fortunate in having Germaine Brée teach contemporary literature during the years from 1961 to 1973 and Eugène Vinaver teach medieval romance as a visiting professor of French and English from 1966 to 1970, imaginative scholars from whom students caught the excitement of learning. Germaine Brée published ten books and directed nearly fifty dissertations while she was at Wisconsin, and Vinaver published *The Rise of Romance* and a new edition of *The Works of Sir Thomas Malory*. Julian Harris and F. Douglas Kelly were authorities on the *Chanson de Roland* and medieval romance, while Alfred Glauser studied a variety of authors from Rabelais to Victor Hugo. Hélène Monod-Cassidy and Merle Perkins specialized in eighteenth-century literature, and in the period of the nineteenth century W. T. Bandy wrote on Baudelaire, Samuel Rogers on Balzac, Herbert Gochberg on Musset, and Lorin Uffenbeck on Chateaubriand. In the field of Italian Joseph Rossi published books on literary criticism and Italo-American relations, and Robert Rodini wrote on Renaissance drama.

German ranks among the five best departments in this country for the excellence of its faculty and the effectiveness of its graduate program. In the fifties scholarship in German at Wisconsin was strongest in phonetics, with Roe-Merrill Heffner publishing *General Phonetics* and Martin Joos *Acoustic Phonetics,* but by 1974 the chief scholars were in literature. Max Baeumer, a scholar of wide learning, is a member of the Institute for Research in the Humanities. Reinhold Grimm, Alexander Hohlfeld Professor, is a distinguished critic of modern literature and probably the foremost authority on Brecht. Jost Hermand, a Vilas Research Professor, has published a dozen books and many articles on literature and art of the last two centuries. The tradition of Goethe scholarship at Wisconsin is carried on by Ian Loram, department chairman, and by Valters Nollendorfs, editor of the journal *Monatshefte*.

The Department of Scandinavian Studies is the oldest in the United States and one of the very best. Einar Haugen, the leading Scandinavian scholar in America, taught Norwegian and Old Norse at Wisconsin from 1931 to 1964, when he went to Harvard. Here he published his major work, *The Norwegian Language in America,* and translated *Voyages to Vinland.* His successor, Harald Naess, is editor of the journal *Scandinavian Studies* and author of *Knut Hamsun og Amerika.*

J. Thomas Shaw, who became chairman of Slavic Languages in 1962, edited *The Letters of Alexander Pushkin* and *Pushkin's Rhymes* and in 1974 was president of the American Association of Teachers of Slavic and East European Languages. His colleague Xenia Gasiorowska has published studies on contemporary Russian and Polish literature, especially *Women in Soviet Fiction: 1917-1964.*

The Department of Spanish and Portuguese, which consistently ranks as one of the three best in the United States, achieved an international reputation for its Seminary of Medieval Spanish Studies, where Antonio Solalinde and after 1937 Lloyd Kasten directed the preparation of a comprehensive dictionary of Old Spanish and publication of the history of the world and other works written for Alfonso the Wise. Kasten is also editor of the *Luso-Brazilian Review,* the only journal in this country devoted to the study of Brazilian and Portuguese literature, culture, history, and politics. Among the leading scholars in medieval and Renaissance Spanish literature have been J. Homer Herriott, Mack Singleton, and Mary Elizabeth Brooks. Antonio Sanchez-Barbudo, a Vilas Professor, and Birute Ciplijauskaite, a member of the Institute for Research in the Humanities, are authorities on modern Spanish literature, and Eduardo Neale-Silva and Earl Aldrich on the literature of Spanish America.

Four departments which did not exist in 1949 have since been created and have helped to make the University of Wisconsin a center for studying the languages and literature of Asia and Africa. The Department of Hebrew and Semitic Studies grew from one professor with thirty students in its first year, 1955, to five professors with four hundred students in 1974. The chairman from the beginning, Menahem Mansoor, received his graduate training at London and Dublin and has served as president of the Midwest branches of the American Oriental Society and the Society of Biblical Literature. His many publications include books on the Dead Sea Scrolls, readers in modern Hebrew and Arabic, and, with his staff, *A*

Political and Diplomatic History of the Arab World: 1900-1967, of which seven volumes have been published and eight more are scheduled for 1975.

The Department of Indian Studies, founded in 1959, changed its name in 1973 to the Department of South Asian Studies. The main emphasis is on the subcontinent of India, but the department also reaches out to include other regions of South Asia. With federal, state, and foundation support, the South Asian Area Center at Madison has developed one of the best programs of South Asian studies in the United States, and its faculty has produced a whole series of textbooks and teaching materials in Hindi, Urdu, Tamil, Tibetan, and other languages. The Buddhist Studies program has proved particularly successful. A. K. Narain is a distinguished historian, author of *The Indo-Greeks,* and Robert E. Frykenberg is an authority on the history of South India.

The Department of Chinese, which began in 1962 with one professor, Kuo-p'ing Chou from Yenching University, became in 1967 the Department of East Asian Languages and Literature, offering courses in Chinese, Japanese, and Indonesian. By 1974 it had eleven professors. Tse-tsung Chow, now chairman, is author of *The May Fourth Movement: Intellectual Revolution in Modern China.* The department sponsors the *Wisconsin China Series* and *Wen-lin: Studies in the Chinese Humanities.*

African Languages and Literature, established in 1963, emphasizes not only languages but also oral traditions and written literature in Arabic, Swahili, Hausa, Xhosa, Zulu, and other tongues, and includes literature written by Africans in French and English. The department has the most comprehensive program of its kind in the United States, and its faculty has carried out significant research projects throughout Africa. One of its early distinguished professors was A. C. Jordan, a black poet and novelist from South Africa who was also an authority on African languages and oral traditions. The present faculty includes Lyndon Harries, a scholar in Swahili language and literature, Neil Skinner in Hausa, Edris Makward in Senegalese and contemporary African literature, Daniel Kunene in the Bantu languages, and Harold Scheub in African oral narratives.

THE History of Science Department became a leader in its field under the direction of Marshall Clagett, author of *Greek Science in Antiquity, The Science of Mechanics in the Middle Ages,* and *Archimedes in the Middle Ages.* He served as president of the History of Science Society and founded the Institute for Research in the Humanities.

A brilliant philosopher at the Institute for Research in the Humanities was Julius R. Weinberg, whose works ranged from *An Examination of Logical Positivism* to *A Short History of Medieval Philosophy*. The long-standing emphasis on ethics at the University of Wisconsin was continued by A. Campbell Garnett in *The Moral Nature of Man* and *Religion and the Moral Life* and by Marcus G. Singer in *Generalization in Ethics*. In a different branch of philosophy, Albert G. Ramsperger published *Philosophies of Science*.

THE University of Wisconsin Press, directed by Thompson Webb, Jr., provides an essential service by publishing scholarly work in the humanities. It can be proud of its distinguished books on the history of science by Clagett and other authorities. Generations of students have read Agard on the Greeks and *Classics in Translation* by MacKendrick and Howe. They use Haugen's *Norwegian-English Dictionary* and Heffner and Joos on language, books on Russian literature by Xenia Gasiorowska and J. T. Shaw, on Italian by Robert Rodini and Joseph Rossi, and on Spanish by Earl Aldrich, Mary Elizabeth Brooks, J. Homer Herriott, Eduardo Neale-Silva, and Mack Singleton. The Press has published studies on English literature by Helen White, Ruth Wallerstein, Madeleine Doran, Mark Eccles, John Enck, James Nelson, Robert Presson, Eric Rothstein, Richard Schwartz, and Paul Wiley, and on American writers by Harry Clark, Henry Pochmann, L. S. Dembo, E. N. Feltskog, and Merton Sealts. Men and women from many fields in many universities have contributed to knowledge and understanding with the expert help of the University of Wisconsin Press.

CHAPTER 13

The University and the Arts, 1949-1974

JONATHAN W. CURVIN

"I look forward to an America," declared John F. Kennedy during a commemorative service for poet Robert Frost at Amherst College in 1963, "which will not be afraid of grace and beauty . . . an America which will reward achievement in the arts as we reward achievement in business and statecraft. I look forward to an America which will steadily enlarge cultural opportunities for all our citizens. And I look forward to an America which commands respect throughout the world not only for its strength but for its civilization as well."[1]

President Kennedy thus anticipated what soon came to be popularly called a nationwide "cultural explosion," manifest by extraordinary bursts of creative energies in all the arts. Even more impressive than the external evidence of regional playhouses, art museums, and concert halls has been the widespread interest and enthusiastic support which the American public has accorded to artists and the cultural ideals they represent. The Rockefeller Brothers Panel Report on the *Future of Theatre, Dance, Music in America* (1965) documented this expansion, and called attention to the "unparalleled opportunity for the arts and the nation, particularly since it occurs at a moment when a surge of vitality in the arts themselves has brought their needs and their delights to the attention of the national consciousness, as never before. . . ."[2] On September 29, 1965, President Johnson was to sign into law authorization for the establishment of a National Foundation on the Arts and the Humanities, thereby assuring the arts of financial support by the federal government.

The signs of cultural progress have prompted a general reassessment of the breadth and quality of arts training in colleges and universities. Con-

A member of the University of Wisconsin-Madison faculty since 1948, Jonathan W. Curvin currently holds a joint appointment in the departments of Communication Arts and Theatre and Drama. He has been editor of the *Educational Theatre Journal*. He has taught courses and conducted research in American drama, theatre and film. He has served as director of the University Theatre, and staged more than fifty productions on the campus, a number of them collaboratively with the Dance Division and the School of Music.

tributors to two important studies, *The Arts in Higher Education,* published by the American Association for Higher Education, and *The Arts on Campus: The Necessity for Change,* edited by Margaret Mahoney, express serious concern.[3] They are, however, in common agreement that the universities have the potential to become powerful agents for vitalizing the role of the arts in American society, and that they are uniquely equipped for the task.

First of all, as democratic institutions they seek to better the lives of all their students, rather than of merely an elite few. When in the university community the many modes of artistic expression are made readily accessible to everyone, they can exert their widest and most beneficial influence. Universities, being dedicated to free inquiry, are hospitable to change and experiment. The arts no less than the sciences thrive in an environment where original ideas may be tested and new discoveries made. And finally, the universities—"magnetic centers of intellectual life," in Stephen Spender's phrase—with their traditions of humanistic scholarship, can explore meaningful relationships between the creative arts and other academic disciplines, and thereby convey an awareness of the arts as being both relevant and necessary for educated men and women.

WITH its expanding commitments to high standards of artistic endeavors, the University of Wisconsin-Madison has achieved eminence as art patron and as a source of learning in the arts in ways wholly compatible with the University's general goals "to provide an environment in which faculty and students can discover, examine critically, preserve and transmit the knowledge, wisdom and values that will ensure the survival of the present and future generations with improvement in the quality of life."[4]

From the evidence available to Merle Curti and Vernon Carstensen for their history of the University up to 1925, one might not have predicted a flowering of the arts on the Madison campus, although the authors did cite some few early developments to suggest that a seedbed had been planted: the organization in 1910 of the influential Wisconsin Dramatic Society by Thomas H. Dickinson of the English Department; the extension of programs within the School of Music in 1915-1916; and the establishment in 1925 of the Department of Art History and Appreciation.[5] Yet as late as 1950 the Committee on Functions and Policies urged improvements in the University's cultural programs, which then appeared to be lagging conspicuously behind those more directly identified with vocational training.[6]

During the past quarter-century, however, the arts on the campus have experienced dynamic growth and greatly increased their range of effectiveness. Thousands of students have found at the University an atmosphere congenial for cultivating their aesthetic tastes, and opportunities to exercise their talents for creative expression. By its fostering of the arts the University has clearly come to recognize a vitally important obligation to its students and to the future well-being of American society.

The fact that instruction in different art forms at the University is entrusted to various academic departments should not imply that each art exists insulated from the others, or suggest that departmental barriers prevent interrelationships or weaken a feeling of common purpose. Allocation of disciplines to departments, traditional practice in the University, has proven administrative advantages. An alternative structure, such as that of a school or college devoted exclusively to the fine and performing arts, although not uncommon in some universities, would not necessarily serve as well at Wisconsin. Nor has the departmental system made for separatism or created antagonistic artistic dominions. Students are quite free and are encouraged to acquire a variety of aesthetic experiences. Faculty members conduct interdepartmental studies that bring together colleagues and students of different areas of interest; and departments regularly collaborate and assist one another in instructional projects, experiments, and performances.

Indicative of the wide curricular distribution of art and art-related subjects, it might be noted that primitive art is taught in the Anthropology Department, environmental aesthetics in Urban and Regional Planning, and African art in Afro-American Studies. Aesthetics, social problems in contemporary art, and philosophy of the arts are all established courses within the province of the Philosophy Department. Aspiring student authors may practice their craft in creative writing courses offered in the Department of English, and the literary arts also engage the foreign language, Classics, and Comparative Literature departments, and the School of Journalism.

An average of 1,300 University students enroll each academic year in the two survey courses of the Art History Department, where they discover the vast heritage of man's creative achievements in architecture, painting, and sculpture. Through the experience they are enabled to appreciate works of the visual arts as sources of personal enjoyment and as keys to the better understanding of whole civilizations, whether of the ancient past or of modern technological society. Some fifty more specialized courses for undergraduate majors and advanced degree candidates allow more concentrated focus upon the arts of particular epochs and nationalities, European, Asian and American.

Periodically the Department of Art History has invited distinguished art historians to the campus to conduct the endowed Rojtman Graduate Seminar and to lecture to the public. Guests have included Sir John Summerson, director of the Soames Museum in London, Sir Anthony Blunt of the Courtauld Institute, Lloyd Goodrich of the Whitney Museum of American Art, and Carl Nordenfalk, director of the National Museum, Stockholm.

When in 1949 William Kiekhofer, then chairman of the University of Wisconsin Centennial Committee, suggested the desirability of a fine arts building to "house all the art treasures of the University, present and prospective," the prospects were not encouraging for securing state funds for so ostensibly a nonessential luxury. Nevertheless, President E. B. Fred and the Board of Regents foresightedly initiated plans. From the beginning stages to its eventual completion, James Watrous of the Art History Department worked tirelessly on behalf of an art museum that would be worthy of the University.

In 1958 came heartening support. Results of a campuswide poll showed that all colleges and departments of the University endorsed an art museum for first priority among new buildings recommended for financing through private funds. Four years later the Thomas Brittingham Trusts donated $1,000,000 toward the project, and the University of Wisconsin Foundation opened a campaign to secure the additional $2,500,000 required.

The opening in 1970 of the Elvehjem Art Center on the lower campus was an event of more than commemorative significance. Largely financed through voluntary contributions by alumni and friends, this handsome structure testified to a wide public interest in art and the belief that a museum of this kind could be an active force both within and beyond the University community. Millard F. Rogers, its first director, stressed the multiple functions of the center: "to enhance studies in the humanities (art, music, history, English, languages, social and political sciences, etc.); to provide research facilities (study collections, an art reference library, a print and drawing center); to offer educational forays into the past and suggest the future through its permanent collections and exhibitions."[7]

For prospective artists and teachers of art, the Art Department in the School of Education provides many varied opportunities for studio practice in the visual arts, under the guidance of such gifted professional artist-teachers as Donald Anderson, Warrington Colescott, Robert Grilley, Harvey Littleton, Dean Meeker, John Wilde, and others, whose award-winning works have been shown in prestigious exhibitions in the United States and abroad.

In the spring of 1974, in celebration of the 125th anniversary of the founding of the University, the Elvehjem Art Center collaborated with the

Art Department in an exhibiton of representative works by faculty members. The quality of the drawings, ceramics, glass and metal works, etchings, paintings, engravings, mosaics, lithographs, and photographs on display in the galleries spoke eloquently for the individual talents of the Madison faculty, and the remarkable diversity of instruction available to students in the Art Department.

The move in 1969 from restricted quarters in the Education Building to spacious facilities in the new Humanities Building made it possible for the department substantially to augment its course offerings, while the transfer of its departmental library to the Kohler Library in the nearby Art Center assured a close-knit relationship between studio practice and scholarly research.

THE School of Music, an integral part of the University of Wisconsin-Madison since 1894, besides serving its primary function, "to graduate educated musicians," has contributed extensively to the public's enjoyment of fine music. In its academic policies the school subscribes to the principles of liberal education. It has neither concentrated exclusively upon applied music and performance, nor wholly confined itself to historical and theoretical studies, but rather has maintained a judicious balance between the two extremes.

In order to meet increasing student demands, the School of Music during the chairmanship of Samuel Burns between 1952 and 1964 added several accomplished instrumentalists to the faculty, among whom were Donald R. Whitaker (trumpet); John Barrows (French horn), and Harry B. Peters (bassoon). Bettina Bjorksten, Dale Gilbert, and Samuel Jones joined the vocal-instruction staff, and Karlos Moser came to teach and produce opera.

Music appreciation courses in the history of music, the symphony, opera, and quartet were opened for nonmajors and immediately attracted large enrollments. These courses afforded the singular advantage of having musical literature interpreted "live" in the classroom by such resident artists as pianist Gunnar Johansen and the members of the Pro Arte Quartet. Paul Badura-Skoda, the jazz pianist Cecil Taylor, and harpsichordist Alice Ehlers have all at one time been resident members of the faculty, too, while the composer Alec Wilder and the late Duke Ellington have been stimulating guests for brief visits.

As the School of Music grew, the problems of finding adequate instructional space became ever more acute. In the 1960s members of the faculty, dispersed throughout the campus in no fewer than thirteen annexes and twelve additional temporary locations, were virtually isolated from one another. Coordinated programs suffered as a result.

The school's transfer to the new Humanities Building in 1969 ended a period of makeshift arrangements and centralized activities under one roof. In addition to nine classrooms equipped for music recording and reproduction, there are in Humanities thirty-eight teaching studios for individual instruction and 115 practice rooms. Three large rooms, each having specifically designed acoustical properties, are used for rehearsals of band, symphony, and vocal choruses. Facilities for public concerts include Mills Concert Hall, seating 800, a smaller chamber-music auditorium, and Eastman Hall for organ recitals. The building, in 1974, accommodated a faculty of fifty-three and 450 undergraduate and graduate music majors; and it will be capable of serving the future needs of a contemplated 600 students and a staff of seventy.

The venerable Music Hall, the school's former center, was extensively renovated to meet requirements of the Opera Workshop. Under the directorship of Karlos Moser, opera production on the Madison campus has developed with conspicuous success in recent years. Nearly fifty different works have been performed since the early 1960s. In keeping with the experimental goals of the workshop, its repertoire has included many rarely staged operas. The aim has been to extend the range of operatic acquaintance beyond the already familiar, and to introduce to audiences a rich variety of historical and contemporary forms. One workshop season might typically include a production of *La Traviata* from the standard repertoire, and a more exotic work like Stravinsky's *Oedipus Rex;* or the popular nineteenth-century *Tosca* and the seventeenth-century *L'Incoronazione Di Poppea,* which most audiences would presumably be seeing and hearing for the first time. Several productions have represented combined efforts. Joining forces, the faculties and students in music and theatre have realized mutual benefits from collaborative presentations as diverse as *My Fair Lady* and Verdi's *Macbeth.*

Some of the School of Music performance organizations are composed of members of its faculty. Among these, the famous Pro Arte Quartet has been affiliated with the school for more than thirty years. The Wingra Woodwind Quintet, formed in 1965, and the Wisconsin Brass Quintet, in 1972, have gained wide popular approval. Seven major choral groups, the University Symphony, Chamber and String Orchestras, the Wind Ensemble, Symphonic Band, Concert and University Bands, all provide student musicians with invaluable performing experience in public concerts. A close alliance has been formed between the School of Music and the Madison Civic Music Association, parent organization of the Madison

Symphony Orchestra and Madison Civic Opera. Faculty members who perform in the leading chairs of the orchestra or in operatic roles not only lend status to these musical enterprises, but clearly affirm their genuine interest in the cultural prosperity of the wider community.

THE arts of dramatic production on the campus, which for long had been associated with the Department of Speech (retitled in 1970 as the Department of Communication Arts), attained independent recognition in 1973 upon the formation of a new department, that of Theatre and Drama, within the Humanities Division of the College of Letters and Science. Departmental autonomy coincided with the opening in Vilas Communication Hall of two fully equipped playhouses; one having a "thrust" stage and a seating capacity of 321, the other a highly flexible "open space" experimental theater. Backstage facilities, including ample dressing rooms, shop space, and storage areas, are so arranged as to allow performances to go on simultaneously in both theaters. Adjacent are several rehearsal rooms, an extensive costume laboratory, and classrooms especially fitted for instruction in acting, directing, and the design arts.

Study of theatrical art and the public presentation of plays share a common incentive, "to contribute to American cultural life by educating scholars, teachers, artists and audiences. . . ."[8] Theater is seen as a composite art of the written drama, acting, scenic elements, and performance before an assembled audience. As Ronald E. Mitchell, director of the University Theatre from 1942 to 1967, has aptly said: "Plays can give pleasure when read and thought about. They give a great deal more if, at the same time, they are imaginatively heard and seen, and more still if they are realized to be events, at a specific time, in a specific place, with people about."[9]

The curriculum of the Department of Theatre and Drama reflects this comprehensiveness. Courses that deal with the texts of European, British, and American dramatic literature are allied to studies in the historical development of theaters as cultural institutions in the Eastern and Western worlds, and are supplemented by critical and theoretical studies. In laboratory courses—acting, stage direction, scenic and lighting design—students develop the skills required to bring the dramatic text to full stage realization. Graduate work entails advance research in one of these areas, the literary-critical, the historical, or the creative.

When A. C. Scott, authoritative scholar in oriental drama and theatrical techniques, joined the department's faculty in 1964, he instituted an

Asian Theatre Program, having as one of its components the annual production of an Asian play with a student cast. This program has uniquely served its intention of "opening the eyes of successive generations of Wisconsin students to fresh concepts of form and self-discipline in their theatre studies, while at the same time leading them toward a better understanding of an important aspect of Asian culture and society."[10]

The extensive production program of the University Theatre, formerly known as the Wisconsin Players, annually draws more than 18,000 theatergoers to a series of major and studio presentations and is carefully integrated with the academic mission of the department in order to furnish a genuine learning experience for audiences and participants. Consistent with the belief that direct involvement in the theatrical process can be of cultural value for anyone, all students, whether or not they are departmental majors, are always welcome to take part in University Theatre activities. Many productions enlist the special talents of students of music, dance, and communication arts to demonstrate theater art as a synthesis of expressive modes.

The University Theatre, fortunate in being relieved of the severe economic pressures which plague the commercial theater, is happily free to venture beyond producing only works which have an obvious box-office appeal. Its productions have embraced a great diversity of dramatic forms, theatrical styles, historical periods, and civilizations: of ancient Greece (*The Trojan Women*); of Rome (*The Menaechmi Twins*); the Middle Ages (*From the Creation to the Nativity*); Elizabethan England (*King Lear*); nineteenth-century Russia (Chekhov's *Uncle Vanya*); twentieth-century France (*The Madwoman of Chaillot*, by Jean Giraudoux); and contemporary America (*Death of a Salesman*).

IT has been estimated that between 1955 and 1973, the number of dance companies in the United States increased from 178 to 550, indicative of the unprecedented popularity the art of dance has recently gained.

Dance has likewise flourished at the University, "not only as a creative art, manifested in the twentieth-century evolution of dance forms, but as a significant expression of each individual's life and education."[11] Ever since Margaret N. H'Doubler's pioneer work in dance education at the University in the 1920s, the Dance Division of the Department of Physical Education for Women has earned an international reputation as a center for study and for performance training. Many graduates have danced and choreographed professionally, or occupied responsible teaching posts in colleges and universities from coast to coast. The department was first in the nation to award undergraduate degrees in dance education, as well as the first to set up a curriculum for advanced degrees, which now includes the doctorate.

The root strength of dance as studied and performed at the University derives from the philosophical convictions about the art which H'Doubler first articulated. She insisted that dance should be regarded not as an unnatural acitivity or an imposed technique, but rather as having an intimate relation to natural expression. So defined, as "the specific art form of human movement," dance cannot be treated as a narrowly prescribed subject, but as one with basic values for all liberally educated men and women.

The experienced faculty members of the Dance Division have adopted a flexible curriculum and methods of instruction which allow the fullest scope for the creative potential of the individual student. They have made important explorations during recent years in the field of dance therapy, confirming through practice at the Mendota State Hospital and other institutions the beneficial effects of dance movement for the emotionally disturbed. Frequent master classes and demonstrations conducted by such renowned professional artists as Alwin Nikolais, José Limón, Martha Graham, and Merce Cunningham have greatly enhanced the academic program.

Public performances by student and faculty dancers constitute an integral part of the Dance Division's syllabus. Group and solo recitals, lecture demonstrations, special performances for children—all have been effective means for promoting wide general interest in the art. The current producing organization, the University Dance Repertory Theater, regularly stages originally choreographed works, both in Madison and on tours to other communities; and student dancers frequently appear in University Theatre and Opera Workshop productions.

W HETHER or not, as some have claimed, our twentieth-century culture is dominated by the "image media," there is little doubt of a significant change in academic attitudes toward the motion pictures. Once dismissed by the intelligentsia as vulgar and aesthetically worthless, films have come of age and have justified their serious study as a major artistic expression of modern times.

The artistic values of the motion picture were recognized at the University as early as the 1930s, when Fredrick Buerki and William Troutman of the Speech Department arranged for showings of foreign-language films in the auditorium of Bascom Hall. Theirs was the first university-sponsored film program in the United States, and the origin of the popular "movie-time" series that since 1940 has been in continuous operation in the Memorial Union Play Circle.

When eventually in the 1960s the University sanctioned the addition of two courses in film theory and history to the curriculum of the Speech Department, the art of the film won status as a legitimate subject for academic study. By 1973 the Communication Arts Department, with a much enlarged teaching staff, had more than tripled the number of film courses offered on both the undergraduate and graduate levels.

The Wisconsin Center for Theatre Research, which is jointly sponsored by the Department of Communication Arts and the State Historical Society, received in 1969 a munificent gift — the invaluable United Artists collection of film materials. Corporate records, nearly 1,750 feature films, 1,500 short subjects, 500 cartoons, 2,000 television episodes, 1,000 pressbooks, with 165,000 negatives and still photographs, make this collection an unexcelled research source. The films are constantly used for classroom instruction in several courses, and students may arrange for their private showings at the Film Archive in the State Historical Society Building. WHA-TV has secured permission to borrow from the collection for the public broadcast of programs illustrating developments in motion picture history.

Serious student interest in films has by no means been confined to the classroom. Undergraduates on their own initiative have formed many active film societies and arranged showings of both popular and more esoteric works. Members of the Wisconsin Film Society, oldest of its kind in the country, have even on occasion managed to publish reputable film studies and to subsidize production of original experimental films.

THE Wisconsin Union Theater, opened in 1939, has during more than three decades remained an imposing cultural landmark on the University campus. The beauty of its location on the Lake Mendota shore and the graceful simplicity of its architectural lines harmonize well with the function of the theater as a center for the performing arts. Nearly 5,000,000 people have attended events there. Madison residents, whether temporary or permanent, have come to look upon theatergoing at the Union as one of the most agreeable experiences the city affords.

Each year University students, assisted by the Union Theater director, plan the programs for the upcoming season and arrange bookings of music concerts, dramatic and dance performances, film showings, and other special events. Consistently these programs have opened a window on the cosmopolitan world of artistic achievements; they have featured American talents of the highest rank, and illustrious artists from the far corners of the world. In a single representative Union Theater season audiences have been privileged to enjoy performances of a touring Broadway musical, the London Bach Society, the Chinese Opera Theater, the Leningrad Philharmonic Orchestra, and the Topeng Dancers of Bali.

The Union Theater has, in addition, provided an exceptionally fine stage for student dramatic productions. It has been made available, too, for performances by civic groups, the Wisconsin Ballet Company, and the Opera Guild, and for concerts by high school bands, orchestras, and choral groups.

No account of the University's role in sponsoring the arts would be complete without reference to the far-reaching influences of its extension services. These, in the honored tradition of sharing the resources of the University with Wisconsin citizens everywhere, have done much to stimulate artistic expression and enjoyment in communities far distant from Madison.

A perennial conduit of cultural enlightenment, the University's radio broadcasting station, WHA, celebrated in 1969 its 50th anniversary of dedicated public service. Superior dramatic and musical programs, lectures, and discussions by artists and critics have always been featured in its broadcast schedules. Completion in the early 1950s of the state FM network increased the broadcast range of WHA radio to the furthest borders of the state and beyond, and brought the artistic benefits of the station to new and substantially larger listening audiences than ever before.

Out of the first tentative experiments with television broadcasting in 1954 from improvised studios in the old Chemical Engineering Building on the Madison campus evolved station WHA-TV, and the establishment in 1972 of the Wisconsin-Extension Telecommunications Center in Vilas Communication Hall. Here are located four television studios — two of them operated by the Department of Communication Arts for the teaching of television production, and two studios operated by the University of Wisconsin-Extension.

WHA-TV (Channel 21), affiliated with the Wisconsin Educational Television Network, the Central Educational Network, and the national

Public Broadcasting Service, has maintained the finest standards of non-commercial programming in all subject-areas, social, political, and educational. As for the allegiance of Channel 21 to the arts, this is fully demonstrated by the scope and quality of its programs of classical and popular music, opera and ballet, the graphic arts, and dramatic and cinematic presentations.

The eminent painter, John Steuart Curry, was appointed by the Department of Agricultural and Extension Education of the College of Agriculture as the University's first artist-in-residence in 1936. Working in his studio on the campus, Curry sensitively recorded on his canvasses Wisconsin scenes he had observed. He traveled throughout the state, encouraging the talented he discovered among its residents. Native artists, he advised, would do well to seek their subjects in their own immediate surroundings. His own fine painting, "Wisconsin Landscape," exemplified this faith in indigenous sources. A strong creative personality, Curry inspired respect and affection. He amply justified by his own example the concept of a resident artist who would serve as a cultural influence beyond the campus boundaries. After a two-year interval following Curry's death in 1946, the College of Agriculture invited as his distinguished successor in the post the Chicago-born artist, Aaron Bohrod, who was to remain at the University until his retirement in 1974.

The University Extension Division has initiated and administered a number of effective model programs in order to vitalize the arts for Wisconsin young people and adults. Establishment of the Department of Music in Extension in 1950 both assured continuity for existing services and made possible experiments with new methods of arousing interest in music and encouraging active participation in musical organizations. Similarly, Extension's Department of Art, created in 1953, bolstered the statewide visual arts programs. The Wisconsin Theatre Association under Extension auspices has directly advised and assisted community theater groups, promoted original playwriting, and conducted numerous discussion groups, conferences, and practical workshops.

The staff of University-Extension Arts has been particularly successful in arranging for opera and theater study tours. In making possible the experience of attending performances of the Lyric Opera of Chicago, the Tyrone Guthrie Theatre in Minneapolis, or Lincoln Center in New York, Extension has served well to cultivate what is so essential to a society's cultural maturity: audiences of taste and discrimination.

The quarterly journal, *Arts in Society,* which University Extension has published since 1958, illustrates yet another important dimension. Dedicated to "the augmenting of the arts in society and to the advancement of education in the arts, particularly in the field of adult education," *Arts in*

Society has attracted international attention. Its contributing authors include an impressive number of leading artists, critics, scholars, and administrators, who have offered in its pages most insightful commentaries on various aspects of modern arts and culture.

The University's School of Business has astutely recognized that if the proliferating arts organizations in the United States—arts councils, museums, art centers, and performance groups—are to thrive, their growth must be carefully tended. Besides artistry they require skilled management and soundly based fiscal policies. Sensing the need for personnel especially trained to deal with the unique and often highly complex managerial probems of arts institutions, the Graduate School of Business in 1969 originated a carefully structured career program in arts administration. This innovative program is designed to prepare qualified men and women who will "understand the special needs and conditions of work within the arts," and who will be "knowledgeable and sympathetic to the needs of the arts and at the same time understand those elements of fund raising, personnel, accounting, business law, marketing methods and the like needed in the field."[12]

D URING the academic year 1973-1974 a committee of faculty and students representing several departments and organizations made plans for a program of arts events which in the University's 125th anniversary year would illustrate in a comprehensive way the vitality of the arts on the Madison campus. These plans came to fruition in April 1974, with a four-day festival entitled "Artscape: An Introduction to the Arts at UW-Madison."

The "Artscape" committee invited the public to have a voice in discussions of timely problems and needs of the visual and performing arts in the Madison community, and to attend current University exhibits and performances. These included an outdoor showing and sale of students' art works, and the previously mentioned Art Department faculty exhibit at the Elvehjem Art Center. The Wisconsin Institute for Intermedia Studies co-sponsored with the Communication Arts and Theatre and Drama departments a special circular cinema project, a novel experiment in creating a "kinetic environment" and an unusual aesthetic experience by combining various film and video resources. There were screenings of students' films and of special television programs. Students of the Asian Theatre Program performed a Japanese drama, *The Twilight Crane,* in the Open Theatre, Vilas Hall, while the Madison Theatre Ensemble, an independent student organization, presented an original rock opera in the

Memorial Union. The Wisconsin Ballet Company staged the American première of the Dada ballet, *Relache,* and graduate students of the New Dance Ensemble featured a new work by Gerda Zimmerman, guest choreographer in the Dance Division. The Contemporary Improvisation Group, in dual concert with the Vilas Contemporary Players, introduced music its own student members had composed. Other components of the School of Music, the U.W. Madison Wind Ensemble, the Concert and University Bands, also performed. African and Afro-American Studies offered a diversified program of African art, dance, drama, music, and poetry.

In retrospect, this panoramic "Artscape" may be viewed as more than a passing show to divert the public on an April week-end. Of larger value and significance, it epitomized the talent, creative energy, and united purpose that sustain the arts throughout the University in the 1970s.

The cumulative evidence of how the arts have developed over the past twenty-five years (clearly not as an expedient response to the boom of a "cultural explosion") may readily be documented by statistics of course enrollments, faculty employment; new subjects, programs, buildings, and physical facilities.

The arts in the University today, however, draw their real source of strength from the well of old ideas and traditional Wisconsin beliefs as to the educational rights of the individual.

Harold Taylor, an assistant professor of philosophy at the University in the 1940s, and thereafter president of Sarah Lawrence College, has recalled his class in philosophy of the arts at Wisconsin. The only requirement for admittance was that the student be practicing one of the arts. The enrollees, while not, according to Taylor, "great performers," did share a "common concern for the practice of the arts," which took them to "new areas of experience where they found things for themselves which could not be found in any other way."[13]

Relatively few undergraduates at the University expect to follow careers as painters, sculptors, actors, writers, musicians, or dancers. Those who do may continue their training in graduate programs. On occasion there appears the rare, extraordinarily gifted young artist who shows promise of a brilliant professional future. The University, "cradle of all talent," has room for all. Room as well for the majority of students, not in a practical sense artistically creative at all, but who at the University of Wisconsin-Madison may cultivate a lively and informed appreciation of the arts for their own inherent values and delights.

It has been wisely said that a civilizing education cannot aim or wish to produce a nation composed exclusively of saints, philosophers, and artists; but it ought to aim at producing one in which every educated man and woman can to some extent participate in the experience of the saint, the philosopher, and the artist.[14]

NOTES

1 Nicholas Schneider and Nathalie S. Rockhill, comps. and eds., *John F. Kennedy Talks to Young People* (New York, 1968), pp. 49-50.
2 Quoted by Lewis B. Mayhew, "The Arts and Access to Higher Education," in *The Arts in Higher Education,* ed. Lawrence E. Dennis and Renate M. Jacob (San Francisco, 1968), pp. 105-6.
3 Mayhew, "The Arts and Access"; Margaret Mahoney, ed., *The Arts on Campus: The Necessity for Change* (New York, 1970).
4 College of Letters and Science, University of Wisconsin-Madison, *Bulletin,* 1974-76, p. 4.
5 Merle Curti and Vernon Carstensen, *The University of Wisconsin,* vol. 2 (Madison, 1949).
6 *History Digest: Bulletin of the University of Wisconsin* (Madison, 1971), p. 38.
7 From an address to the Madison Art Association, May 20, 1968, at Spring Green, Wisconsin.
8 Letters and Science, *Bulletin,* 1974-76, p. 267.
9 From a statement presented to the Department of Communication Arts, June 3, 1971.
10 The Artscape Program, April 1974, p. 9.
11 Dance Division, University of Wisconsin-Madison, *Dance* (Madison, 1967), p. 5.
12 Graduate School of Business, University of Wisconsin-Madison, *Graduate Education in Arts Administration* (Madison, 1972).
13 Harold Taylor, "Symposium Statement," *Arts in Society,* vol. 3, no. 1 (1965), p. 8.
14 Joseph Wood Krutch, "Creative America," in The National Cultural Center, *Creative America* (New York, 1962). Krutch here paraphrases President George Shuster of Hunter College.

CHAPTER 14

The "Wisconsin Idea" Expanded, 1949-1974

CLAY SCHOENFELD

FLOWERING from seeds planted and roots let down during the preceding fifty years, the University of Wisconsin-Madison's outreach activities expanded during the 1949-1974 era to bear new fruits of extension, public service, and youth/adult education programs and consultations throughout the state, the nation, and the world. They were all part of a commitment that had come to be called the Wisconsin Idea, characterized by Charles R. Van Hise in 1904 as a pledge to make "the beneficent influences of the University available to every home in the state,"[1] more recently by a 1949 Faculty Functions and Policies Report as the concept of "a community of scholars making itself as useful as possible."[2]

In the whole history of adult education, James Creese has written, no development has had more importance than this implementation of university outreach on the part of the University.[3] Indeed, the University has, in the words of the late Frank P. Graham, "taught the university world that the university of the people has the responsibility of taking the university — the professors, the books, the skills, the findings of research, the interpretations, the insights, the forums, and the publications to the people — as far as feasible, of making all resources of the university available to the people beyond the college walls."[4] In recognition of this distinctive tradition, the "select missions" assigned the University of Wisconsin-Madison by the University System Board of Regents in January 1974 included "providing public service by application of the results of scholarly and scientific inquiry for the benefit of society, and meeting the continuing educational needs of the public through coordinated statewide outreach programs, in accordance with its designated Land-Grant status," and "encouraging

Clay Schoenfeld is joint professor of journalism and mass communication and wildlife ecology, chairman of the Center for Environmental Communications and Education Studies, and director of Inter-College Programs, and Summer Sessions. He was former assistant to the president, assistant to the dean of University Extension, and assistant to the director of the University Center System. He is the author of *The University and Its Publics*, and *The American University in Summer*, and the co-author of *University Extension*.

cooperative use of its resources by state and national agencies and continuing extensive participation in statewide, nationwide, and international programs."[5]

In its broadest sense, the Wisconsin Idea had come to be an institutional state of mind which viewed the University not as a place but as an instrument. In the spirit of the Idea, campus leaders sought to identify public problems, to stimulate public awareness and concern, to interpret public educational needs to the University, to focus University skills and resources upon them, and thence to translate University insights into a wide range of formal and informal educational service activities throughout Wisconsin and beyond.[6]

While their forms had become many, varied, and often combined, U.W.-Madison outreach programs in recent years could be usefully categorized as follows: (1) the formal geographic dispersion of regular credit courses and curricula through Extension centers and off-campus classes; (2) relatively formal noncredit institutes, conferences, clinics, and workshops, such as the Graduate School of Banking and the Summer Youth Music Clinics; (3) educational media, such as books, bulletins, films, and radio-TV; (4) a wide range of relatively informal public service programs, such as the research-dissemination activities of the Sea Grant Program, and the educational-telephone-network (ETN) refresher instruction conducted by the Medical School for Wisconsin doctors; and (5) consultations with communities, government agencies, schools, businesses, and nations by expert faculty, such as the work of the University-Industry Research Program, the Office of Undergraduate Orientation, and the Land Tenure Center.

Over the years U.W.-Madison had developed five principal instrumentalities to help carry on its Wisconsin Idea missions: (1) a General Extension Divison, incorporating two-year Extension centers; (2) an Agricultural Extension Service, in cooperation with Wisconsin counties and the U.S. Department of Agriculture; (3) WHA Radio-TV and the University Press; (4) various special offices, individuals, and programs associated with appropriate departments, such as the Geological and Natural History Survey and the State Laboratory of Hygiene; and (5) several overseas-programs offices. Since 1970 many of these outreach instrumentalities and arrangements once indigenous to U.W.-Madison had been expropriated or modified to a great or lesser degree by the University Central Administration, although Extension's major resource base continued at Madison. Implemented imperceptively, an emerging system outreach provost concept could make the drift even more definite, divorcing outreach from its historic close association with U.W.-Madison resources and U.W.-Madison from appropriate constituencies.

All such clouds were not on the sun, however, in 1956-1957, when the

General Extension Division marked its fiftieth anniversary as the oldest and largest such arm in the country. That event provides a convenient hook on which to hang an account of a key element of the Wisconsin Idea in action, U.W.-Madison General Extension.

But first, a bit of background. In other chapters we have seen how the close of World War II, like the end of World War I, corresponded with a change in University commands. The presidency passed to Edwin Broun Fred, who had been on the campus since 1913 as bacteriology professor, dean of the Graduate School, and dean of the College of Agriculture. The new dean of Extension was Lorenz H. Adolfson, who had been a member of the Extension political science staff since 1937. They were both Wisconsin Idea enthusiasts. Together they fashioned what scholars generally consider the ingredients of an effective university outreach process: clear-cut statements of the university outreach misson, a commitment to outreach on the part of all echelons and personnel, a direct two-way channel between Extension specialists and residence departments, a symbiotic relationship between research and outreach, coordinated extension administration, a suitable reward system for outreach duties, an outreach curriculum both responsible for institutional standards and responsive to public needs, effective teaching techniques and materials, adequate financing, and working relationships with community groups and agencies.[7]

What is more, the climate was ripe for fruitful relationships between Wisconsin people and their University.

Externally, the 1945-1958 decade was a period of relative quiescence in Wisconsin politics. Stalwart Republicans held the balance of power in the state capitol, and they dealt relatively generously with their Stalwart Republican friends on the University Board of Regents. Between 1945 and 1958, too, the state was relatively prosperous, the governmental coffers well-filled, and hence legislative largesse came easily. While relinquishing none of its hard-won academic freedom, the University used its privileges with more discretion than in some periods, and consequently did not raise so many hackles on conservative necks. Furthermore, building on wartime prestige and wartime contacts, the University went out of its way to develop programs of direct service to business and industry, paralleling its older programs for labor and agriculture, and these projects paid dividends in terms of support from influential and well-heeled quarters. Championship football and basketball teams may have helped. A convenient centennial celebration focused the attention of state and national educators and journalists on the campus and brought much the same kind of editorial praise which enhanced the Van Hise era. Perhaps most significant of all, the war-

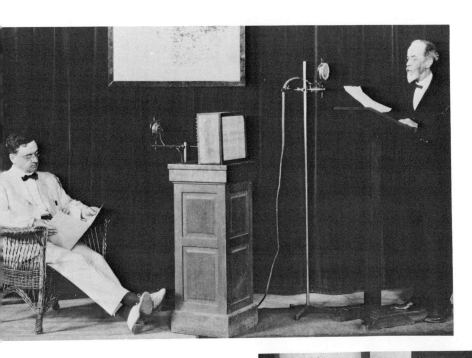

Taking the University to the state in the
Wisconsin Idea was facilitated by pioneering
work in communications. F. M. Terry and
William H. Lighty, shown above in the
broadcasting studio in Sterling Hall about
1923, were among those who gave the University "the oldest station in the nation."
Today, telephone lines extend University resources throughout the state with an Educational Telephone Network, and (right)
SEEN, the Statewide Engineering Education
Network which utilizes both ETN and an
electrowriter which transmits video as well as
audio lesson materials.

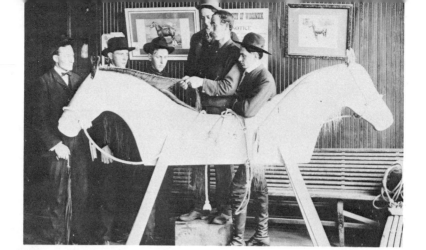

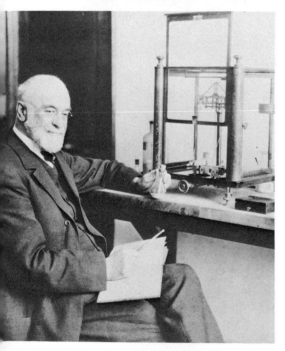

University extension efforts opened with a focus on agriculture, the Farm Short Course in 1886, and the Farmer's Institutes, which drew 50,000 their first year. All manner of farm arts and sciences were taught. Above, students learn to braid a horse's mane in 1918. Among the earliest contributions from University science to the state was the butterfat test developed by Stephen M. Babcock, left. As extension broadened its concerns its focus included urban problems. The Parent-Child Education program for welfare families in Milwaukee was a 1974 example (below).

time emphasis on training and the postwar G.I. Bill gave a tremendous impetus to public interest in higher education, and brought to Madison strong demands for varied educational services in many directions.

Internally, with fairly adequate funds to allocate for salaries, buildings, research projects, service programs, and student agencies, the University was protected from those bickerings and back-stabbings which arise largely out of short rations. Senior faculty members returned from wartime assignments with platoons of outstanding young recruits in tow. The housing and the promotions to hold them in Madison were forthcoming, not to mention the continuing presence of the University's lakeshore location. Postwar students initially were less inclined to "raise hell" than their predecessors. Grants and revenue-producing programs made many University subdivisions less vulnerable to political control. Enough professors were "University minded" to keep schools and departments from riding off in all directions. And "that plaque on the wall" was a continuing shield against reactionaries.

"We stand," hence said E. B. Fred confidently in 1945, "at the threshold of a new era. . . . More and more people are using the services of the University."[8]

It is indeed true that the 1945-1958 period saw a new spirit—or more correctly, a revivified spirit—characterize the University of Wisconsin-Madison campus. A half-century before, the University had set for itself a noble purpose and a practical function—the Wisconsin Idea. With this principle as its guide, the University moved with increasing momentum toward a fuller realization of earlier dreams, that a great university with its extraordinary equipment and its congregation of teachers and scholars would consider and provide for the part-time adult student, of varying circumstances of life.[9] Adult education came into its own as a co-equal with undergraduate instruction, its aim to inspire grown-ups to be something more than they were and to do their work better. At its best in Wisconsin, it led to "constantly increasing richness of life, better appreciation of what life offers, greater satisfaction in the use of the mind and body, and better understanding of the rights and duties of one's fellow man."[10] In so doing, the Wisconsin Idea projected the University as never before into the life of the state, and projected the people of the state as never before into the life of the University.

All five of the campus outreach instrumentalities were in high gear. With its agents in every county, Agricultural Extension was helping work a near-miracle in increasing farm production in Wisconsin. WHA, a pioneer in educational radio, was moving into video of equally high quality. Many of the campus schools and colleges were developing specialized outreach instrumentalities. Sponsored by federal agencies and private foundations, expert Wisconsin faculty members were engaged in international development programs from Alaska to Zanzibar.

THE epitome of the Wisconsin Idea, U.W.-Madison's General Extension Division was organized in its fiftieth anniversary year, 1956-1957 around twenty-three academic departments: Art Education, Chemistry, Commerce, Economics-Sociology-Anthropology, Education, Engineering, English, French-Italian, Geography, German, History, Journalism, Law, Library Methods, Mathematics, Music, Pharmacy, Photography, Physical Education, Political Science, Psychology, Spanish, and Speech.[11] Each of these disciplines was represented within the division at the least by a one-man department and at the most by staffs of up to ten instructors, who in turn were closely tied to their mother departments in residence. In addition, such subjects as botany, zoology, social work, classics, astronomy, geology, and miscellaneous languages were covered by ad hoc relationships with residence professors.

Some of these departments were concerned almost exclusively with correspondence study. Others operated across the board as professional bureaus in the fields of their competency; these "applied studies agencies" included Education, Political Science, Economics and Sociology, Psychology, Engineering, Law, Journalism, Pharmacy, German, and Spanish.

Beyond the academic departments and their integral service bureaus were seven free-wheeling interdepartmental agencies: Information and Program Services, Lectures and Concerts, Audio-Visual Instruction, the Wisconsin Idea Theatre, Community Development, the Industrial Management Institute, and the School for Workers. Operating on the flanks were six administrative service departments: the business office, field organization, editorial services, library, photographic laboratory, and auxiliary services.

Tying the whole organization together were four "general staff" officers in correspondence study, the freshman-sophomore center program and credit classes, informal instructional services, and field. Specific public relations responsibilities were shared by an assistant to the director and a director of editorial services. The Milwaukee Extension Division operated outside the division organization and reported directly to Adolfson.

The division in 1956-1957 thought of itself as being concerned with the direct extension of University work through a college credit program on both the undergraduate and graduate levels; with broad adult education programs; and with cooperative services for other state and local agencies, for the University, and for federal agencies. This outreach was effected through six core programs:

1. Correspondence study. The original function of the division, correspondence study was still the bulwark of Extension. There were 477 courses in all, from high school math to professional library methods. Currently active enrollments stood at more than 93,000 — 8,423 in U.W. courses, 85,000 in USAFI courses under a contract unjeopardized by the otherwise strained relations with the Department of Defense.

2. Special classes. Where correspondence study represented direct extension of University instruction by mail, special classes represented direct extension via periodic classroom assemblies throughout the state. There were 225 such classes — 81 for credit, 144 in noncredit areas.

3. The center program. Rising in the depression and flourishing immediately after World War II, the center system had shaken down to eight "community colleges" in Green Bay, Kenosha, Manitowoc, Marinette, Menasha, Racine, Sheboygan, and Wausau, providing one- and two-year University programs for young people otherwise unable to begin their college careers.

4. Institutes. The fastest-growing area of adult education work at Wisconsin was a wide range of conferences and short courses tailored to meet the need of professional and functional groups in the state. Fourteen Extension units held 229 such institutes with a combined attendance of 29,859.

5. The Milwaukee Extension Division. The Milwaukee Extension Division had become in every sense a metropolitan college, ensconced in its own new building and dreaming of the day when it would be a Lake Shore College. Reality was to exceed expectations in 1956-1957: together with the State Teachers College at Milwaukee, Milwaukee Extension became University of Wisconsin-Milwaukee, a major center of undergraduate and graduate instruction, urban-oriented research, and metropolitan public services.

6. Special services. Besides the more or less formal types of outreach already outlined, the Extension Division was involved in a multiplicity of public-service programs which can only be described adequately by looking briefly at the bureaus directly concerned.

The Bureau of Information and Program Services was the old "package library" bureau established to promote the public study of questions of the day by supplying packets of authentic and well-balanced study materials, and the basic purposes of the bureau continued to be, for the most part, elaborations in modern form of that original goal. The bureau distributed

9,000 packets and 10,000 sets of materials on group leadership and program planning. In addition it acted as the executive office for the Wisconsin High School Forensic Association.

The Bureau of Lectures and Concerts, another old bureau, offered "lyceum" programs for schools and civic groups, off-campus concerts by U.W. artists and bands, off-campus lectures by faculty personnel, and various other cultural programs. Its audience was estimated at 982,000.

The Department of Music picked up where E. B. Gordon had left off in the 1920s. Its mission was "to provide a broad music program to aid the esthetic and cultural growth of the state, developing and enriching the cultural activities in local schools, communities, and regions."

The Wisconsin Idea Theatre was the revival of the old Bureau of Dramatic Activities, and served as an agency for coordinating creative efforts throughout the state in theater and creative writing.

The Bureau of Community Development, already alluded to, was a wide-ranging office charged with assisting Wisconsin communities in their efforts to find adequate and satisfactory means for improving their social and economic conditions. The bureau was concerned largely with regional development programs and the attraction of new industries to small towns.

The Industrial Management Institute was the servant of the businessman. It held 113 conferences and seminars for top management and supervisory personnel.

The School for Workers was the servant of labor. It held nine institutes for laboring people, plus forty-six special classes and ten short-courses.

The Bureau of Audio-Visual Instruction maintained a film library for schools, conducted a teacher-training program, produced sound motionpictures and kinescopes, and supplied the campus with audio-visual aids. According to the state superintendent's 1956 annual report, 323,933 Wisconsin public school children watched BAVI films.

The Bureau of Government assisted Wisconsin public officials directly in improving governmental administration through research projects, institutes, manuals, and consultative services. The Bureau of Industrial Psychology helped Wisconsin industry develop general procedures in applied psychology. The Bureau of Sociology and Social Work "brought new knowledge and findings to public and private agencies."

Extension Services in Engineering, Law, Journalism, Pharmacy, Education, German, and Spanish acted as the operational agencies for making available to professional people throughout the state the resources and skills of their counterpart University departments and schools.

Together, all of these units sought, in the words of Dean Adolfson, "to make the University an integral and dynamic part of the life of the state in every way possible within the limits of available resources."[12]

In 1956-1957, as for most of the preceding fifty years, what gave General Extension its character at U.W.-Madison were two key characteristics—indigenousness and flexibility. Always at home in its surroundings, always ready to close up this program and expand that project, the division was distinguished by these activities and trends:[13]

1. The fastest growing area of adult education work was the wide range of institutes and conferences tailored to meet the specific needs of professional and functional groups in Wisconsin.

2. The entire correspondence-study program was undergoing critical survey and experimentation.

3. General adult education programs were growing constantly as people recognized the need for "lifelong learning."

4. The Extension Center program appeared to have stabilized at eight centers outside of Milwaukee, with most of them emerging as very strong regional "outposts" of the University and in a real sense as "community colleges."

5. The division recognized educational television as an intimate and essential part of its activities and was on the air with a series of experimental programs.

6. Research in the social sciences was being made an integral part of Extension activities in order to capitalize on the unique field facilities of the division.

7. The field organization of the division was undergoing a thorough analysis and realignment.

8. Since the end of World War II, off-campus graduate programs had been growing steadily.

9. The division was constantly refining the processes of self-analysis and budgeting.

10. Key explorations were underway with Agricultural Extension to determine how best to make the total extension services of the University available to the people of the state.

THOSE last explorations gradually became operational. In 1965, during the presidency of Fred Harvey Harrington, the University's outreach underwent a massive reorganization with an aim better to coordinate programs, personnel, and urban-oriented problem-solving.

The Extension centers became a separate entity under a chancellor,

Adolfson. In a remarkable demonstration of community-University team-work, nine new two-year center buildings had gone up since 1960 in Menasha, Green Bay, Kenosha, Manitowoc, Wausau, Marinette, Marsh-field, Racine, and Sheboygan. (The Green Bay Center was about to be-come a four-year University of Wisconsin-Green Bay and the Racine and Kenosha Centers a four-year U.W.-Parkside.)

A new amalgamated U.W.-Extension emerged under another chan-cellor, Donald McNeil, incorporating General Extension, Agricultural Extension, WHA Radio-TV, and the Wisconsin Geological and Natural History Survey.

The Center System and Extension developed discrete faculties, giving the two instrumentalities more autonomy and flexibility, but somewhat less empathy for the strengths and needs of the mother campus. Extension's academic resources became channeled through three principal divisions: Professional and Human Development, Economic and Environmental De-velopment, and Educational Communications. For meeting the educa-tional needs of both urban and rural citizens, the new combined U.W.-Extension was probably at the time without a peer in the country.

In a recent representative year, for example, the more than eight hundred Extension faculty members served an estimated one of every four state residents. Over 72,000 people attended institutes and workshops associated with continuing education programs, for which fees were charged. Extension served an additional 15,642 graduates and under-graduates in off-campus credit and independent study courses. WHA's School of the Air reached 70 percent of the state's elementary students through the state FM radio network. County-based faculty members scheduled over a half-million consultations to serve youth, women, busi-nessmen, farmers, and community leaders. Over 20,000 group meetings and field tours were scheduled to serve a clientele interested in such diverse subjects as entomology, medicine, plant pathology, black history, drug abuse, poultry science, school curriculum, dairy marketing, pollution control, consumer protection, and community leadership.[14]

What this massive modern implementation of the Wisconsin Idea meant can probably best be portrayed in the words of a 1972 U.W.-Extension document describing typical citizens involved in typical ways with their University:[15]

— A doctor and nurse from Beloit returned to the classroom last winter to review ways they could work more effectively as a team for pediatric care. They were among the more than 14,000 health professionals in Wisconsin who are now involved in continuing education programs.

— A Milwaukee businessman was recently given a certificate indicating he had trained as a volunteer in counseling probationers. He is one of 700 in Milwau-kee, Madison, Racine, Appleton and Beloit who have become involved in a new probation volunteer counseling program.

— An Oneida County homemaker got the final cure for a mild case of cabin fever when she attended the early June College Week for Women on the Madison campus. She and 1,479 other Wisconsin homemakers took home a "bushel" of ideas and inspirations destined to reshape their personal lives, families and communities.

— A former mayor of Milwaukee recently earned his eightieth credit hour through Independent Study. He is one of nearly 10,000 students who each year earn University of Wisconsin credit through correspondence study.

— An Ashland third grader listens to an instructional radio program each Wednesday morning. She is one of 312,000 Wisconsin elementary students who each week attend WHA Radio's School of the Air as a supplement to regular classroom instruction.

— A farmer in Brown County can use a push-button phone to punch in some information relative to questions about his farm loan. Within seconds a com-puter returns an electronic answer which is programmed to sound like a human voice. His job—running a family farm—is one of 6,000,000 that depends on the prosperity of Wisconsin agriculture and related agri-business.

— Each Wednesday a Beaver Dam lawyer takes a brown bag lunch and joins his fellow attorneys in a local hospital conference room to participate in a state-wide seminar sent out over the Educational Telephone Network. He's one of 15,000 Wisconsin adults who have now "returned to school" by way of ETN, pegged the "world's biggest party line."

— An Eau Claire County 4-H member led a crew of local teenagers in a work project to spruce up a town hall. She is among the over 60,000 Wisconsin 4-H'ers who, in addition to their regular educational projects, are providing strong community leadership to meet head-on such serious problems as pollution and drug use.

— Community leaders in Marion gathered last fall to celebrate the rejuvenation of their Marion Millpond area. Marion is one of five Wisconsin communities that have "cured or taken off the critical list" their "sick" lakes during the last two years, with the help of a crack Inland Lakes Renewal Team.

— Washington County farmers are concerned about developing more effective animal waste management and manure recycling programs. The county agri-cultural Extension agent sets up a specialized team of an Extension animal waste management engineer, the county soil conservationist and the agri-cultural stabilization director to make recommendations to help farmers qualify for government environmental assistance.

Public service activities were not alone the province of Extension; public service continued to be an accepted role of residence faculty members. The University Committee in 1974 offered the regents examples of such "sub-stantial activities" as the following:

Economists Commons, Witte, and Groves contributed much to Wisconsin's innovative labor and tax laws and programs from before 1920 until their deaths. In the last decade or more Lampman and others in the department have again and again served on state and national commissions. Young (Political Science) served in the administration of Governor Rennebohm; Knight (Business), in the administration of Governor Vernon Thomson; and Adamany (Political Science) and Jordahl (Urban and Regional Planning) in Governor Patrick Lucey's administration.

Matthews was a leading expert in ballistic identification and did much of the work that led to the establishment of the State Crime Laboratory. Stovall, director of the State Laboratory of Hygiene located on the Madison campus, had a major role in improving the health of all Wisconsin citizens through his efforts at the Laboratory and his work with the Medical School here. Daniels devoted many years in the later part of his life to the study of the utilization of solar energy in inexpensive ways suitable for developing countries.

Research and public service have so overlapped in Agriculture that it is not practical even to begin an enumeration.

Three faculty members, White, Ingraham, and Fellman, have given great service to faculties throughout the nation by serving as president of the national AAUP.[16]

The data are evidence of a vibrant philosophy at work: to deliver campus educational skills and resources to individuals, groups, organizations, and agencies for use in meeting personal aspirations and in solving societal problems; to bring back to the campus those essentail public insights and impulses that enliven teaching and stimulate research; to build those public appreciations that keep open the doors to broad educational opportunities and free inquiry at the highest order of an institution of learning.

Resident instruction, research, outreach services — these were not adversaries but friends, inextricably linked as the tripartite mission of, particularly, a land-grant institution. Each supported the other. Two examples: growing out of long-time University research in the ecological and social problems of lakes and streams, Wisconsin's landmark Water Resources Management Act of 1965 was drafted by professors and graduate students in seminars; extension professors in turn implemented the act by schooling county boards in its zoning requirements. Again, brought to the campus by a farmer and his extension agent, a sick cow became the focus of biochemical research that led to the discovery of the invaluable anticoagulants Dicumarol and Warfarin. In turn, revenues from the two drugs, generated through Wisconsin Alumni Research Foundation patents, came back to the University to support more research programs. And it all started with a cow that ate too much sweet clover, and an extension agent linking soil and seminar. Less dramatic yet no less significant examples of the interplay of teaching, research, and extension came to be legion, as U.W.-Madison expanded the Wisconsin Idea.

Thus had the campus of the outreach university come to be coextensive with the borders of the broad community whose people provide its support or inspiration. As P. P. Claxton said long ago, "Wherever men and women labor in the heat, or toil in the shadows, in field or forest, or mill or shop or mine, in legislative halls or executive offices, in society or in the home, at any task requiring an exact knowledge of facts, principles, or laws, there the modern university sees both its duty and its opportunity."[17] In turn, said Adolfson more recently, as the university "moves out to the people and comes to grips with the people's problems, it is certain the people, in turn, will bring to the university the support it needs for survival in these difficult times."[18]

This is extension, this is public service, and this is the Wisconsin Idea expanded.

WITH the coming of the merger of the University of Wisconsin and the former state teachers colleges, officially consummated in 1974, the status of U.W. Extension came in for subtle yet significant change. It was no longer exclusively the strong right arm of U.W.-Madison; it was a University System instrumentality, charged with energizing and coordinating the outreach activities of not one but twenty-seven campuses. Meanwhile the campuses themselves were asked to cease and desist from arranging independent outreach programs other than those involving credit instruction or self-supporting fees.[19]

From one perspective, all this was remarkable evidence of the leadership role of the Madison campus at work, expanding the Wisconsin Idea philosophy first to U.W.-Milwaukee, then to Green Bay and Parkside, and then to other campuses. From another perspective, it was as if U.W.-Madison's distinguished Graduate School had suddenly ceased to be the intimate instrumentality of the Madison faculty. By 1974 Madison faculty committees were discussing ways to try to restore U.W.-Madison/U.W.-Extension relationships in the interest of effective public service of high quality.

The U.W.-Madison University Committee in 1974 expressed concern "that in an effort to coordinate statewide functions, some of the traditional outreach programs will be eliminaed or removed from the control of the Madison campus," and urged that "the teaching, research, and outreach functions of such programs be again united."[20] A special U.W.-Madison Outreach Functions Committee noted the same year that "it is the ever-evolving knowledge base of the Campus that provides substance for Extension," and cautioned that "it is an uneconomical use of the state's limited funds to build an Extension faculty unrelated to and duplicative of Campus resources."[21]

Whether the system outreach pattern will presage a Wisconsin Idea of new dimensions or its attrition remains for future historians to interpret. Hopefully they will record that U.W.-Madison developed those academic energies and administrative arrangements that assured the continued interplay of a progressive state with its premier campus.

The words of the new University outreach provost, Wilson B. Thiede, were encouraging: "As soon as a strong, free, and independent extension system has been planned, the first admonition must be to relate it closely to the residence teaching and research sources, in order to build the university and serve the public in the great American Land Grant tradition."[22]

NOTES

1 Charles R. Van Hise, Speech to Wisconsin Press Association, Madison, Wisconsin, February 20, 1905, quoted in Chester Allen, "University Extension in Wisconsin," mimeographed (Madison, 1944), p. 3.

2 Committee on University Functions and Policies, *Second Report, Internal Survey* (Madison, 1949), p. 96.

3 James Creese, *The Extension of University Teaching* (New York, 1941), p. 56.

4 Frank Graham, "Higher Education and Public Service," in *Higher Education for American Society* (Madison, 1949), p. 119.

5 Board of Regents of the University of Wisconsin System, "Select Mission of the University of Wisconsin-Madison," January 1974.

6 L. H. Adolfson, "Extension Theory and Practice," *Proceedings of the National University Extension Association* (Bloomington, Ind., 1945), p. 72.

7 Theodore Shannon and Clarence A. Schoenfeld, *University Extension* (New York, 1965), p. 190.

8 *History Digest* (Madison, 1948), p. 16.

9 James C. Egbert, quoted in John Angus Burrell, *A History of Adult Education at Columbia University* (New York, 1954), p. 13.

10 James E. Russell in Burrell, *Adult Education,* p. 13.

11 *University Extension in Wisconsin, 1906-1956: The 50-Year Story of the Wisconsin Idea in Education* (Madison, 1956).

12 *University Extension in Wisconsin* (Madison, 1953), p. 16.

13 *University Extension in Wisconsin* (Madison, 1956).

14 *The Extension Story* (Madison, 1972), p. 5.

15 *Ibid.*

16 University Committee, Statement on the Mission of U.W.-Madison, 1974, p. 7.

17 P. P. Claxton, in *University of Wisconsin Extension News Bulletin* (Madison, March 1926), p. 2.

18 L. H. Adolfson, manuscript in author's files.

19 Board of Regents of the University of Wisconsin System, "Policy Statement on the Organization of University Extension and Outreach," May 11, 1973.

20 University Committee, Statement, p. 9.

21 Phase III Report of the U.W.-Madison Faculty Committee on Outreach Functions, August 1974, p. 10.

22 Wilson Thiede, "Creating a New University Outreach: The Reorganization of Extension," *Educational Record* (Summer 1968), p. 302.

INDEX

Index

Miller, William Snow, 27
Mills, Frederick E., 186
Mills Concert Hall, 242
Mill tax: granting of, 17; as source of income, 21
Milton, John, 229
Milwaukee, Wisconsin, 91
Milwaukee campus: expansion of, 92; funds for, 117
Milwaukee Extension: merged with State Teachers College, 114; mentioned, 105, 116, 258. *See also* Extension Division
Milwaukee Journal, 120
Milwaukee Merger Act of 1955, 106
Milwaukee State Teachers College, 57, 105
The Mind and Art of Jonathan Swift, 229
Minorities, 134, 150. *See also* "Black Strike"
The Miscellany, 11
Missouri, University of, 3
Mitchell, Ronald E., 243
Mitzutani, Satoshi, 211
Modern history: fellowship established for, 27
Modern Humanities Research Association, 229
"Modules," 177
Molecular Biology, Department of, 92, 179
Molecular Biology Building, 82
Monod-Cassidy, Helene, 233
The Moral Nature of Man, 236
Morgan, Theodore, 220
Morrill Land Grant, 11
Mortensen, C. David, 230
Morton, Walter A., 219
Moser, Karlos, 241, 242
Mosse, George L., 224
Mueller, Willard F., 221
Multi-campus system, 117
Multimedia Instructional Laboratory, 177
Munro, Dana: as medievalist, 26
Music, School of: established, 25; curriculum of, 171; growth of, 241; mentioned, 238, 241
Music groups: at University, 242
Musset, 233
The Mute Stones Speak, 230
My Fair Lady, 242

Naess, Harald, 234
Nafzinger, Ralph O., 226

Narain, A. K., 235
Nardin, F. Louise, 49
NASA Orbiting Astronomical Observatory, 198
The Nation, 18
National Academy of Science: membership of U.W. faculty in, 46, 62
National Accelerator Laboratory, 186
National Aeronautics and Space Administration (NASA), 189
National Defense Education Act (NDEA) Fellowships, 175, 226
National Defense Mediation Board: headed by Clarence A. Dykstra, 64
National Foundation on the Arts and the Humanities, 237
National Guardsmen, 135, 150
National Institute of Health: funds for social science of, 219
National Institute of Mental Health, 221, 223
National Museum, Stockholm, Sweden, 240
National Science Foundation, 186, 192, 219, 221, 223, 226
Natural History Survey, 253
Natural Science, 179
Naval Research Laboratory, 189
Neal, N. P., 211
Neale-Silva, Eduardo, 234, 236
Negative income tax program, 220
Nelson, Harold, 226
Nelson, James, 229, 236
Nelson, O. E., 211
Neshek, Milton E., 124
Neurology, Department of, 182
Neurophysiology, Department of, 182
Neurosciences, Department of, 179
Newton, Isaac, 45
New York, 186
Nicolais, Alwin, 245
Nitrogen fixation, 206, 217
Nixon, Richard: and Cambodia, 149
Nobel Peace Prize Lectures, 230
Nobel Prize: winners at University, 46; in Medicine and Physiology, 209; mentioned, 207
Noland Zoology Building, 174
Nollendorfs, Valters, 234
Nominations Committee, 56
Nomura, Masayasu, 210, 211

DESIGNED BY IRVING PERKINS
COMPOSED BY FOX VALLEY TYPESETTING, MENASHA, WISCONSIN
MANUFACTURED BY MALLOY LITHOGRAPHING, INC., ANN ARBOR, MICHIGAN
TEXT AND DISPLAY LINES SET IN BASKERVILLE

Library of Congress Cataloging in Publication Data
Main entry under title:
The University of Wisconsin.
Includes bibliographical references and index.
1. Wisconsin. University — Madison — History.
I. Bogue, Allan G. II. Taylor, Robert, 1916 —
LD6128.U54   378.775'84   74-27306
ISBN 0-299-06840-4